INHUMAN

INHUMAN VOL. 3: LINEAGE. Contains material originally published in magazine form as INHUMAN #12-14 and ANNUAL #1. First printing 2015. ISBN# 978-0-7851-9804-8. Published by MARVEL WORLDWIDE, INC., a subsidiary of MARVEL ENTERTAINMENT, LLC. OFFICE OF PUBLICATION: 135 West 50th Street, New York, NY 10020. Copyright © 2015 MARVEL No similarity between any of the names, characters, persons, and/or institutions in this magazine with those of any living or dead person or institution is intended, and any such similarity which may exist is purely coincidental. **Printed in Canada.** ALAN FINE, President, Marvel Entertainment; DAN BUCKLEY, President, TV, Publishing and Brand Management; JOE QUESADA, Chief Creative Officer; TOM BREVOORT, SVP of Publishing; DAVID BOGART, SVP of Operations & Procurement, Publishing; C.B. CEBULSKI, VP of International Development & Brand Management; DAVID GABRIEL, SVP Print, Sales & Marketing; JIM O'KEEFE, VP of Operations & Logistics; DAN CARR, Executive Director of Publishing Technology; SUSAN CRESPI, Editorial Operations Manager; ALEX MORALES, Publishing Operations Manager; STAN LEE, Chairman Emeritus. For information regarding advertising in Marvel Comics or on Marvel.com, please contact Jonathan Rheingold, VP of Custom Solutions & Ad Sales, at jrheingold@marvel.com. For Marvel subscription inquiries, please call 800-217-9158. **Manufactured between 6/5/2015 and 7/13/2015 by SOLISCO PRINTERS, SCOTT, QC, CANADA.**

10 9 8 7 6 5 4 3 2 1

WRITER
CHARLES SOULE

ARTISTS
RYAN STEGMAN (#12 & ANNUAL #1) &
ANDRÉ ARAÚJO (#13-14)

COLORISTS
RICHARD ISANOVE
WITH RACHELLE ROSENBERG (#12, PGS. 17-20)

LETTERER
VC'S CLAYTON COWLES

COVER ART
RYAN STEGMAN & RICHARD ISANOVE

ASSISTANT EDITOR
CHARLES BEACHAM
EDITOR
NICK LOWE

COLLECTION EDITOR:
SARAH BRUNSTAD
ASSOCIATE MANAGING EDITOR:
ALEX STARBUCK
EDITORS, SPECIAL PROJECTS:
JENNIFER GRÜNWALD & MARK D. BEAZLEY
SENIOR EDITOR, SPECIAL PROJECTS:
JEFF YOUNGQUIST
BOOK DESIGNER:
NELSON RIBEIRO

SVP PRINT, SALES & MARKETING:
DAVID GABRIEL
EDITOR IN CHIEF:
AXEL ALONSO
CHIEF CREATIVE OFFICER:
JOE QUESADA
PUBLISHER:
DAN BUCKLEY
EXECUTIVE PRODUCER:
ALAN FINE

TO PROTECT THE EARTH FROM AN EXTRATERRESTRIAL THREAT, BLACK BOLT, KING OF THE INHUMANS, DETONATED A MASSIVE BOMB IN THE FLOATING INHUMAN CITY OF ATTILAN, CAUSING THE CITY TO FALL AND UNLEASHING A CLOUD OF TERRIGEN MISTS ACROSS THE GLOBE. ONCE RELEASED, THE MISTS AWAKENED SUPERHUMAN ABILITIES IN ANYONE WITH TRACES OF INHUMAN DNA. THOSE WHO SURVIVED EXPOSURE ARE NO LONGER MERELY HUMAN. THEY ARE...

INHUMAN

THE CAPO, LEADER OF THE INHUMAN CORPORATION OF ENNILUX, HAS EXTENDED HIS LIFE FOR CENTURIES BY TRANSFERRING HIS CONSCIOUSNESS INTO NEW HOST BODIES, LEAVING THE OWNERS FOR DEAD. RECENTLY, HIS GENERATION'S CANDIDATE, A YOUNG CHINESE WOMAN NAMED ISO, ESCAPED TO NEW ATTILAN WITH THE HELP OF AN INHUMAN TRACKER NAMED READER.

NOT WILLING TO GIVE UP HIS IMMORTALITY, THE CAPO FOLLOWED THE PAIR, BRINGING THE FULL MILITARY FORCE OF ENNILUX WITH HIM. TO MAKE MATTERS WORSE, MEDUSA, THE QUEEN OF NEW ATTILAN, HAD A FALLING-OUT WITH HER GENERALS AND FLED THE CITY — LEAVING IT MORE VULNERABLE TO ATTACK!

INHUMANS CREATED BY STAN LEE & JACK KIRBY

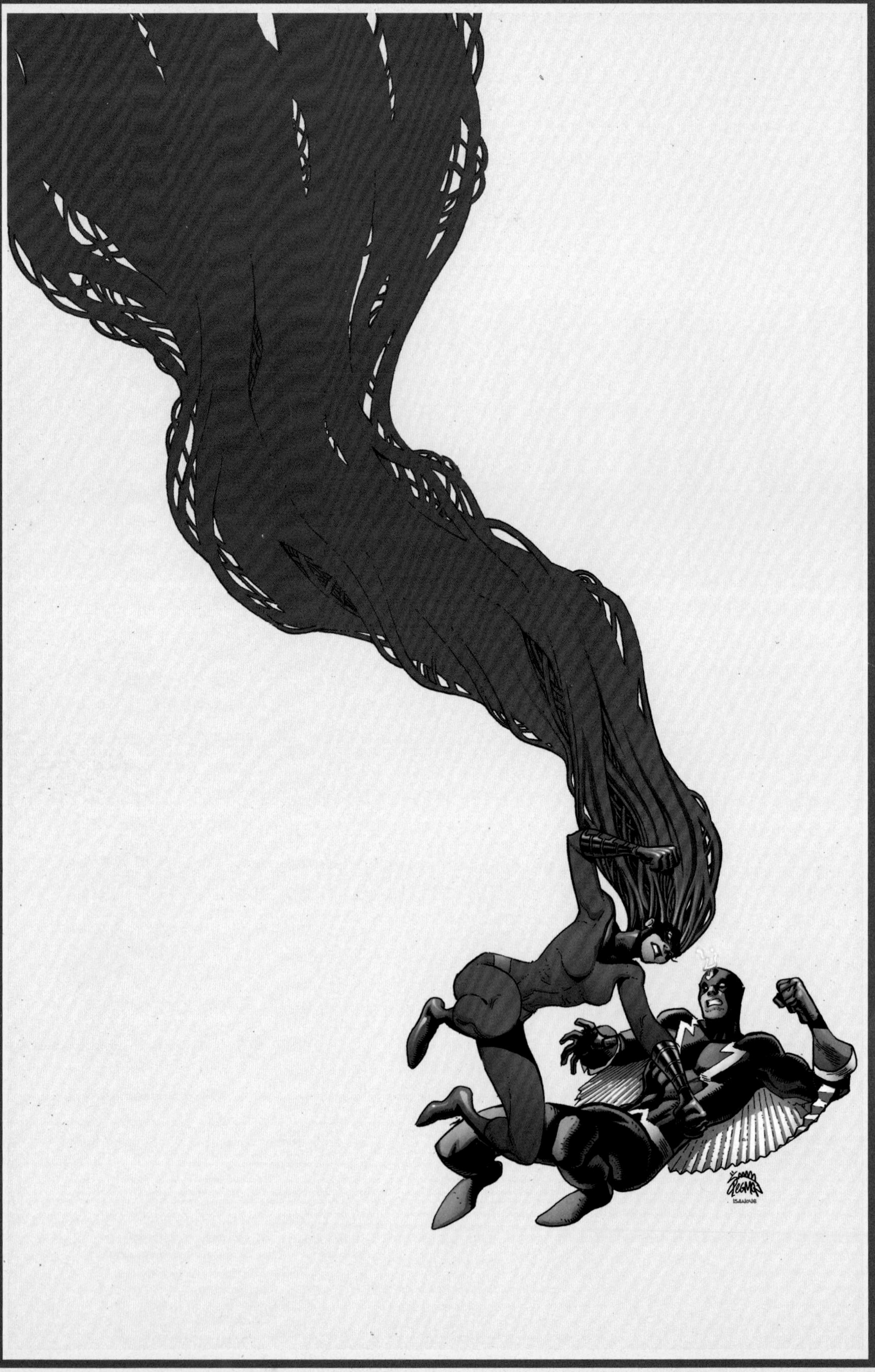

12 PART TWELVE: DISUNION

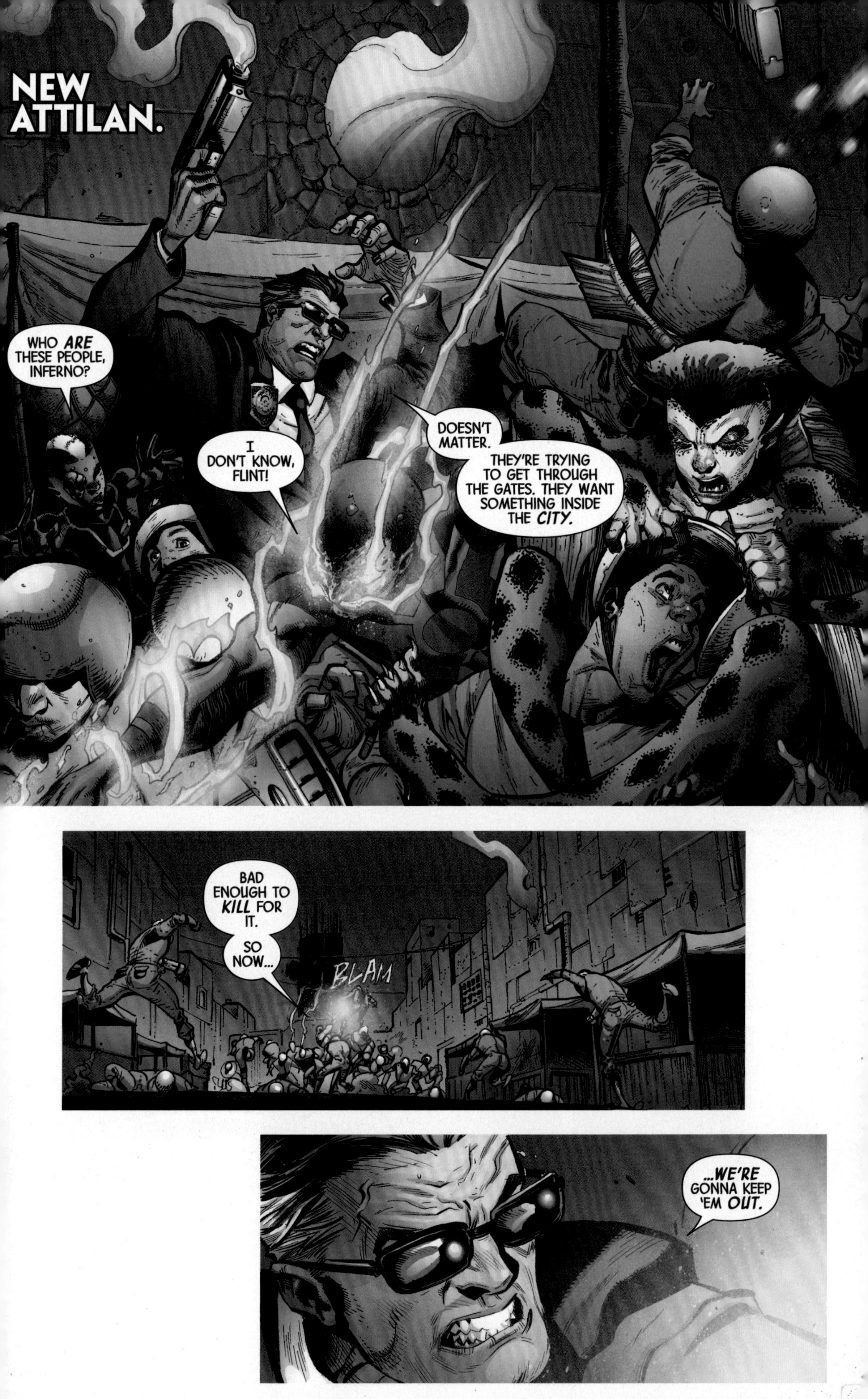
NEW ATTILAN.
WHO ARE THESE PEOPLE, INFERNO?
I DON'T KNOW, FLINT!
DOESN'T MATTER.
THEY'RE TRYING TO GET THROUGH THE GATES. THEY WANT SOMETHING INSIDE THE CITY.
BAD ENOUGH TO KILL FOR IT.
SO NOW...
BLAM
...WE'RE GONNA KEEP 'EM OUT.

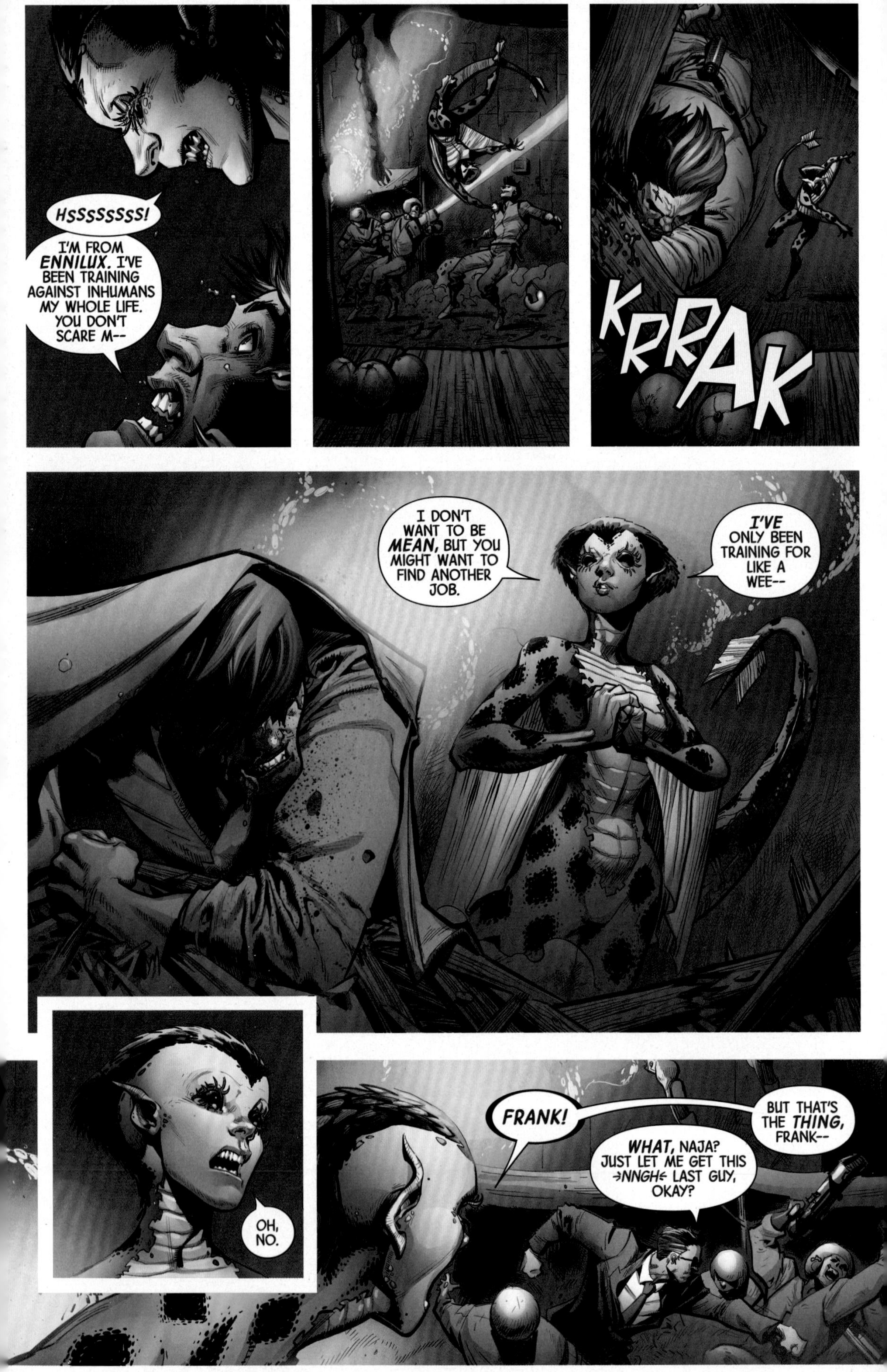
HSSSSSSSS!
I'M FROM ENNILUX. I'VE BEEN TRAINING AGAINST INHUMANS MY WHOLE LIFE. YOU DON'T SCARE M--
KRRAK
I DON'T WANT TO BE MEAN, BUT YOU MIGHT WANT TO FIND ANOTHER JOB.
I'VE ONLY BEEN TRAINING FOR LIKE A WEE--
OH, NO.
FRANK!
WHAT, NAJA? JUST LET ME GET THIS ≥NNGH≤ LAST GUY, OKAY?
BUT THAT'S THE THING, FRANK--

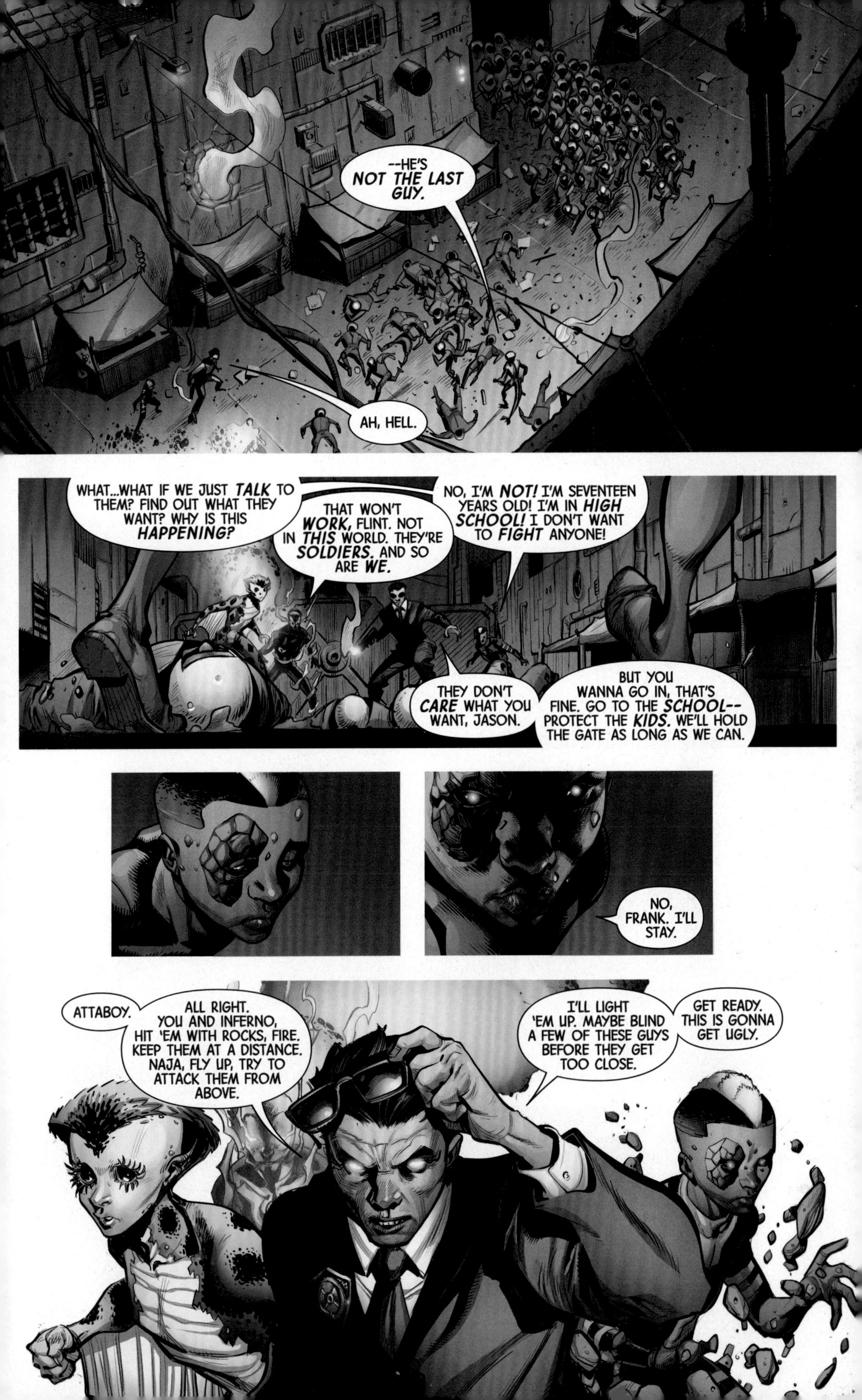
--HE'S NOT THE LAST GUY.
AH, HELL.
WHAT...WHAT IF WE JUST TALK TO THEM? FIND OUT WHAT THEY WANT? WHY IS THIS HAPPENING?
THAT WON'T WORK, FLINT. NOT IN THIS WORLD. THEY'RE SOLDIERS. AND SO ARE WE.
NO, I'M NOT! I'M SEVENTEEN YEARS OLD! I'M IN HIGH SCHOOL! I DON'T WANT TO FIGHT ANYONE!
THEY DON'T CARE WHAT YOU WANT, JASON.
BUT YOU WANNA GO IN, THAT'S FINE. GO TO THE SCHOOL--PROTECT THE KIDS. WE'LL HOLD THE GATE AS LONG AS WE CAN.
NO, FRANK. I'LL STAY.
ATTABOY.
ALL RIGHT. YOU AND INFERNO, HIT 'EM WITH ROCKS, FIRE. KEEP THEM AT A DISTANCE. NAJA, FLY UP, TRY TO ATTACK THEM FROM ABOVE.
I'LL LIGHT 'EM UP. MAYBE BLIND A FEW OF THESE GUYS BEFORE THEY GET TOO CLOSE.
GET READY. THIS IS GONNA GET UGLY.

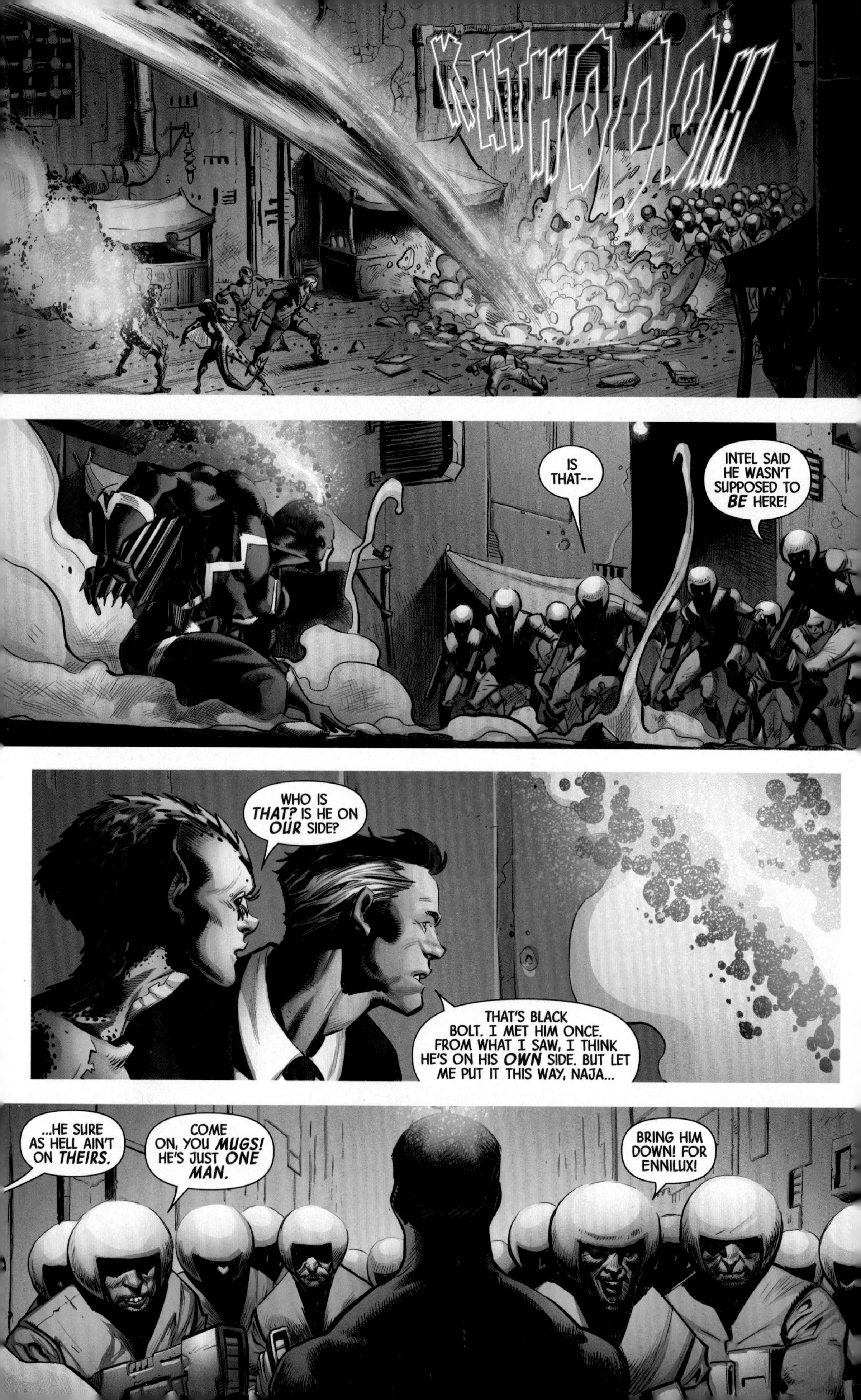
KRATHOOOOM
IS THAT--
INTEL SAID HE WASN'T SUPPOSED TO BE HERE!
WHO IS THAT? IS HE ON OUR SIDE?
THAT'S BLACK BOLT. I MET HIM ONCE. FROM WHAT I SAW, I THINK HE'S ON HIS OWN SIDE. BUT LET ME PUT IT THIS WAY, NAJA...
...HE SURE AS HELL AIN'T ON THEIRS.
COME ON, YOU MUGS! HE'S JUST ONE MAN.
BRING HIM DOWN! FOR ENNILUX!

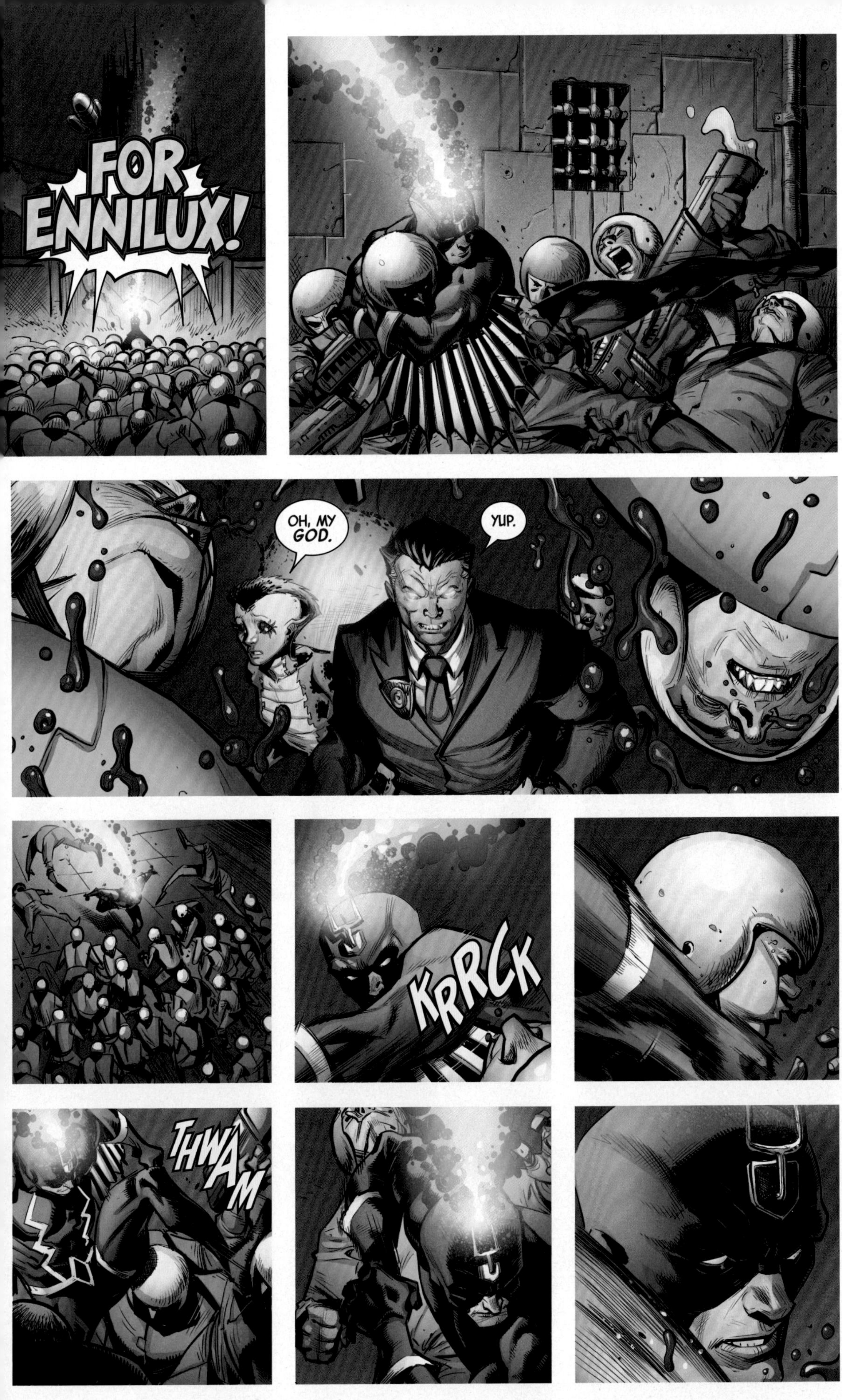
FOR ENNILUX!
OH, MY GOD.
YUP.
KRRCK
THWAM

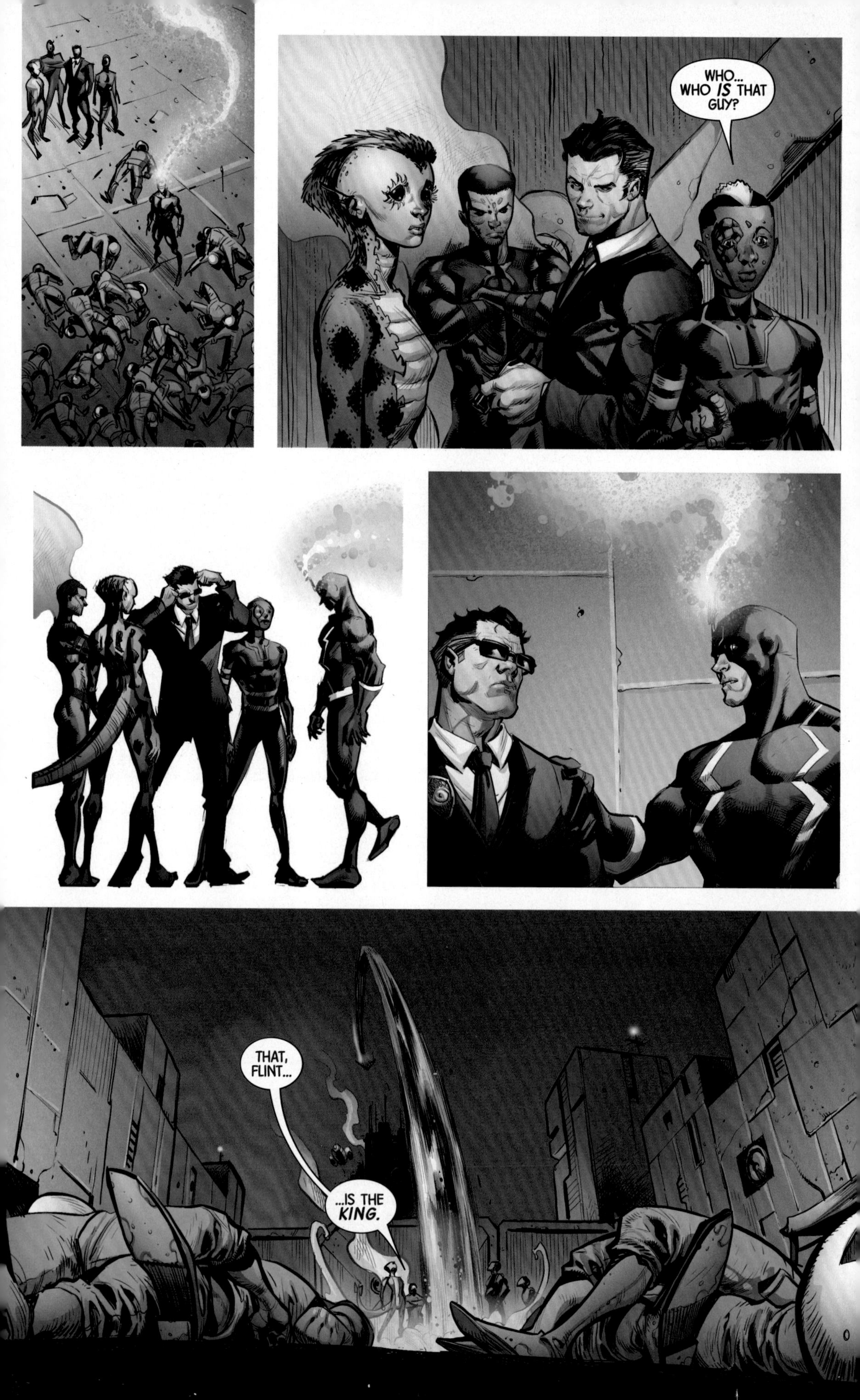
WHO... WHO IS THAT GUY?
THAT, FLINT...
...IS THE KING.

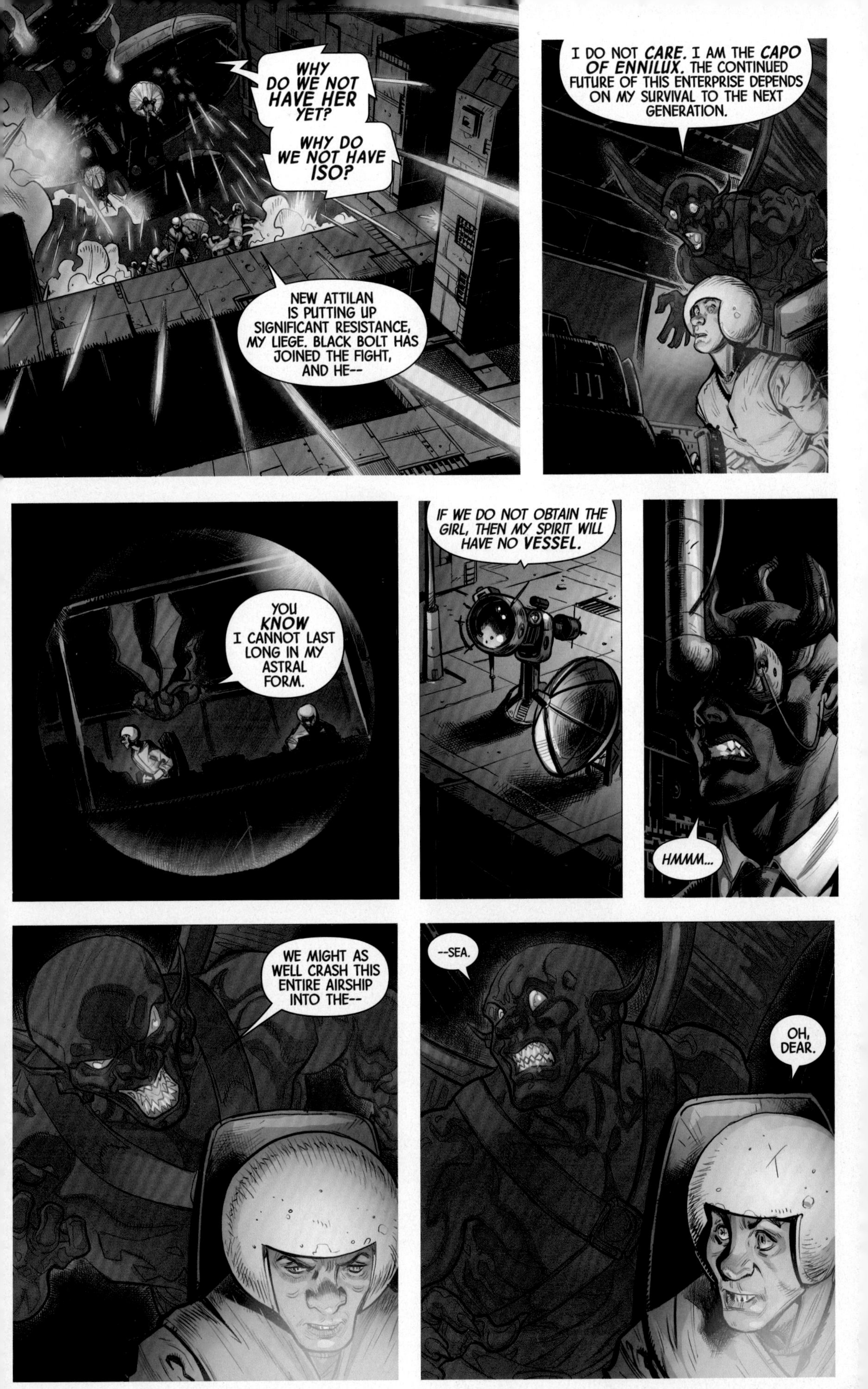
WHY DO WE NOT HAVE HER YET?
WHY DO WE NOT HAVE ISO?
NEW ATTILAN IS PUTTING UP SIGNIFICANT RESISTANCE, MY LIEGE. BLACK BOLT HAS JOINED THE FIGHT, AND HE--
I DO NOT CARE. I AM THE CAPO OF ENNILUX. THE CONTINUED FUTURE OF THIS ENTERPRISE DEPENDS ON MY SURVIVAL TO THE NEXT GENERATION.
YOU KNOW I CANNOT LAST LONG IN MY ASTRAL FORM.
IF WE DO NOT OBTAIN THE GIRL, THEN MY SPIRIT WILL HAVE NO VESSEL.
HMMM...
WE MIGHT AS WELL CRASH THIS ENTIRE AIRSHIP INTO THE--
--SEA.
OH, DEAR.

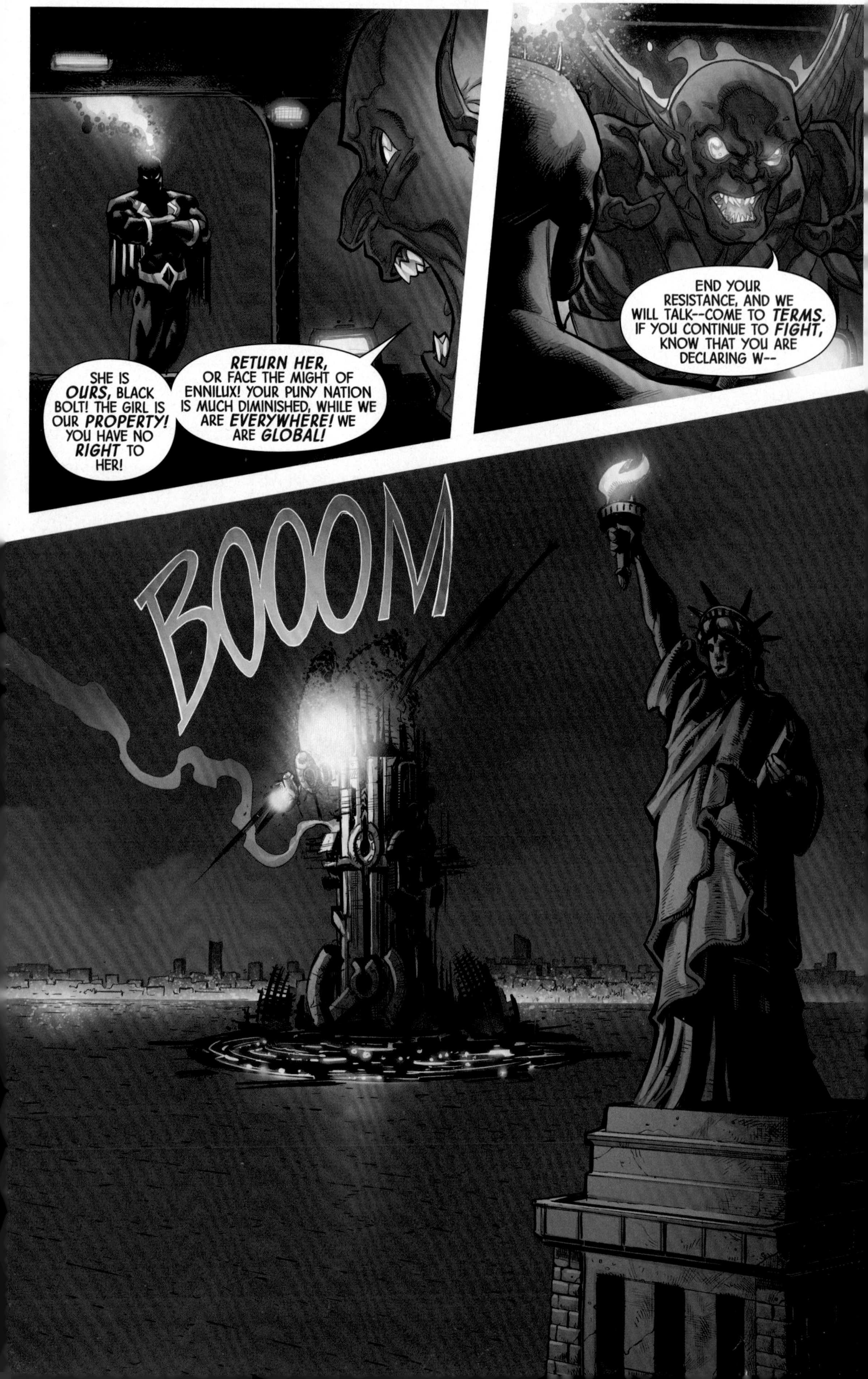
SHE IS OURS, BLACK BOLT! THE GIRL IS OUR PROPERTY! YOU HAVE NO RIGHT TO HER!
RETURN HER, OR FACE THE MIGHT OF ENNILUX! YOUR PUNY NATION IS MUCH DIMINISHED, WHILE WE ARE EVERYWHERE! WE ARE GLOBAL!
END YOUR RESISTANCE, AND WE WILL TALK--COME TO TERMS. IF YOU CONTINUE TO FIGHT, KNOW THAT YOU ARE DECLARING W--
BOOOM

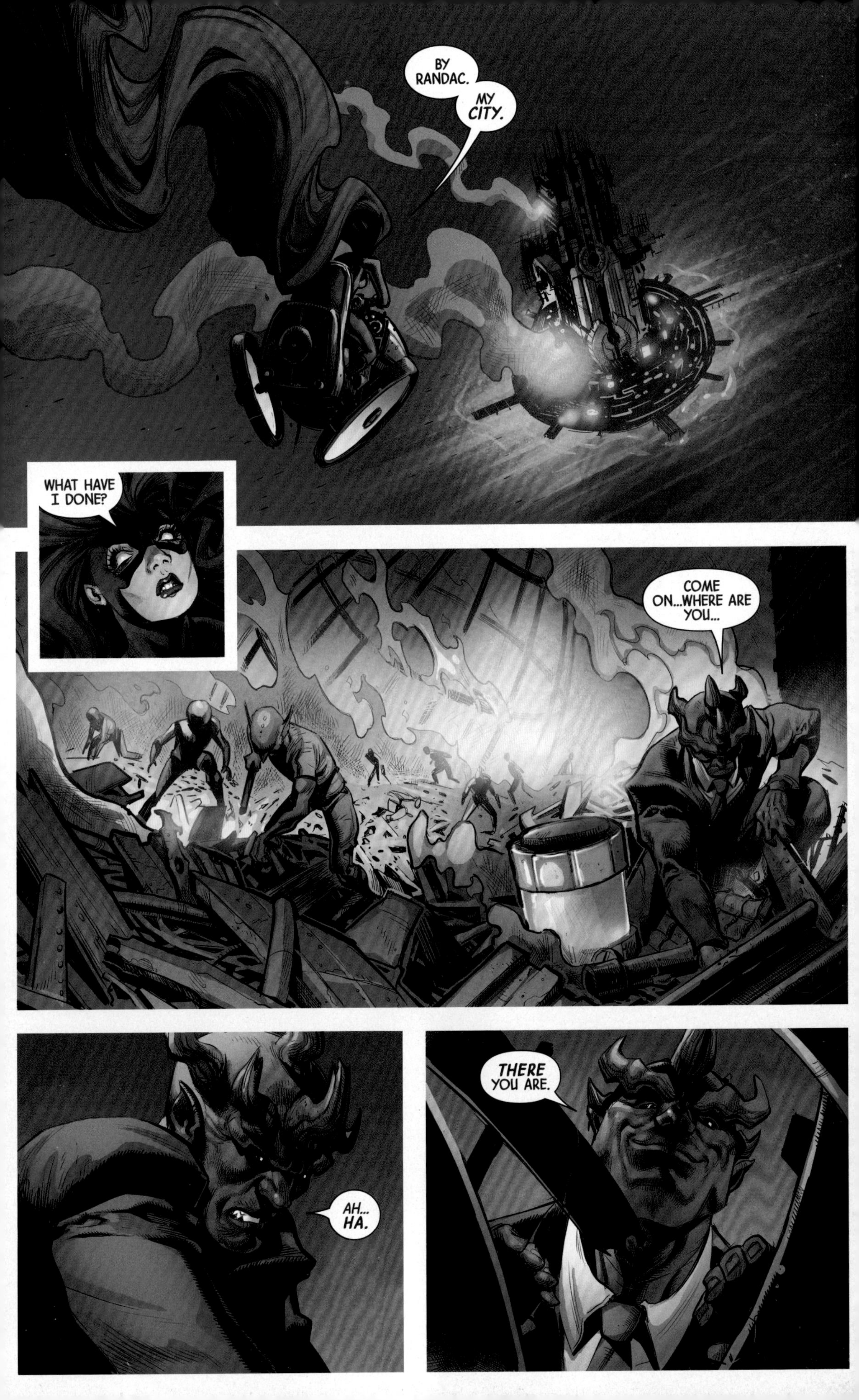
BY RANDAC.
MY CITY.
WHAT HAVE I DONE?
COME ON...WHERE ARE YOU...
AH... HA.
THERE YOU ARE.

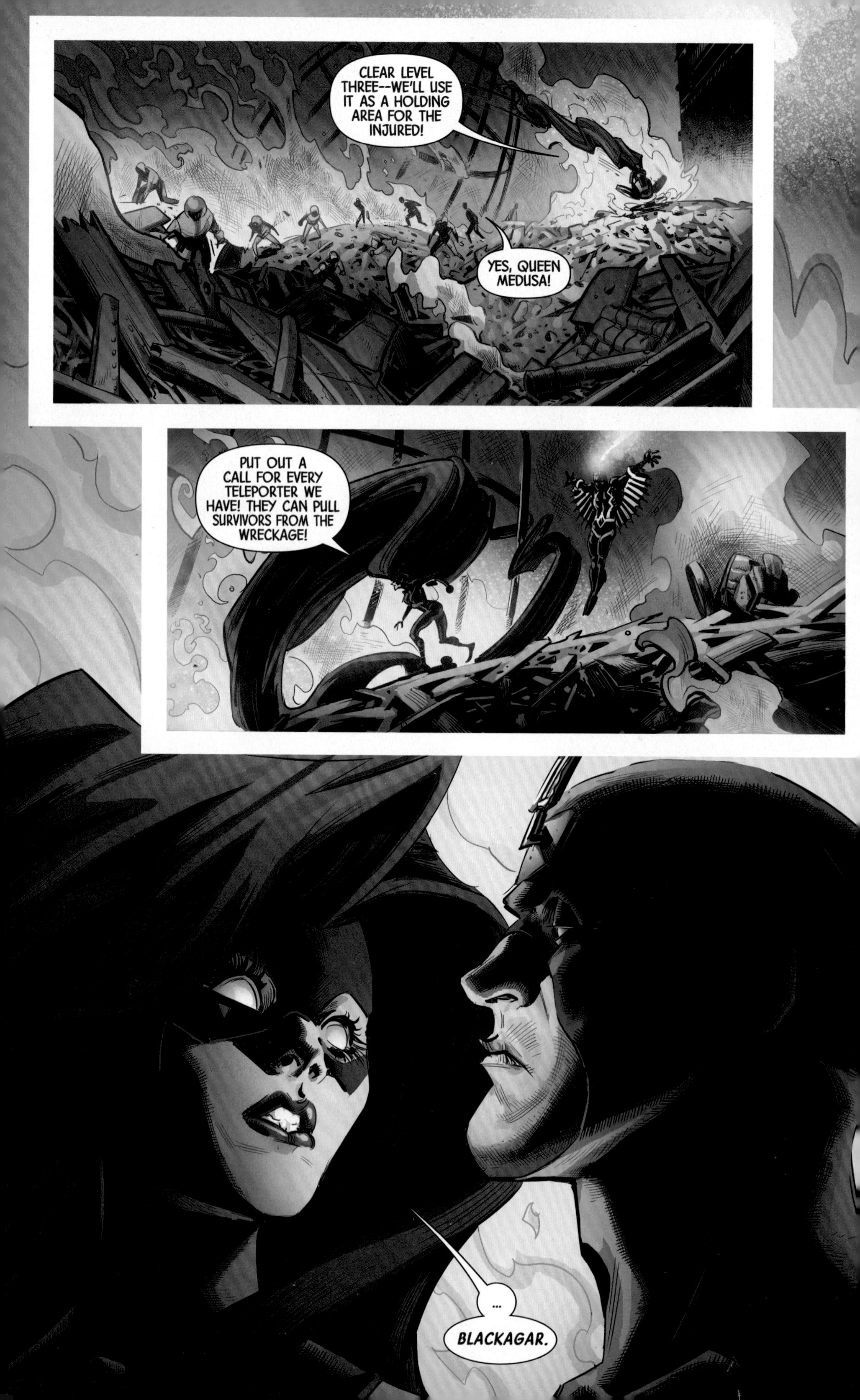
CLEAR LEVEL THREE--WE'LL USE IT AS A HOLDING AREA FOR THE INJURED!
YES, QUEEN MEDUSA!
PUT OUT A CALL FOR EVERY TELEPORTER WE HAVE! THEY CAN PULL SURVIVORS FROM THE WRECKAGE!
...
BLACKAGAR.

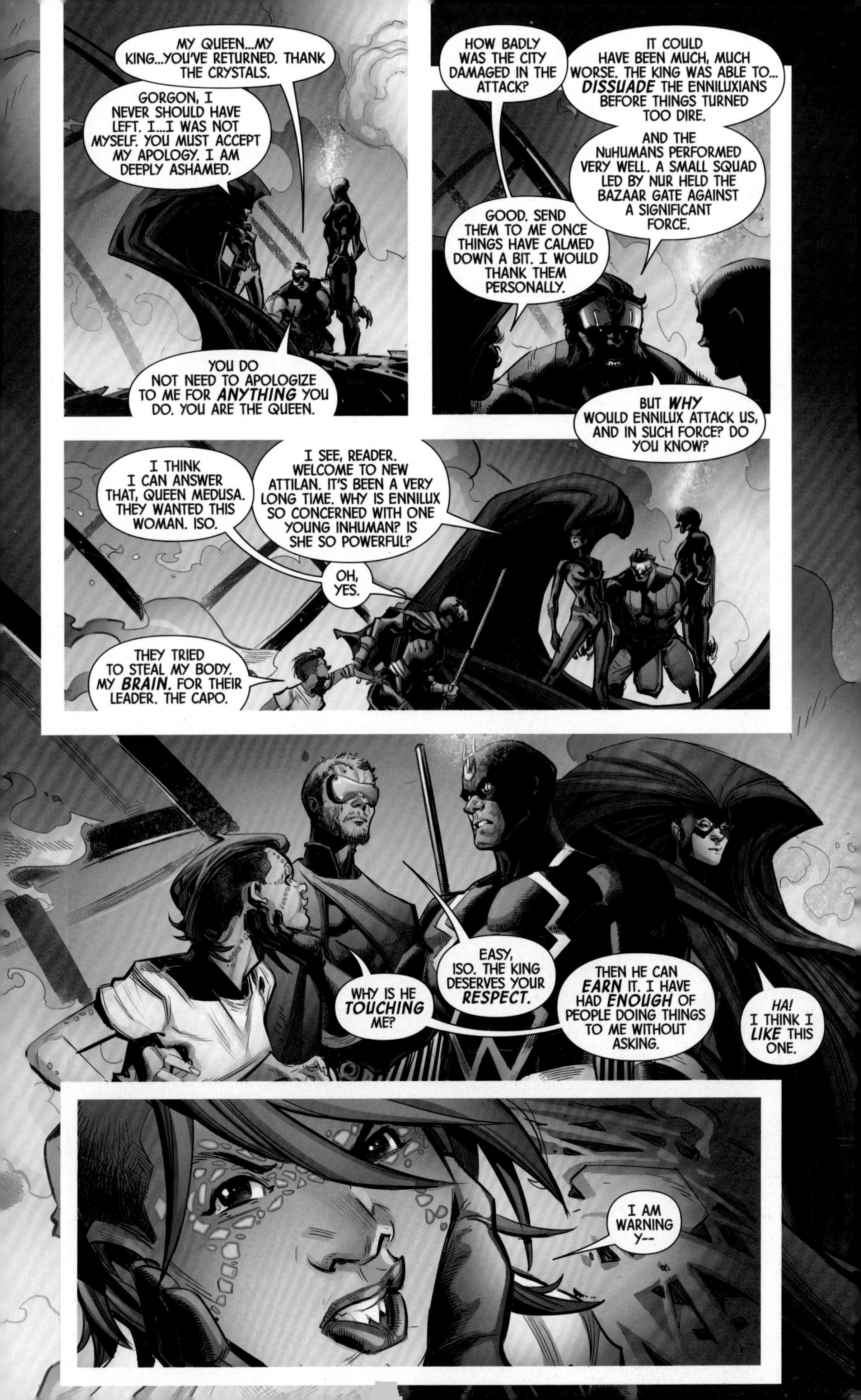
MY QUEEN...MY KING...YOU'VE RETURNED. THANK THE CRYSTALS.
GORGON, I NEVER SHOULD HAVE LEFT. I...I WAS NOT MYSELF. YOU MUST ACCEPT MY APOLOGY. I AM DEEPLY ASHAMED.
YOU DO NOT NEED TO APOLOGIZE TO ME FOR ANYTHING YOU DO. YOU ARE THE QUEEN.
HOW BADLY WAS THE CITY DAMAGED IN THE ATTACK?
IT COULD HAVE BEEN MUCH, MUCH WORSE. THE KING WAS ABLE TO... DISSUADE THE ENNILUXIANS BEFORE THINGS TURNED TOO DIRE.
AND THE NUHUMANS PERFORMED VERY WELL. A SMALL SQUAD LED BY NUR HELD THE BAZAAR GATE AGAINST A SIGNIFICANT FORCE.
GOOD. SEND THEM TO ME ONCE THINGS HAVE CALMED DOWN A BIT. I WOULD THANK THEM PERSONALLY.
BUT WHY WOULD ENNILUX ATTACK US, AND IN SUCH FORCE? DO YOU KNOW?
I THINK I CAN ANSWER THAT, QUEEN MEDUSA. THEY WANTED THIS WOMAN. ISO.
I SEE, READER. WELCOME TO NEW ATTILAN. IT'S BEEN A VERY LONG TIME. WHY IS ENNILUX SO CONCERNED WITH ONE YOUNG INHUMAN? IS SHE SO POWERFUL?
OH, YES.
THEY TRIED TO STEAL MY BODY. MY BRAIN. FOR THEIR LEADER. THE CAPO.
WHY IS HE TOUCHING ME?
EASY, ISO. THE KING DESERVES YOUR RESPECT.
THEN HE CAN EARN IT. I HAVE HAD ENOUGH OF PEOPLE DOING THINGS TO ME WITHOUT ASKING.
HA! I THINK I LIKE THIS ONE.
I AM WARNING Y--

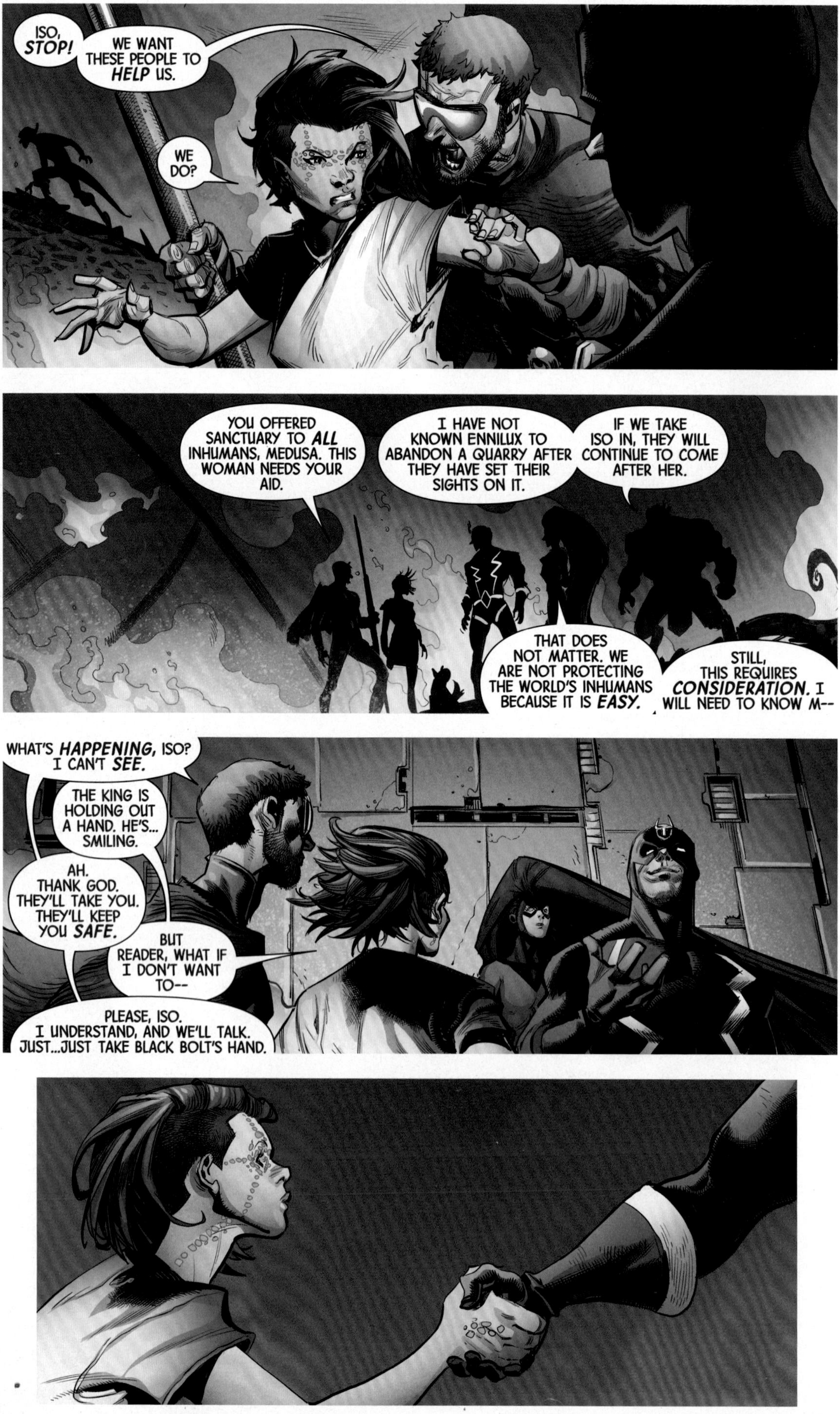
ISO, STOP!
WE WANT THESE PEOPLE TO HELP US.
WE DO?
YOU OFFERED SANCTUARY TO ALL INHUMANS, MEDUSA. THIS WOMAN NEEDS YOUR AID.
I HAVE NOT KNOWN ENNILUX TO ABANDON A QUARRY AFTER THEY HAVE SET THEIR SIGHTS ON IT.
IF WE TAKE ISO IN, THEY WILL CONTINUE TO COME AFTER HER.
THAT DOES NOT MATTER. WE ARE NOT PROTECTING THE WORLD'S INHUMANS BECAUSE IT IS EASY.
STILL, THIS REQUIRES CONSIDERATION. I WILL NEED TO KNOW M--
WHAT'S HAPPENING, ISO? I CAN'T SEE.
THE KING IS HOLDING OUT A HAND. HE'S... SMILING.
AH. THANK GOD. THEY'LL TAKE YOU. THEY'LL KEEP YOU SAFE.
BUT READER, WHAT IF I DON'T WANT TO--
PLEASE, ISO. I UNDERSTAND, AND WE'LL TALK. JUST...JUST TAKE BLACK BOLT'S HAND.

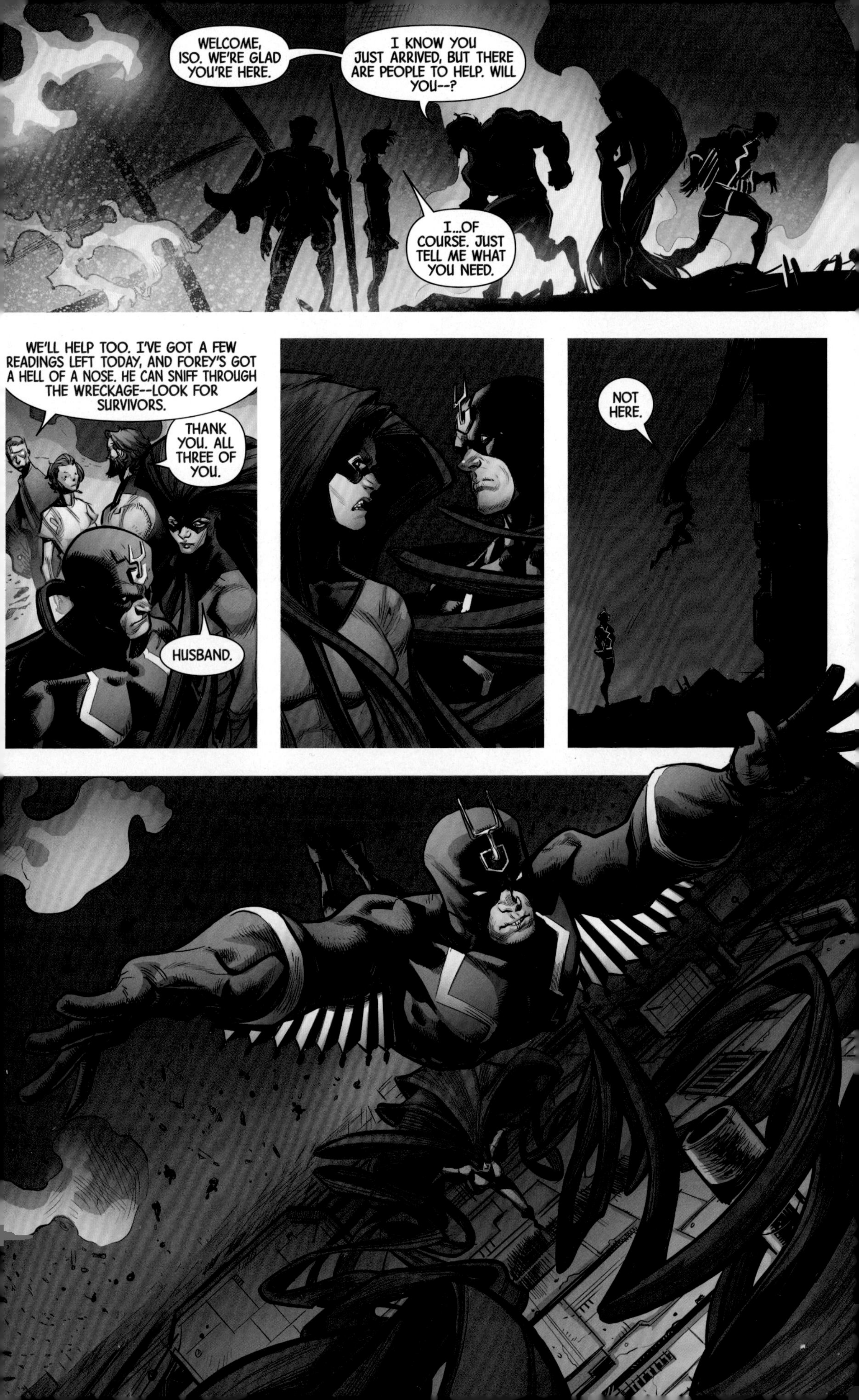
WELCOME, ISO. WE'RE GLAD YOU'RE HERE.
I KNOW YOU JUST ARRIVED, BUT THERE ARE PEOPLE TO HELP. WILL YOU--?
I...OF COURSE. JUST TELL ME WHAT YOU NEED.
WE'LL HELP TOO. I'VE GOT A FEW READINGS LEFT TODAY, AND FOREY'S GOT A HELL OF A NOSE. HE CAN SNIFF THROUGH THE WRECKAGE--LOOK FOR SURVIVORS.
THANK YOU. ALL THREE OF YOU.
HUSBAND.
NOT HERE.

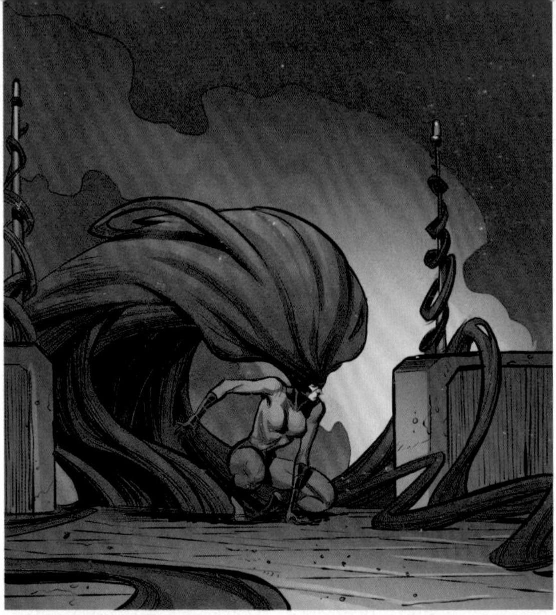

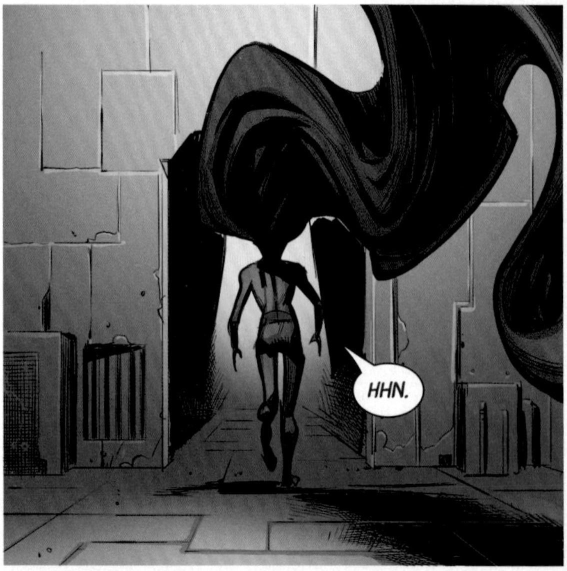
HHN.

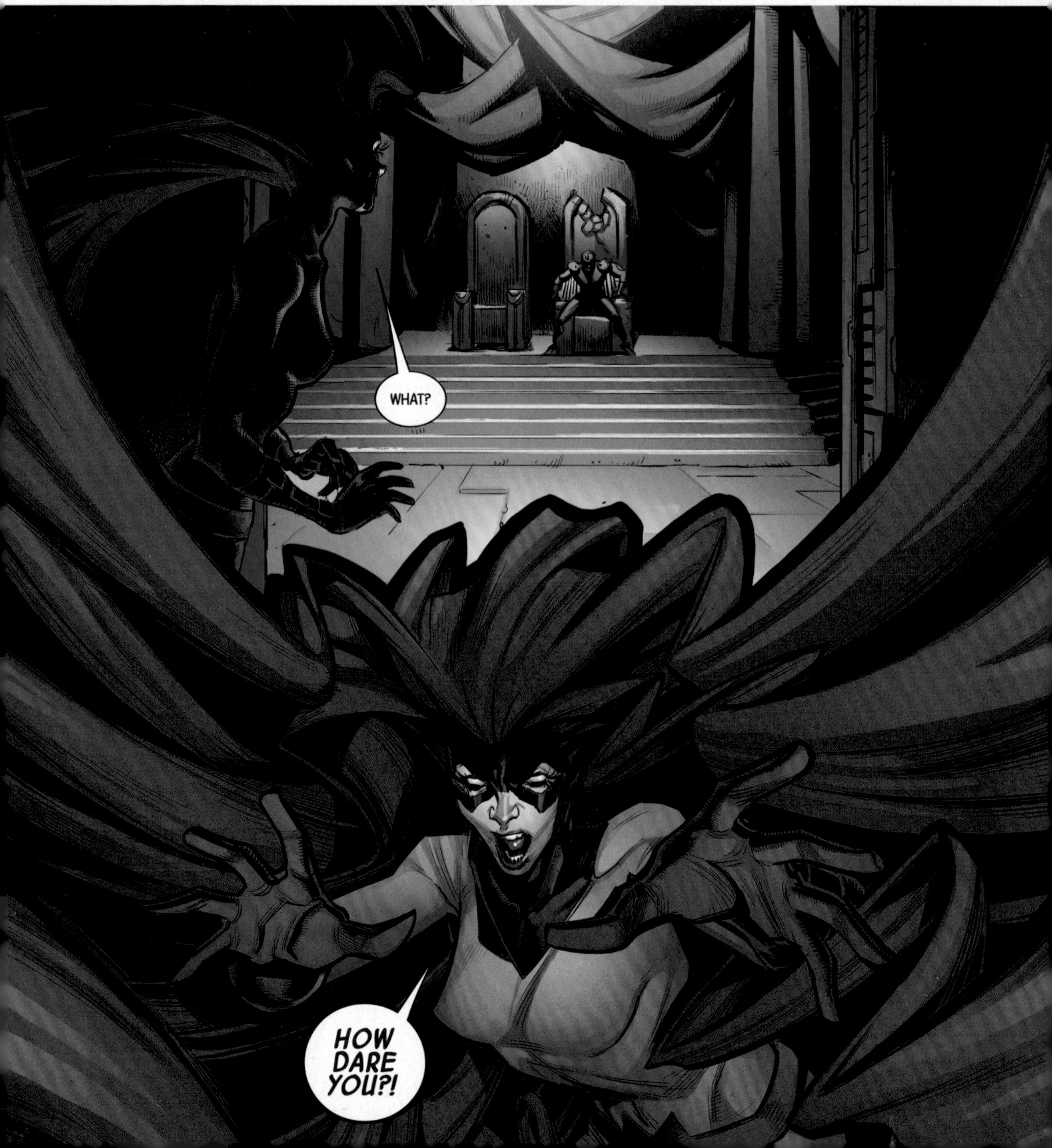
WHAT?
HOW DARE YOU?!

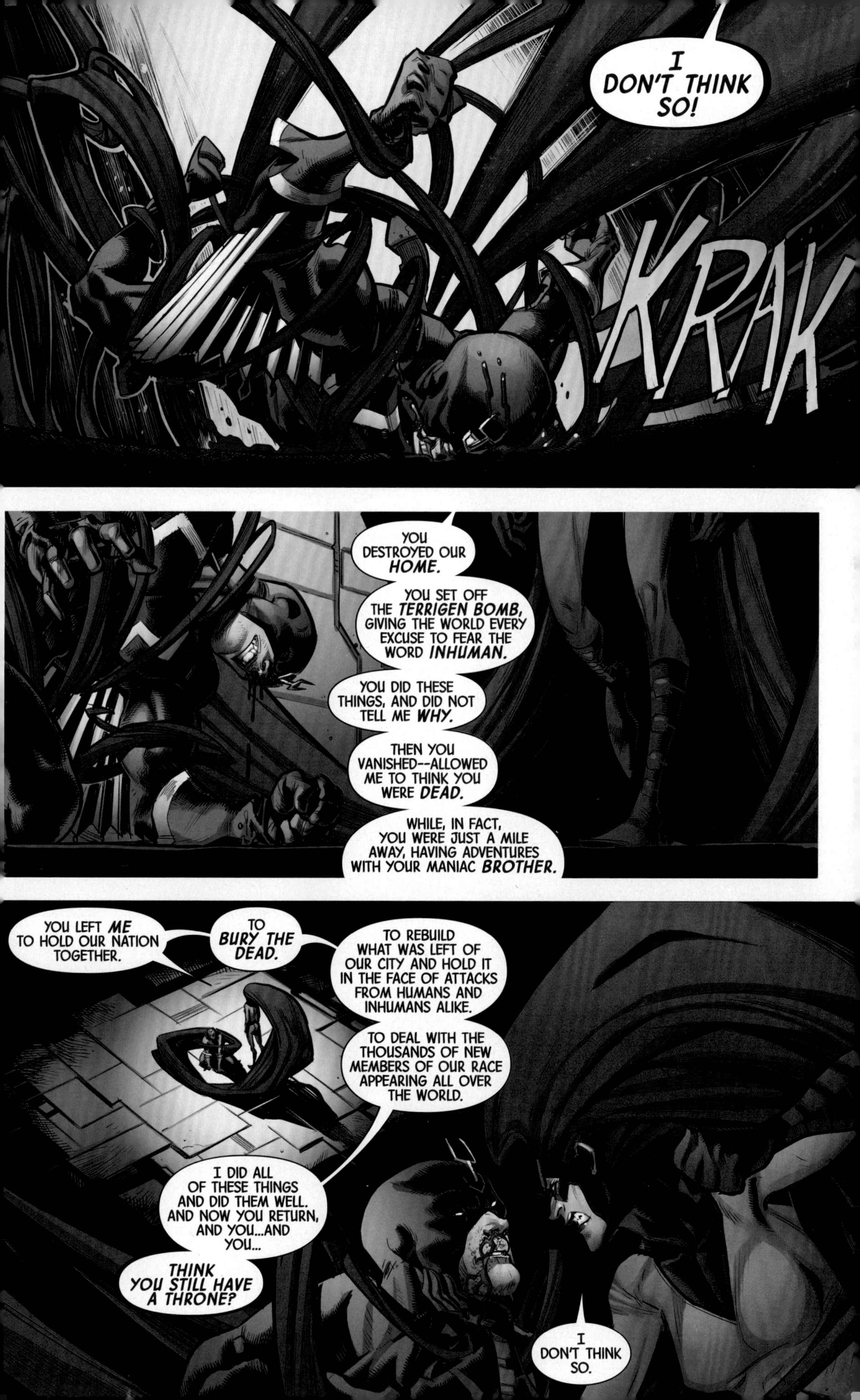
I DON'T THINK SO!
KRAK
YOU DESTROYED OUR HOME.
YOU SET OFF THE TERRIGEN BOMB, GIVING THE WORLD EVERY EXCUSE TO FEAR THE WORD INHUMAN.
YOU DID THESE THINGS, AND DID NOT TELL ME WHY.
THEN YOU VANISHED--ALLOWED ME TO THINK YOU WERE DEAD.
WHILE, IN FACT, YOU WERE JUST A MILE AWAY, HAVING ADVENTURES WITH YOUR MANIAC BROTHER.
YOU LEFT ME TO HOLD OUR NATION TOGETHER.
TO BURY THE DEAD.
TO REBUILD WHAT WAS LEFT OF OUR CITY AND HOLD IT IN THE FACE OF ATTACKS FROM HUMANS AND INHUMANS ALIKE.
TO DEAL WITH THE THOUSANDS OF NEW MEMBERS OF OUR RACE APPEARING ALL OVER THE WORLD.
I DID ALL OF THESE THINGS AND DID THEM WELL. AND NOW YOU RETURN, AND YOU...AND YOU...
THINK YOU STILL HAVE A THRONE?
I DON'T THINK SO.

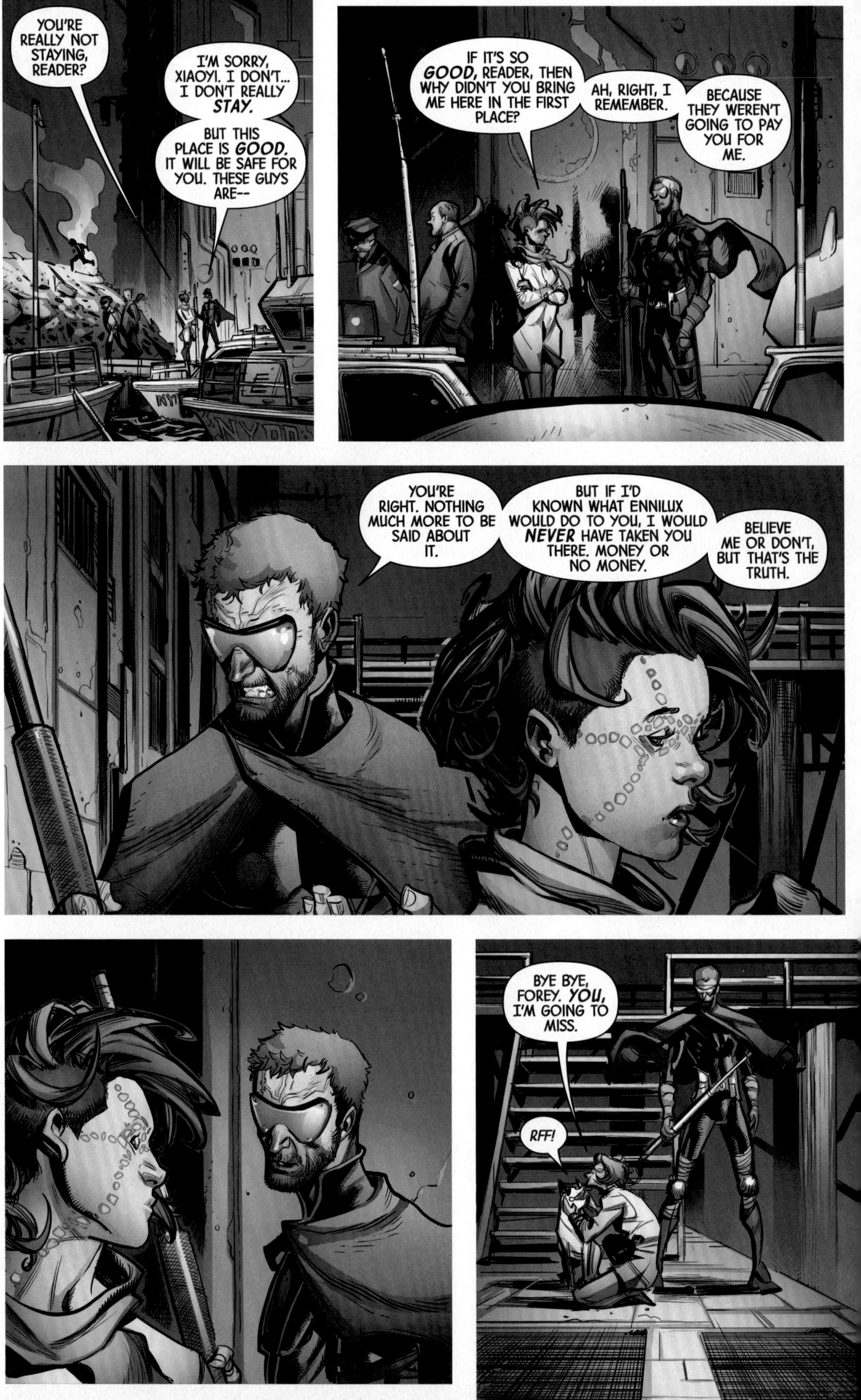
YOU'RE REALLY NOT STAYING, READER?
I'M SORRY, XIAOYI. I DON'T... I DON'T REALLY STAY.
BUT THIS PLACE IS GOOD. IT WILL BE SAFE FOR YOU. THESE GUYS ARE--
IF IT'S SO GOOD, READER, THEN WHY DIDN'T YOU BRING ME HERE IN THE FIRST PLACE?
AH, RIGHT, I REMEMBER.
BECAUSE THEY WEREN'T GOING TO PAY YOU FOR ME.
YOU'RE RIGHT. NOTHING MUCH MORE TO BE SAID ABOUT IT.
BUT IF I'D KNOWN WHAT ENNILUX WOULD DO TO YOU, I WOULD NEVER HAVE TAKEN YOU THERE. MONEY OR NO MONEY.
BELIEVE ME OR DON'T, BUT THAT'S THE TRUTH.
BYE BYE, FOREY. YOU, I'M GOING TO MISS.
RFF!

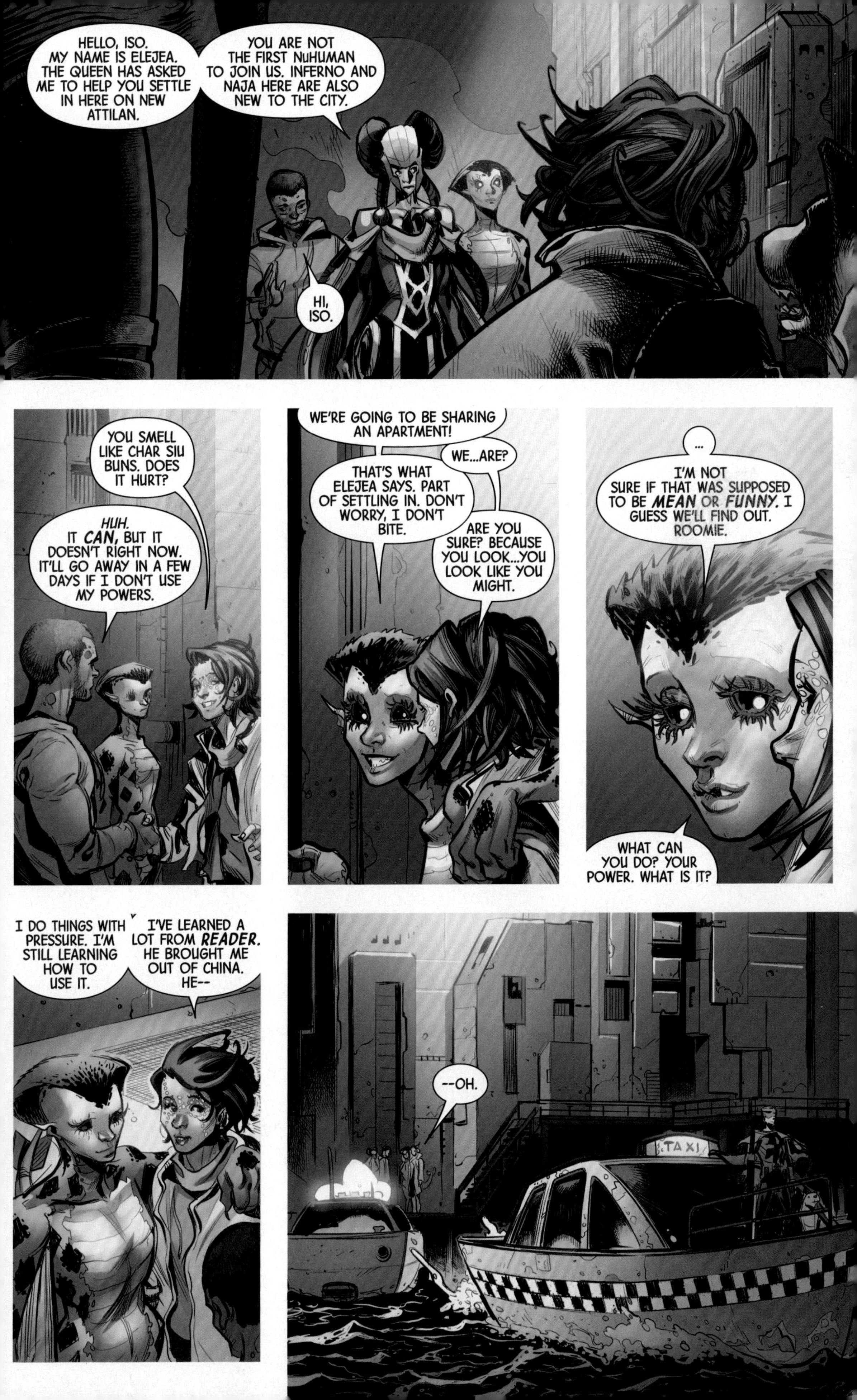
HELLO, ISO. MY NAME IS ELEJEA. THE QUEEN HAS ASKED ME TO HELP YOU SETTLE IN HERE ON NEW ATTILAN.
YOU ARE NOT THE FIRST NuHUMAN TO JOIN US. INFERNO AND NAJA HERE ARE ALSO NEW TO THE CITY.
HI, ISO.
YOU SMELL LIKE CHAR SIU BUNS. DOES IT HURT?
HUH. IT CAN, BUT IT DOESN'T RIGHT NOW. IT'LL GO AWAY IN A FEW DAYS IF I DON'T USE MY POWERS.
WE'RE GOING TO BE SHARING AN APARTMENT!
WE...ARE?
THAT'S WHAT ELEJEA SAYS. PART OF SETTLING IN. DON'T WORRY, I DON'T BITE.
ARE YOU SURE? BECAUSE YOU LOOK...YOU LOOK LIKE YOU MIGHT.
...
I'M NOT SURE IF THAT WAS SUPPOSED TO BE MEAN OR FUNNY. I GUESS WE'LL FIND OUT. ROOMIE.
WHAT CAN YOU DO? YOUR POWER. WHAT IS IT?
I DO THINGS WITH PRESSURE. I'M STILL LEARNING HOW TO USE IT.
I'VE LEARNED A LOT FROM READER. HE BROUGHT ME OUT OF CHINA. HE--
--OH.
TAXI

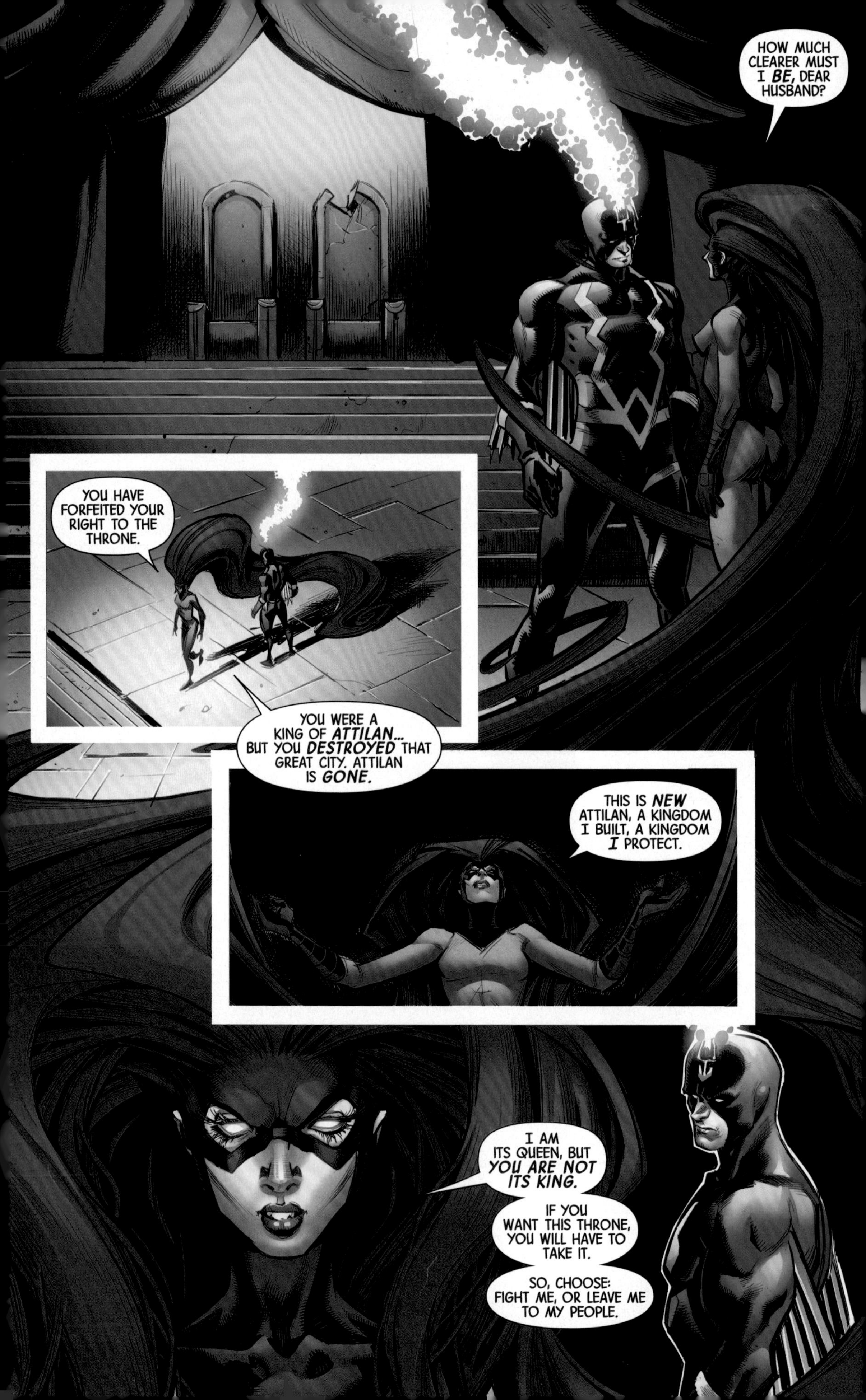
HOW MUCH CLEARER MUST I BE, DEAR HUSBAND?
YOU HAVE FORFEITED YOUR RIGHT TO THE THRONE.
YOU WERE A KING OF ATTILAN... BUT YOU DESTROYED THAT GREAT CITY. ATTILAN IS GONE.
THIS IS NEW ATTILAN, A KINGDOM I BUILT, A KINGDOM I PROTECT.
I AM ITS QUEEN, BUT YOU ARE NOT ITS KING.
IF YOU WANT THIS THRONE, YOU WILL HAVE TO TAKE IT.
SO, CHOOSE: FIGHT ME, OR LEAVE ME TO MY PEOPLE.

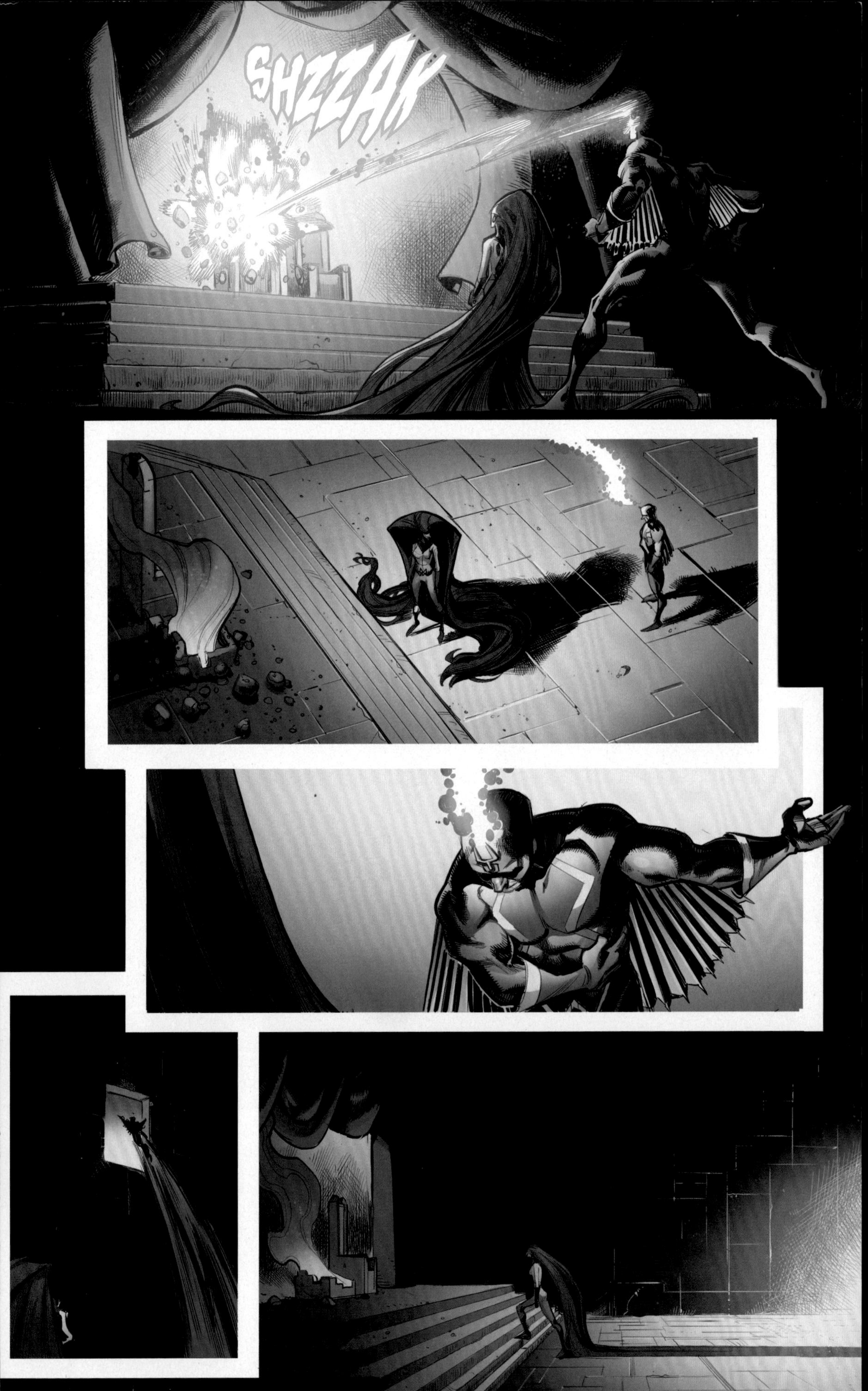
SHZZAK

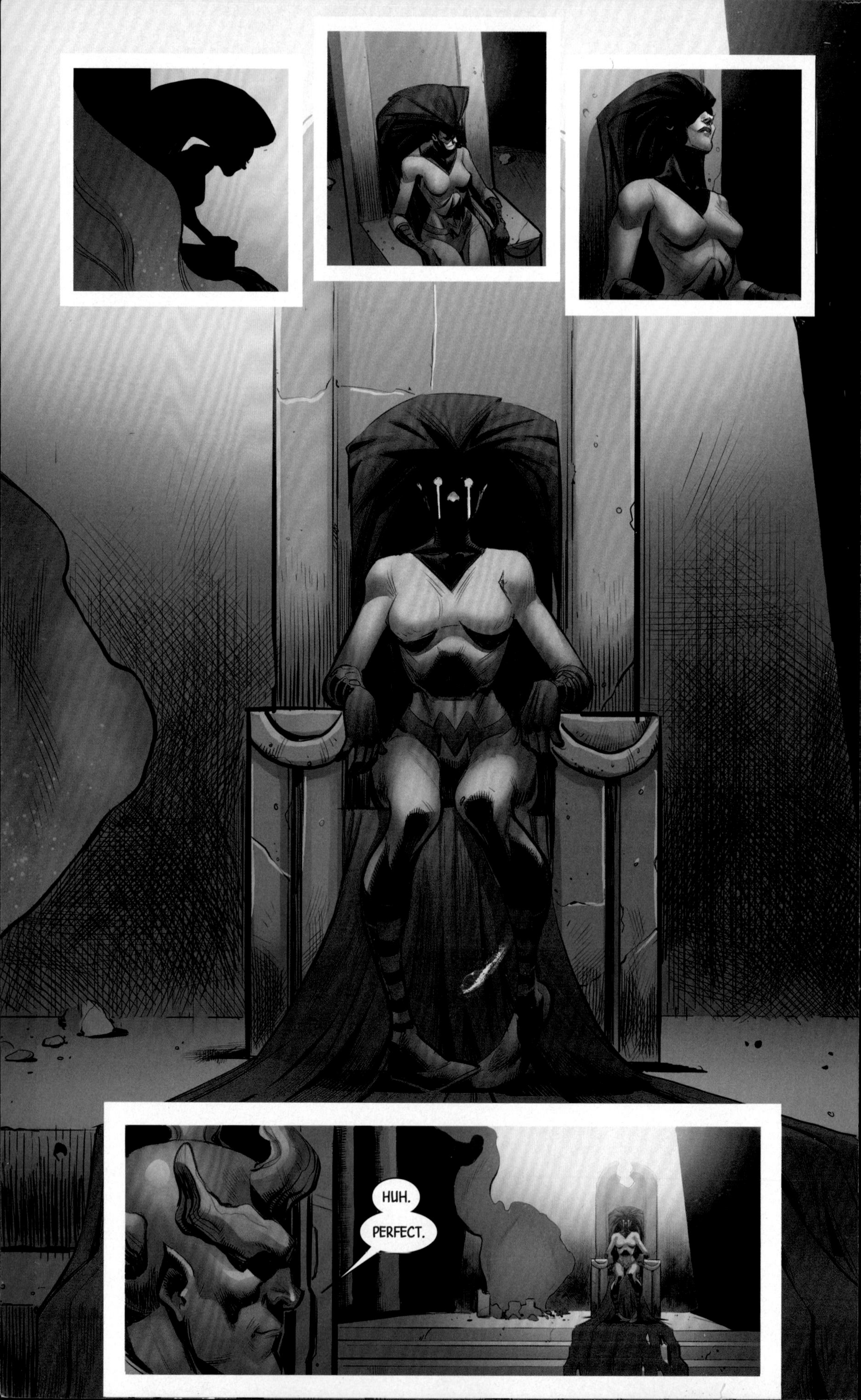
HUH.
PERFECT.

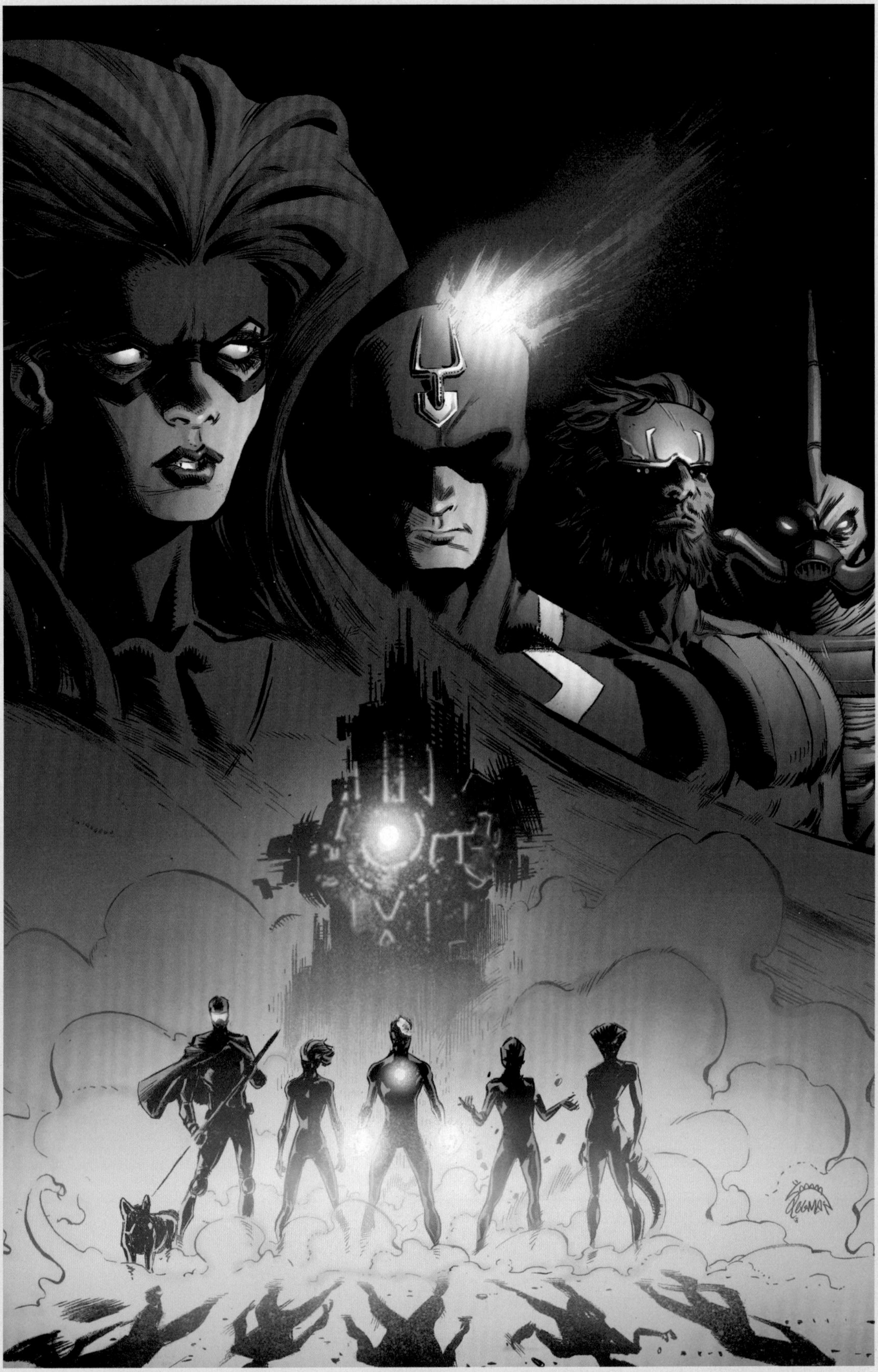

PART THIRTEEN: LINEAGE 13

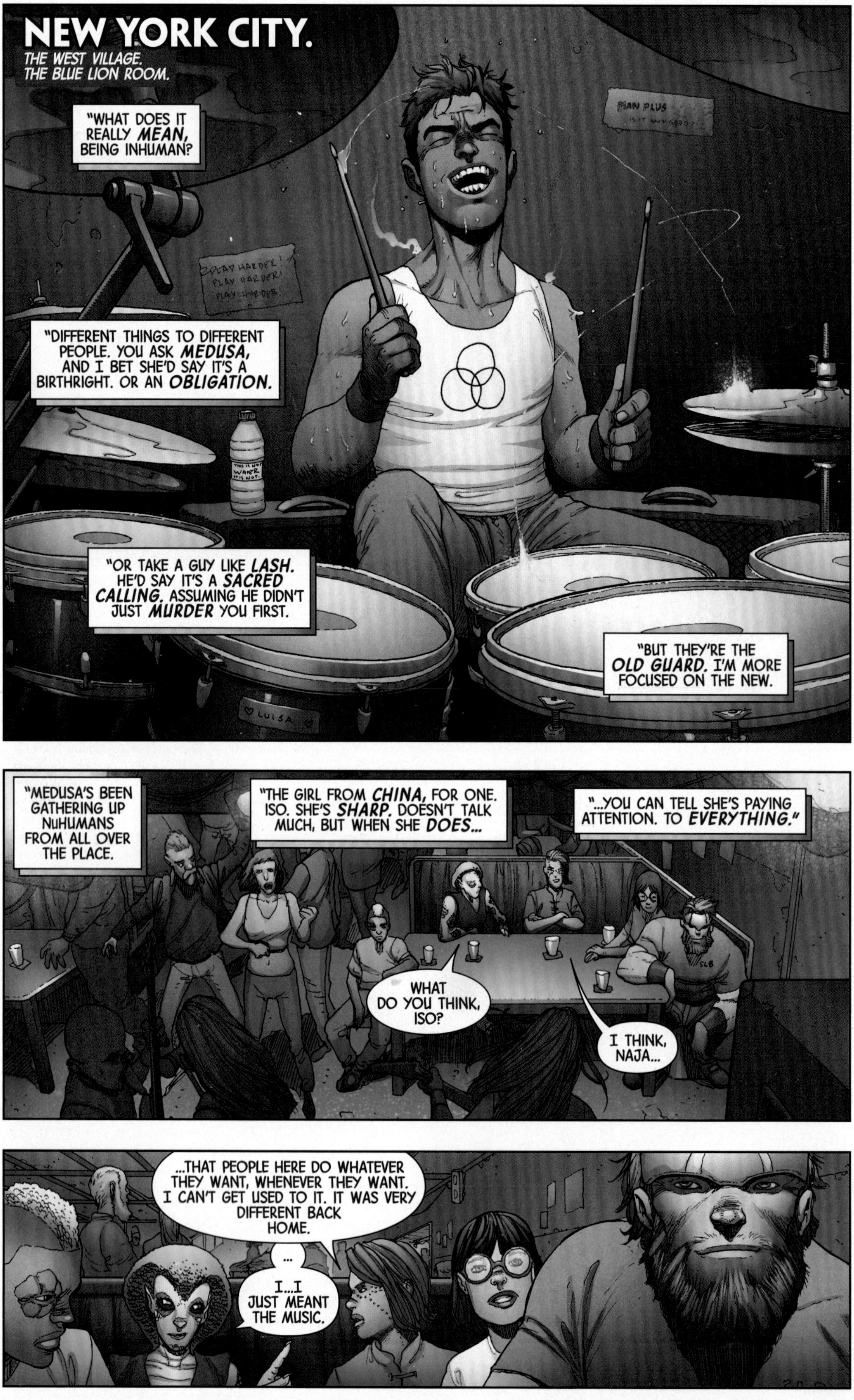
NEW YORK CITY.
THE WEST VILLAGE.
THE BLUE LION ROOM.
"WHAT DOES IT REALLY MEAN, BEING INHUMAN?
PLAY HARDER! PLAY HARDER! PLAY HARDER!
"DIFFERENT THINGS TO DIFFERENT PEOPLE. YOU ASK MEDUSA, AND I BET SHE'D SAY IT'S A BIRTHRIGHT. OR AN OBLIGATION.
"OR TAKE A GUY LIKE LASH. HE'D SAY IT'S A SACRED CALLING. ASSUMING HE DIDN'T JUST MURDER YOU FIRST.
"BUT THEY'RE THE OLD GUARD. I'M MORE FOCUSED ON THE NEW.
LUISA
"MEDUSA'S BEEN GATHERING UP NuHUMANS FROM ALL OVER THE PLACE.
"THE GIRL FROM CHINA, FOR ONE. ISO. SHE'S SHARP. DOESN'T TALK MUCH, BUT WHEN SHE DOES...
"...YOU CAN TELL SHE'S PAYING ATTENTION. TO EVERYTHING."
WHAT DO YOU THINK, ISO?
I THINK, NAJA...
...THAT PEOPLE HERE DO WHATEVER THEY WANT, WHENEVER THEY WANT. I CAN'T GET USED TO IT. IT WAS VERY DIFFERENT BACK HOME.
...
I...I JUST MEANT THE MUSIC.

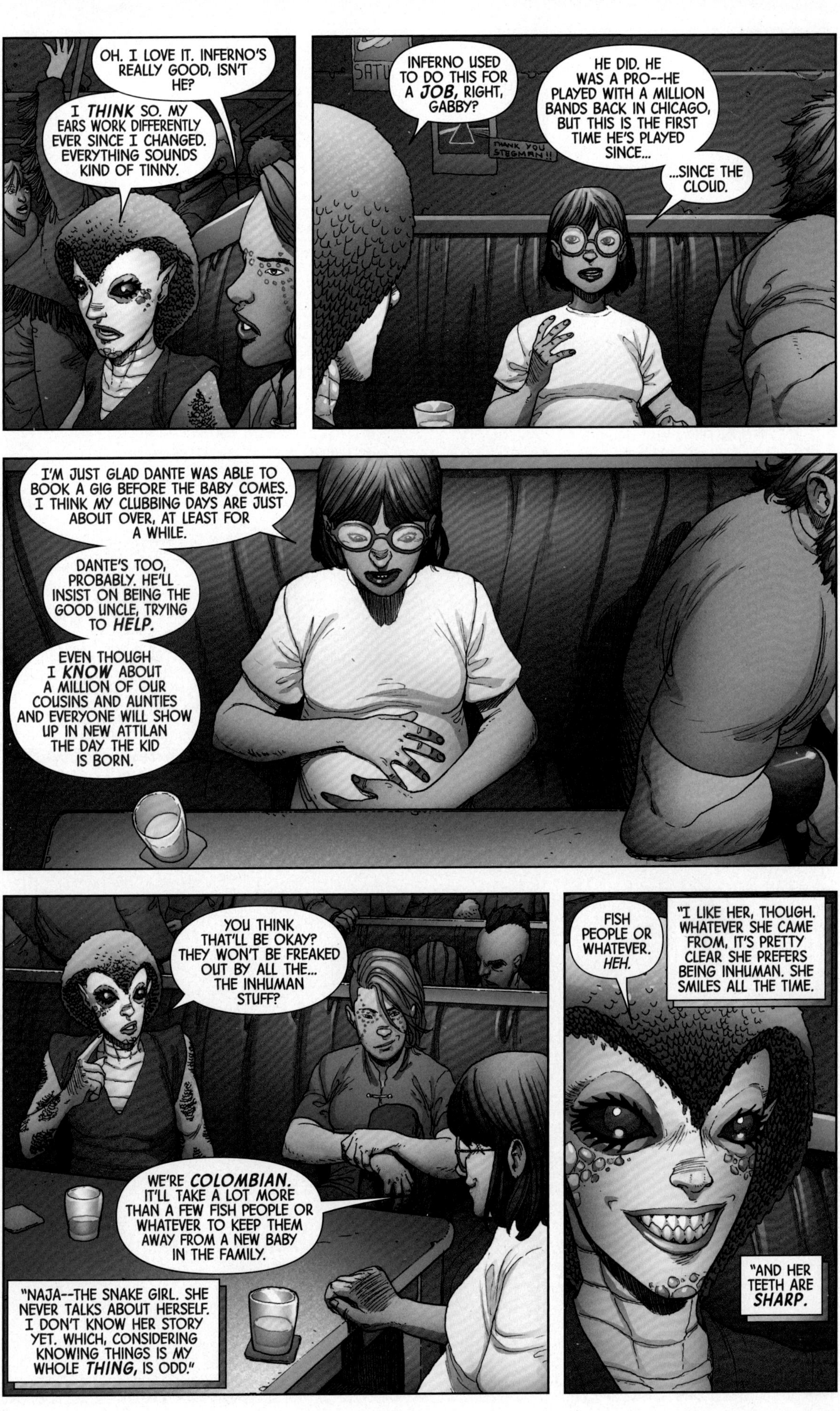

OH. I LOVE IT. INFERNO'S REALLY GOOD, ISN'T HE?
I THINK SO. MY EARS WORK DIFFERENTLY EVER SINCE I CHANGED. EVERYTHING SOUNDS KIND OF TINNY.
SATU
THANK YOU STEGMAN!!
INFERNO USED TO DO THIS FOR A JOB, RIGHT, GABBY?
HE DID. HE WAS A PRO--HE PLAYED WITH A MILLION BANDS BACK IN CHICAGO, BUT THIS IS THE FIRST TIME HE'S PLAYED SINCE...
...SINCE THE CLOUD.
I'M JUST GLAD DANTE WAS ABLE TO BOOK A GIG BEFORE THE BABY COMES. I THINK MY CLUBBING DAYS ARE JUST ABOUT OVER, AT LEAST FOR A WHILE.
DANTE'S TOO, PROBABLY. HE'LL INSIST ON BEING THE GOOD UNCLE, TRYING TO HELP.
EVEN THOUGH I KNOW ABOUT A MILLION OF OUR COUSINS AND AUNTIES AND EVERYONE WILL SHOW UP IN NEW ATTILAN THE DAY THE KID IS BORN.
YOU THINK THAT'LL BE OKAY? THEY WON'T BE FREAKED OUT BY ALL THE... THE INHUMAN STUFF?
WE'RE COLOMBIAN. IT'LL TAKE A LOT MORE THAN A FEW FISH PEOPLE OR WHATEVER TO KEEP THEM AWAY FROM A NEW BABY IN THE FAMILY.
"NAJA--THE SNAKE GIRL. SHE NEVER TALKS ABOUT HERSELF. I DON'T KNOW HER STORY YET. WHICH, CONSIDERING KNOWING THINGS IS MY WHOLE THING, IS ODD."
FISH PEOPLE OR WHATEVER. HEH.
"I LIKE HER, THOUGH. WHATEVER SHE CAME FROM, IT'S PRETTY CLEAR SHE PREFERS BEING INHUMAN. SHE SMILES ALL THE TIME.
"AND HER TEETH ARE SHARP.

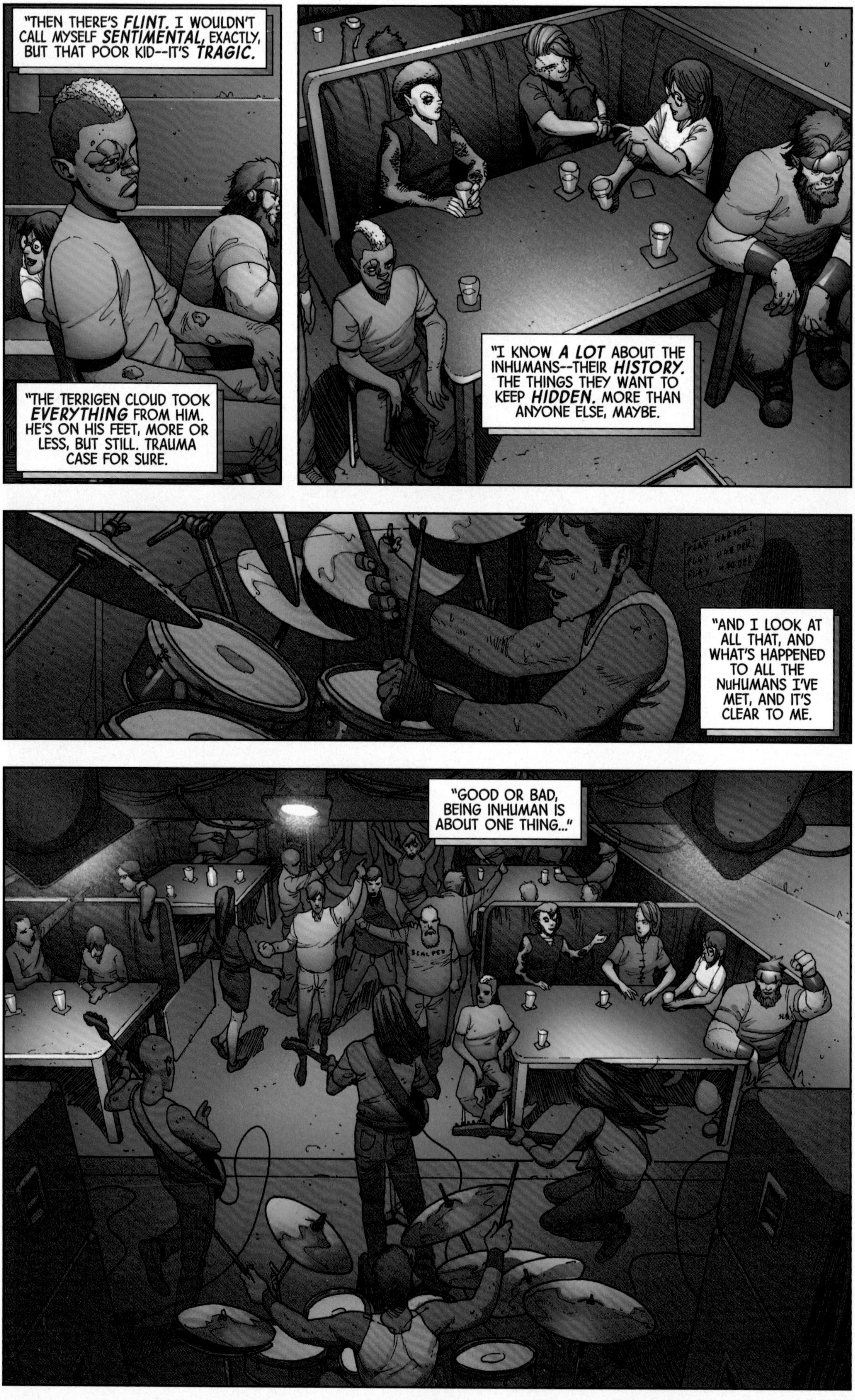
"THEN THERE'S FLINT. I WOULDN'T CALL MYSELF SENTIMENTAL, EXACTLY, BUT THAT POOR KID--IT'S TRAGIC.
"THE TERRIGEN CLOUD TOOK EVERYTHING FROM HIM. HE'S ON HIS FEET, MORE OR LESS, BUT STILL. TRAUMA CASE FOR SURE.
"I KNOW A LOT ABOUT THE INHUMANS--THEIR HISTORY. THE THINGS THEY WANT TO KEEP HIDDEN. MORE THAN ANYONE ELSE, MAYBE.
"AND I LOOK AT ALL THAT, AND WHAT'S HAPPENED TO ALL THE NuHUMANS I'VE MET, AND IT'S CLEAR TO ME.
"GOOD OR BAD, BEING INHUMAN IS ABOUT ONE THING..."

NEW ATTILAN.

...CHANGE.

BUT I BET YOU KNOW THAT MORE THAN MOST, *EH, ELDRAC?*

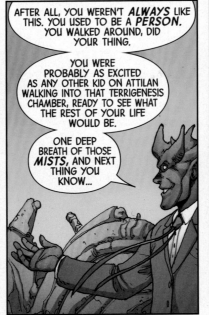

AFTER ALL, YOU WEREN'T *ALWAYS* LIKE THIS. YOU USED TO BE A *PERSON.* YOU WALKED AROUND, DID YOUR THING.

YOU WERE PROBABLY AS EXCITED AS ANY OTHER KID ON ATTILAN WALKING INTO THAT TERRIGENESIS CHAMBER, READY TO SEE WHAT THE REST OF YOUR LIFE WOULD BE.

ONE DEEP BREATH OF THOSE *MISTS,* AND NEXT THING YOU KNOW...

...YOU'RE ARCHITECTURE.

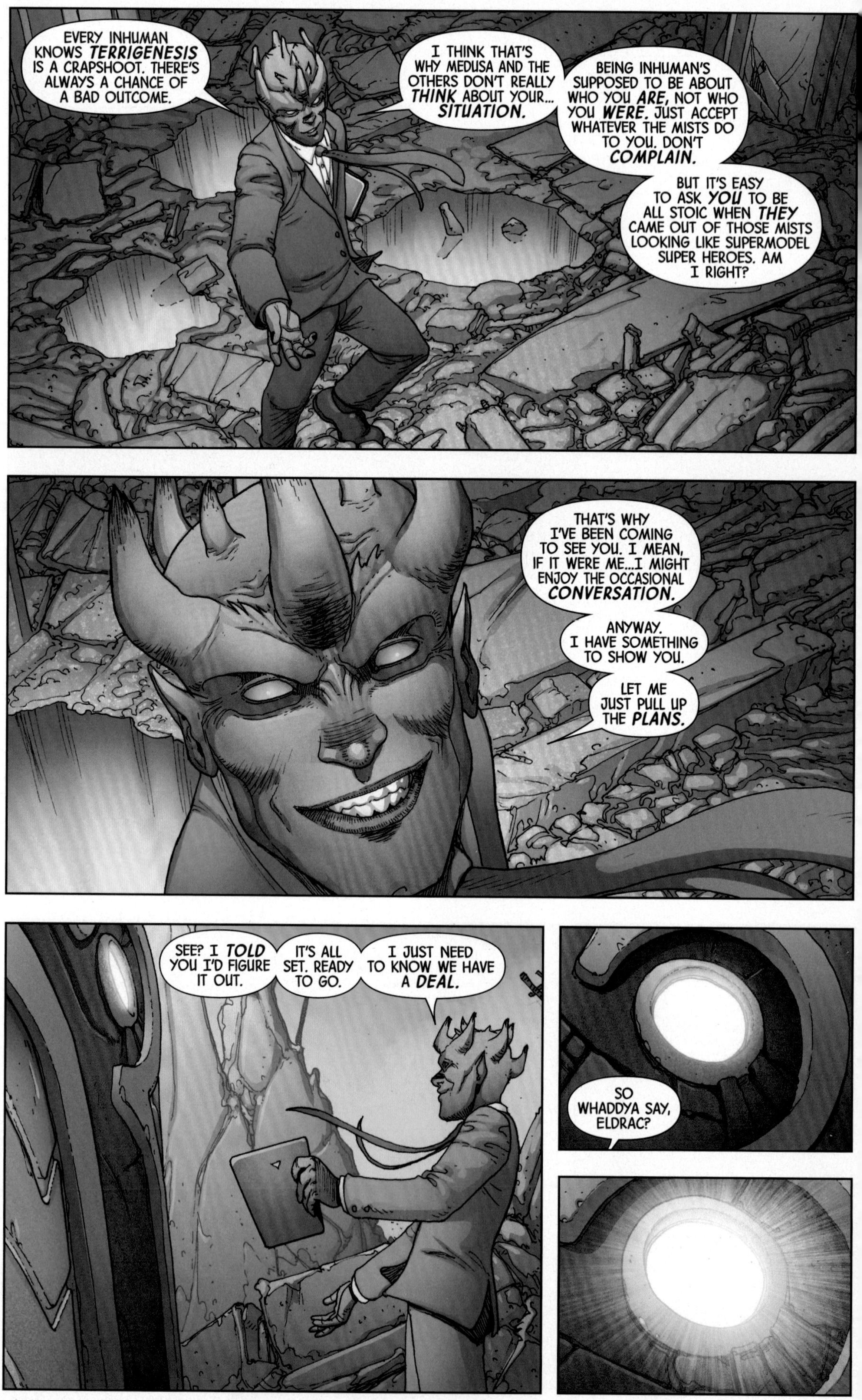
EVERY INHUMAN KNOWS TERRIGENESIS IS A CRAPSHOOT. THERE'S ALWAYS A CHANCE OF A BAD OUTCOME.
I THINK THAT'S WHY MEDUSA AND THE OTHERS DON'T REALLY THINK ABOUT YOUR... SITUATION.
BEING INHUMAN'S SUPPOSED TO BE ABOUT WHO YOU ARE, NOT WHO YOU WERE. JUST ACCEPT WHATEVER THE MISTS DO TO YOU. DON'T COMPLAIN.
BUT IT'S EASY TO ASK YOU TO BE ALL STOIC WHEN THEY CAME OUT OF THOSE MISTS LOOKING LIKE SUPERMODEL SUPER HEROES. AM I RIGHT?
THAT'S WHY I'VE BEEN COMING TO SEE YOU. I MEAN, IF IT WERE ME...I MIGHT ENJOY THE OCCASIONAL CONVERSATION.
ANYWAY. I HAVE SOMETHING TO SHOW YOU.
LET ME JUST PULL UP THE PLANS.
SEE? I TOLD YOU I'D FIGURE IT OUT.
IT'S ALL SET. READY TO GO.
I JUST NEED TO KNOW WE HAVE A DEAL.
SO WHADDYA SAY, ELDRAC?

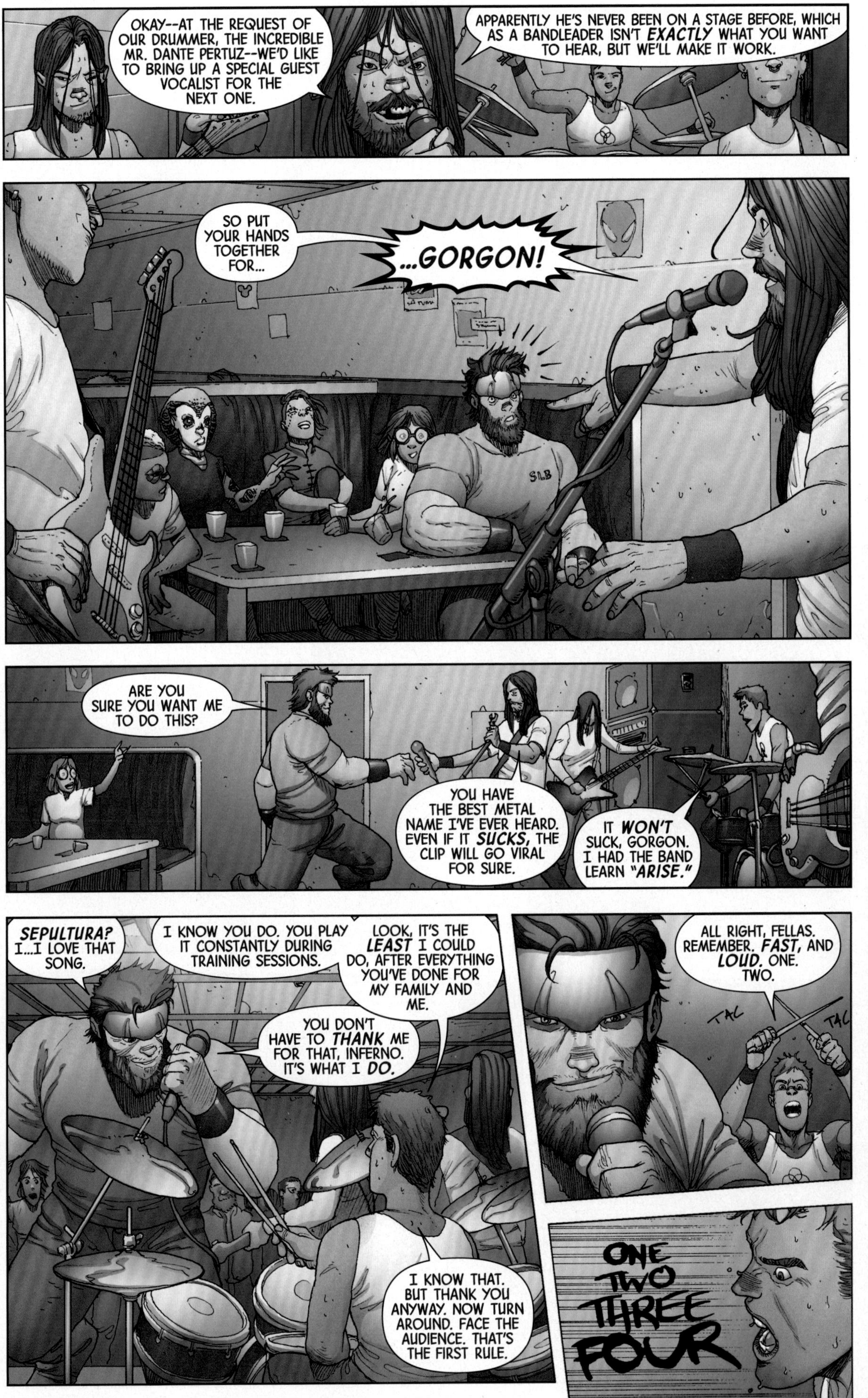
OKAY--AT THE REQUEST OF OUR DRUMMER, THE INCREDIBLE MR. DANTE PERTUZ--WE'D LIKE TO BRING UP A SPECIAL GUEST VOCALIST FOR THE NEXT ONE.
APPARENTLY HE'S NEVER BEEN ON A STAGE BEFORE, WHICH AS A BANDLEADER ISN'T EXACTLY WHAT YOU WANT TO HEAR, BUT WE'LL MAKE IT WORK.
SO PUT YOUR HANDS TOGETHER FOR...
...GORGON!
ARE YOU SURE YOU WANT ME TO DO THIS?
YOU HAVE THE BEST METAL NAME I'VE EVER HEARD. EVEN IF IT SUCKS, THE CLIP WILL GO VIRAL FOR SURE.
IT WON'T SUCK, GORGON. I HAD THE BAND LEARN "ARISE."
SEPULTURA? I...I LOVE THAT SONG.
I KNOW YOU DO. YOU PLAY IT CONSTANTLY DURING TRAINING SESSIONS.
LOOK, IT'S THE LEAST I COULD DO, AFTER EVERYTHING YOU'VE DONE FOR MY FAMILY AND ME.
YOU DON'T HAVE TO THANK ME FOR THAT, INFERNO. IT'S WHAT I DO.
I KNOW THAT. BUT THANK YOU ANYWAY. NOW TURN AROUND. FACE THE AUDIENCE. THAT'S THE FIRST RULE.
ALL RIGHT, FELLAS. REMEMBER. FAST, AND LOUD. ONE. TWO.
TAC
TAC
ONE
TWO
THREE
FOUR

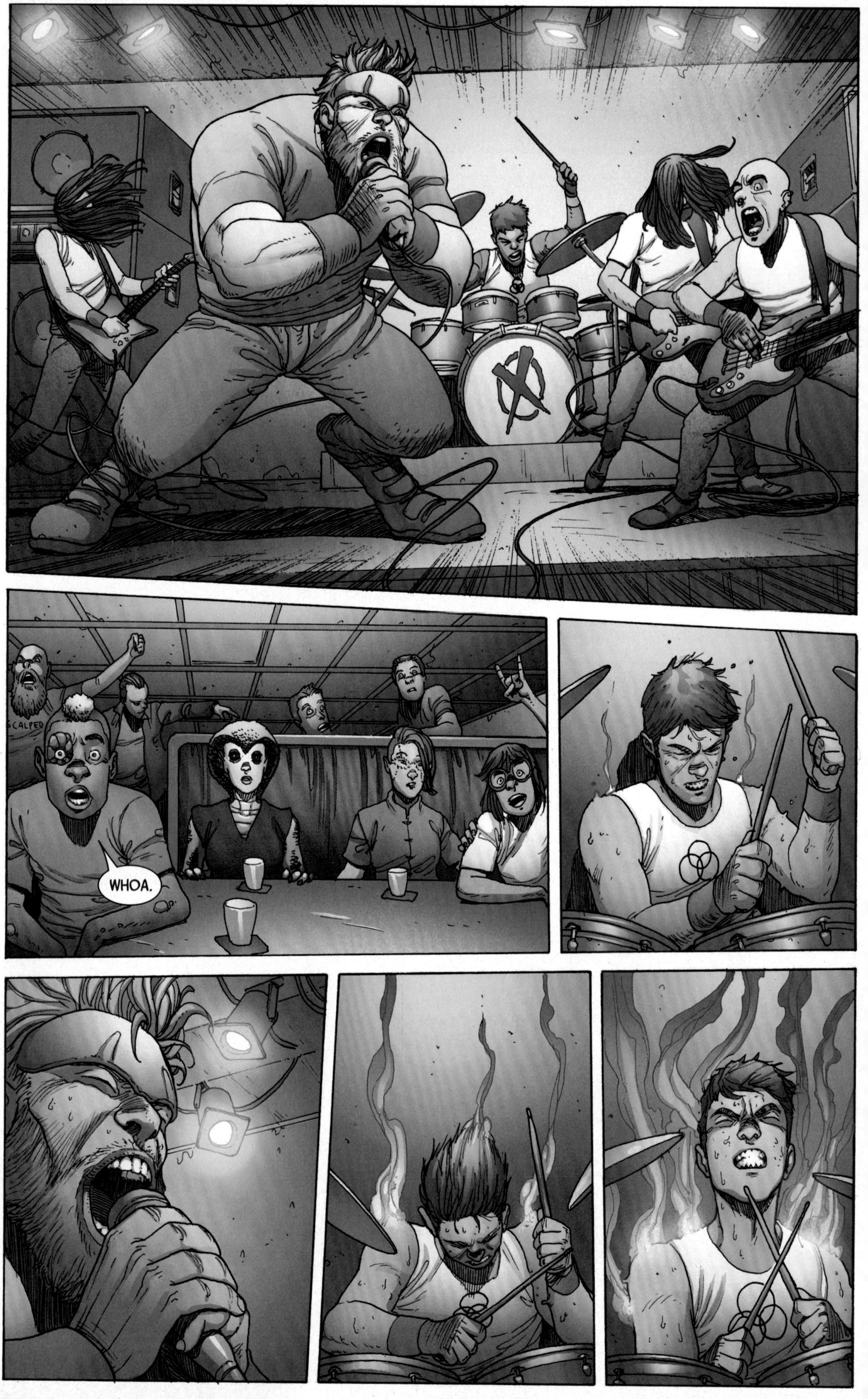
SCALPED
WHOA.

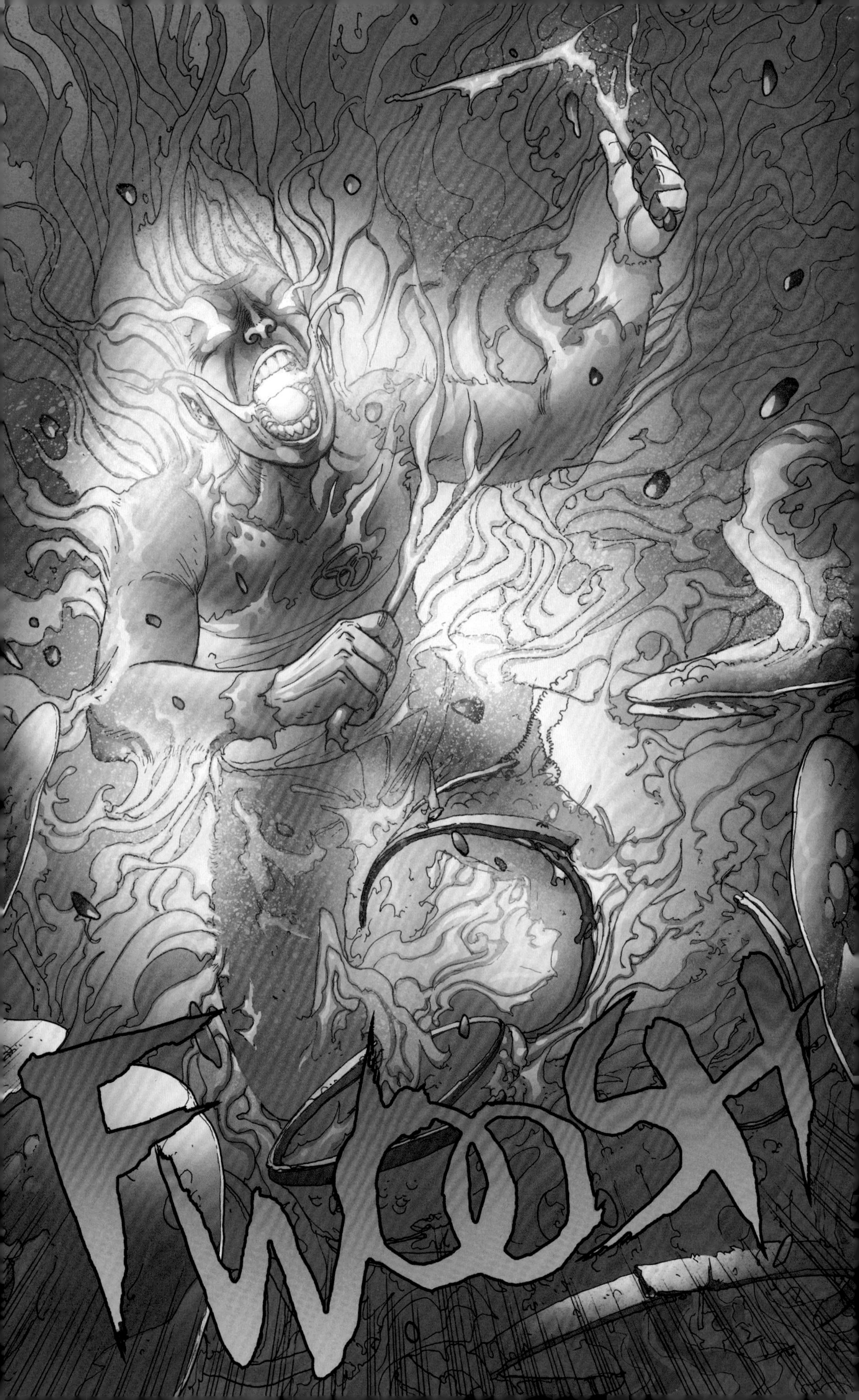
FWOOSH

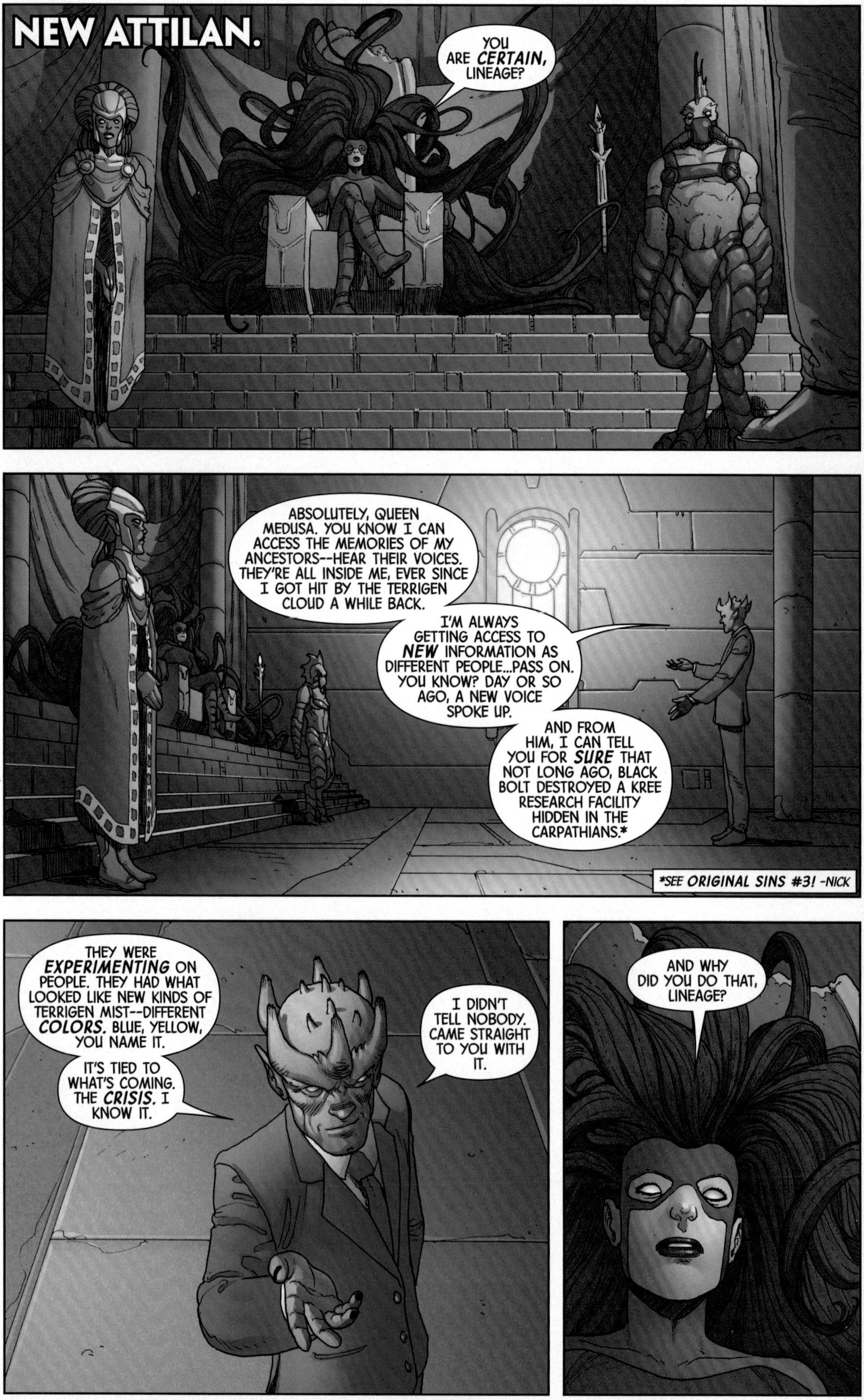

NEW ATTILAN.
YOU ARE CERTAIN, LINEAGE?
ABSOLUTELY, QUEEN MEDUSA. YOU KNOW I CAN ACCESS THE MEMORIES OF MY ANCESTORS--HEAR THEIR VOICES. THEY'RE ALL INSIDE ME, EVER SINCE I GOT HIT BY THE TERRIGEN CLOUD A WHILE BACK.
I'M ALWAYS GETTING ACCESS TO NEW INFORMATION AS DIFFERENT PEOPLE...PASS ON. YOU KNOW? DAY OR SO AGO, A NEW VOICE SPOKE UP.
AND FROM HIM, I CAN TELL YOU FOR SURE THAT NOT LONG AGO, BLACK BOLT DESTROYED A KREE RESEARCH FACILITY HIDDEN IN THE CARPATHIANS.*
*SEE ORIGINAL SINS #3! -NICK
THEY WERE EXPERIMENTING ON PEOPLE. THEY HAD WHAT LOOKED LIKE NEW KINDS OF TERRIGEN MIST--DIFFERENT COLORS. BLUE, YELLOW, YOU NAME IT.
IT'S TIED TO WHAT'S COMING. THE CRISIS. I KNOW IT.
I DIDN'T TELL NOBODY. CAME STRAIGHT TO YOU WITH IT.
AND WHY DID YOU DO THAT, LINEAGE?

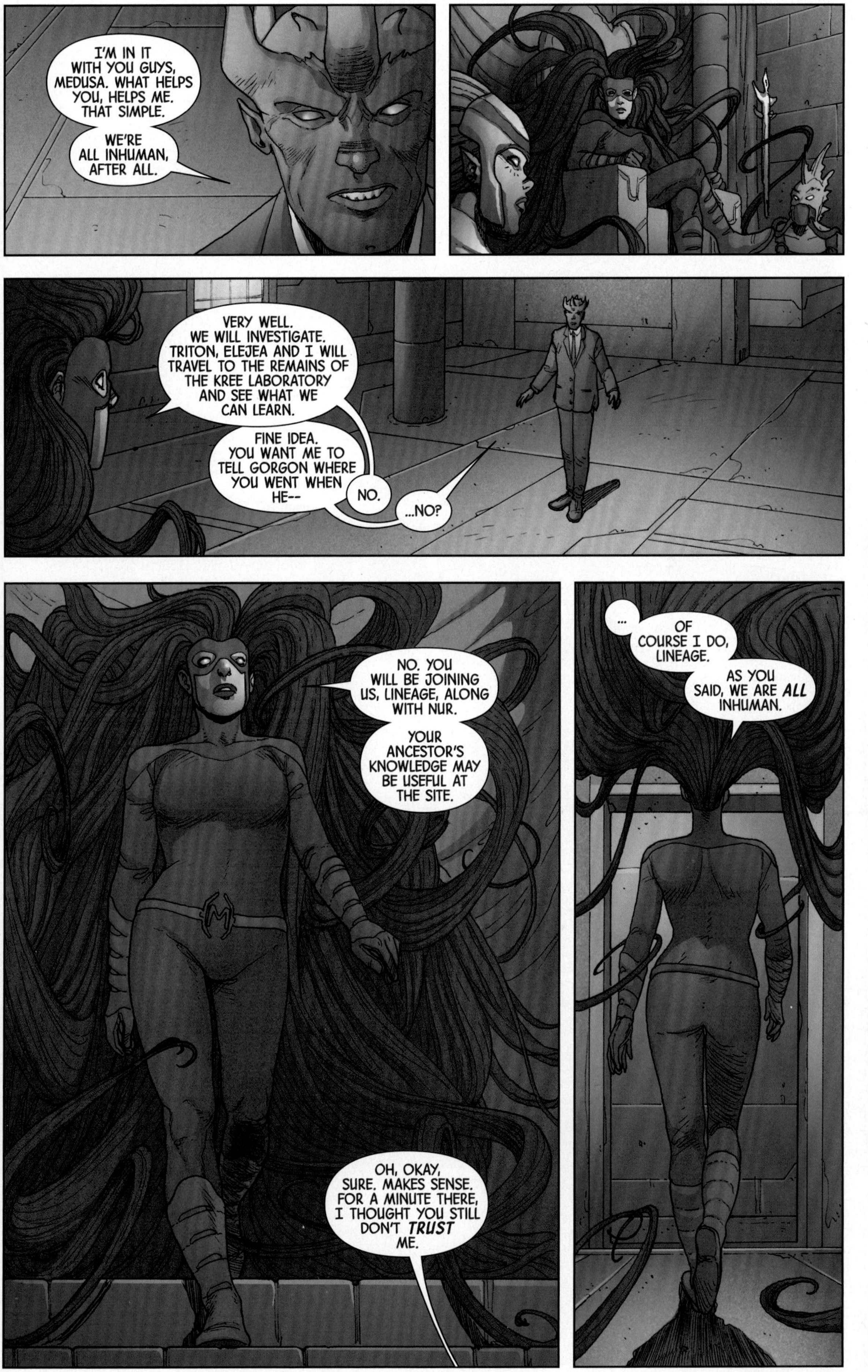
I'M IN IT WITH YOU GUYS, MEDUSA. WHAT HELPS YOU, HELPS ME. THAT SIMPLE.
WE'RE ALL INHUMAN, AFTER ALL.
VERY WELL. WE WILL INVESTIGATE. TRITON, ELEJEA AND I WILL TRAVEL TO THE REMAINS OF THE KREE LABORATORY AND SEE WHAT WE CAN LEARN.
FINE IDEA. YOU WANT ME TO TELL GORGON WHERE YOU WENT WHEN HE--
NO.
...NO?
NO. YOU WILL BE JOINING US, LINEAGE, ALONG WITH NUR.
YOUR ANCESTOR'S KNOWLEDGE MAY BE USEFUL AT THE SITE.
OH, OKAY, SURE. MAKES SENSE. FOR A MINUTE THERE, I THOUGHT YOU STILL DON'T *TRUST* ME.
...
OF COURSE I DO, LINEAGE.
AS YOU SAID, WE ARE *ALL* INHUMAN.

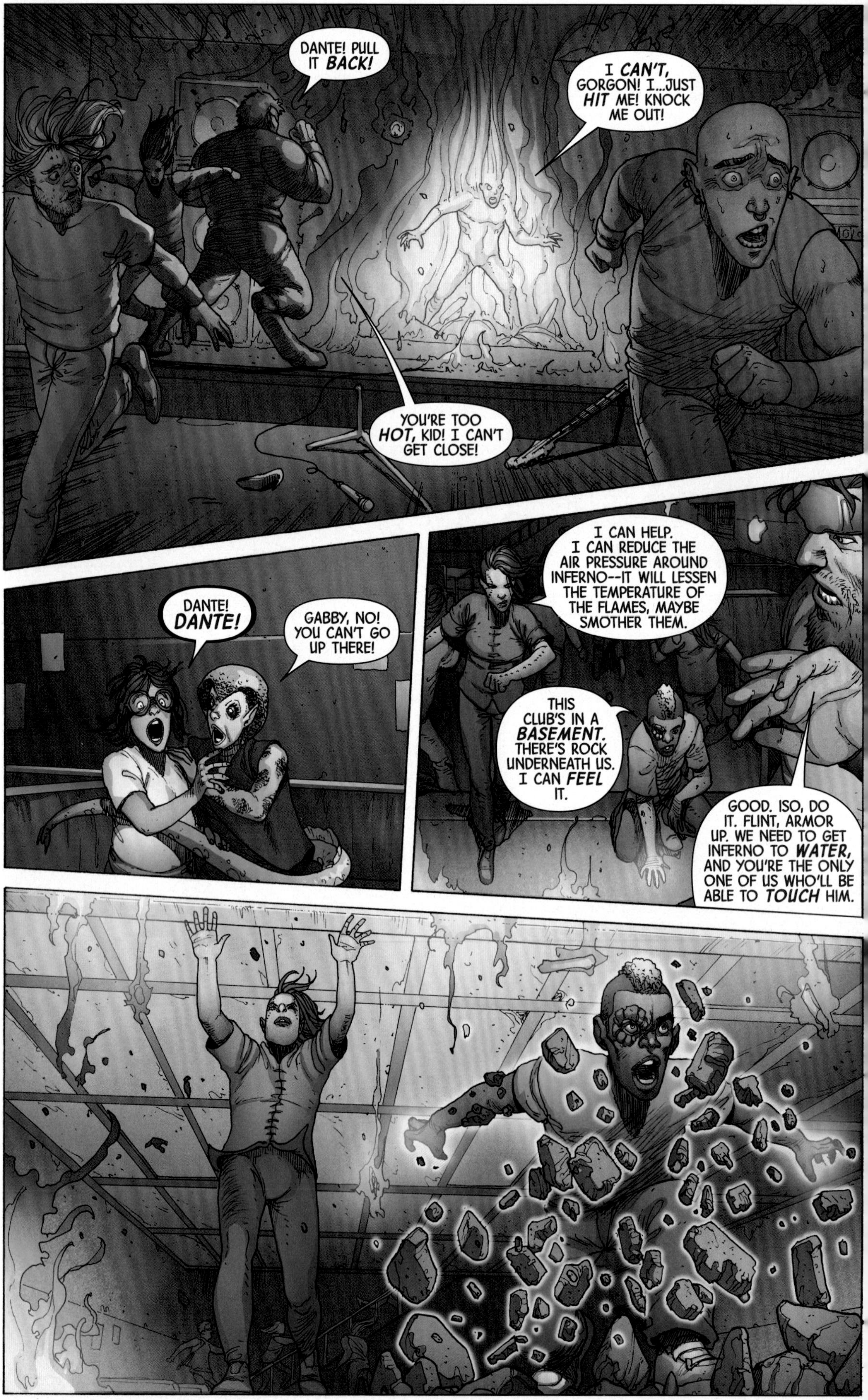
DANTE! PULL IT BACK!
I CAN'T, GORGON! I...JUST HIT ME! KNOCK ME OUT!
YOU'RE TOO HOT, KID! I CAN'T GET CLOSE!
DANTE! DANTE!
GABBY, NO! YOU CAN'T GO UP THERE!
I CAN HELP. I CAN REDUCE THE AIR PRESSURE AROUND INFERNO--IT WILL LESSEN THE TEMPERATURE OF THE FLAMES, MAYBE SMOTHER THEM.
THIS CLUB'S IN A BASEMENT. THERE'S ROCK UNDERNEATH US. I CAN FEEL IT.
GOOD. ISO, DO IT. FLINT, ARMOR UP. WE NEED TO GET INFERNO TO WATER, AND YOU'RE THE ONLY ONE OF US WHO'LL BE ABLE TO TOUCH HIM.

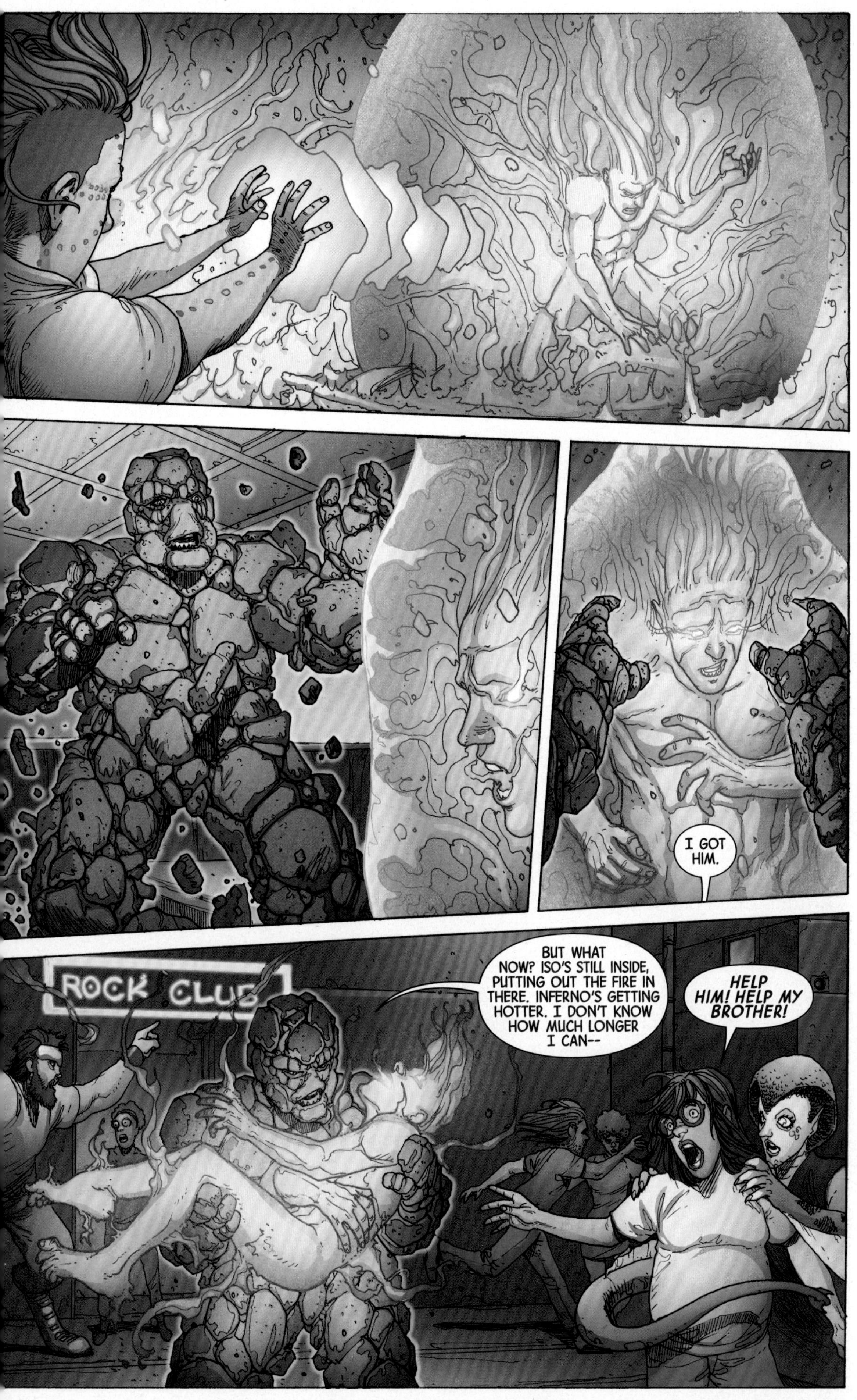
I GOT HIM.
ROCK CLUB
BUT WHAT NOW? ISO'S STILL INSIDE, PUTTING OUT THE FIRE IN THERE. INFERNO'S GETTING HOTTER. I DON'T KNOW HOW MUCH LONGER I CAN--
HELP HIM! HELP MY BROTHER!

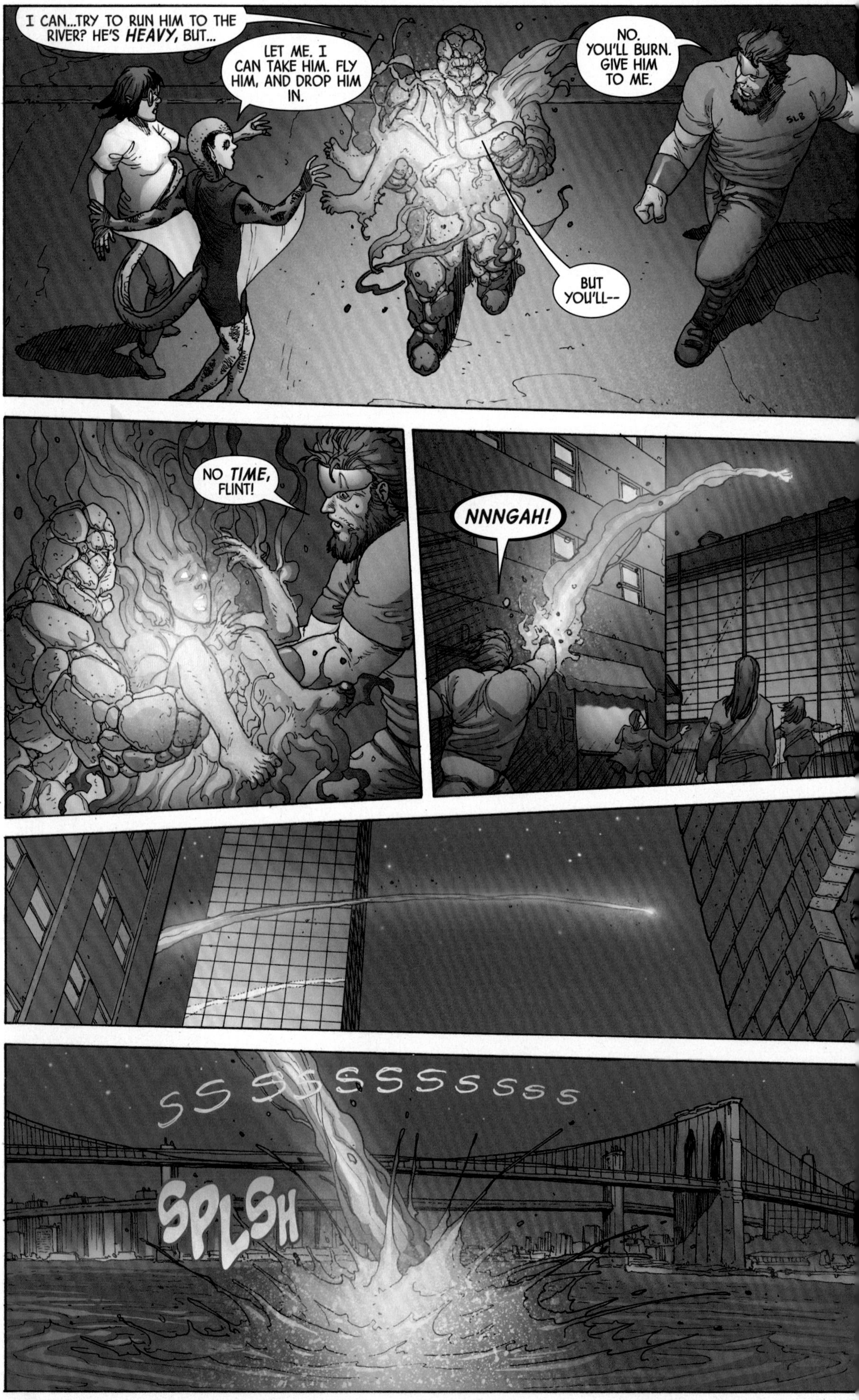
I CAN...TRY TO RUN HIM TO THE RIVER? HE'S HEAVY, BUT...
LET ME. I CAN TAKE HIM. FLY HIM, AND DROP HIM IN.
NO. YOU'LL BURN. GIVE HIM TO ME.
BUT YOU'LL--
SLB
NO TIME, FLINT!
NNNGAH!
SSSSSSSSSSSS
SPLSH

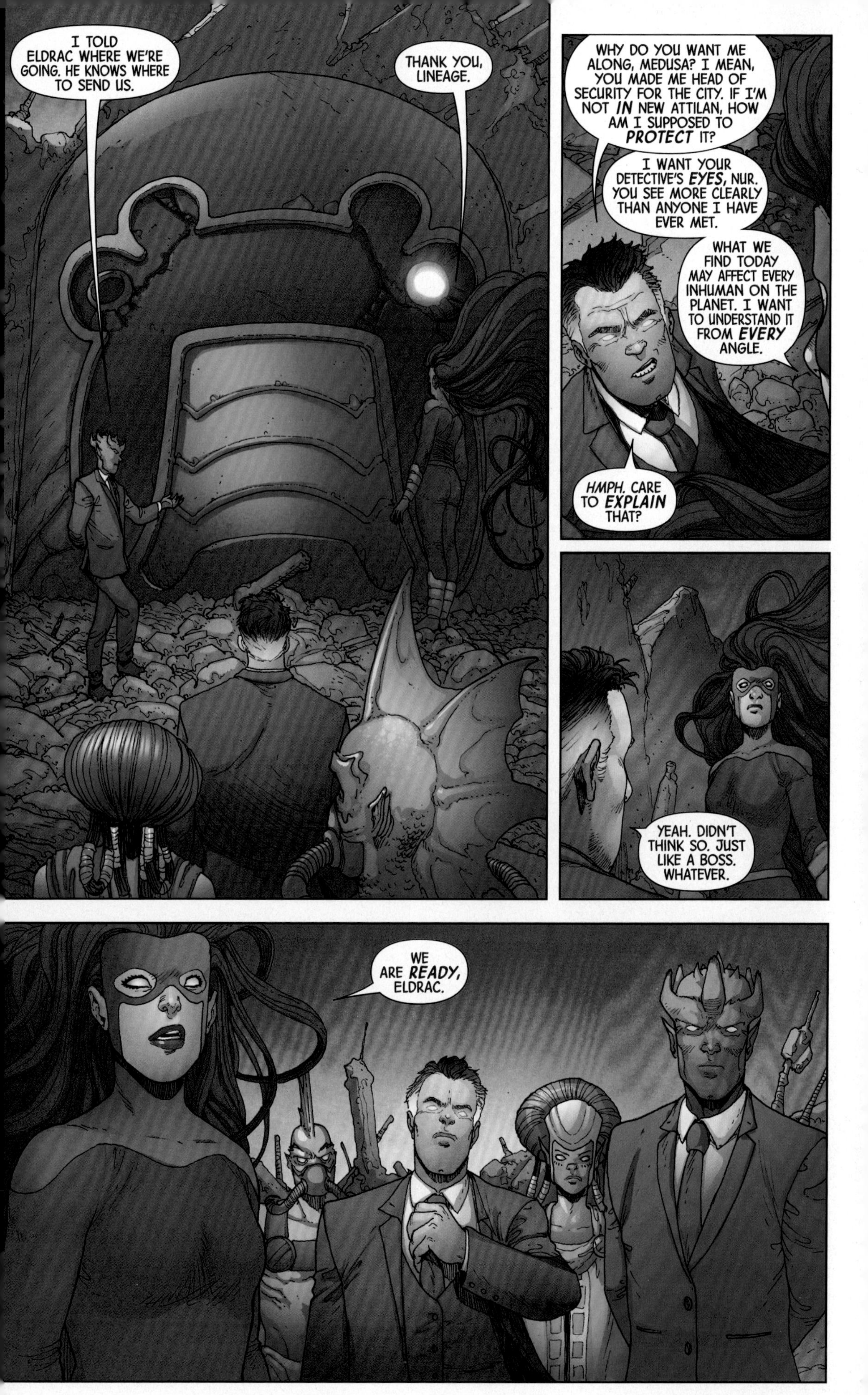
I TOLD ELDRAC WHERE WE'RE GOING. HE KNOWS WHERE TO SEND US.
THANK YOU, LINEAGE.
WHY DO YOU WANT ME ALONG, MEDUSA? I MEAN, YOU MADE ME HEAD OF SECURITY FOR THE CITY. IF I'M NOT IN NEW ATTILAN, HOW AM I SUPPOSED TO PROTECT IT?
I WANT YOUR DETECTIVE'S EYES, NUR. YOU SEE MORE CLEARLY THAN ANYONE I HAVE EVER MET.
WHAT WE FIND TODAY MAY AFFECT EVERY INHUMAN ON THE PLANET. I WANT TO UNDERSTAND IT FROM EVERY ANGLE.
HMPH. CARE TO EXPLAIN THAT?
YEAH. DIDN'T THINK SO. JUST LIKE A BOSS. WHATEVER.
WE ARE READY, ELDRAC.

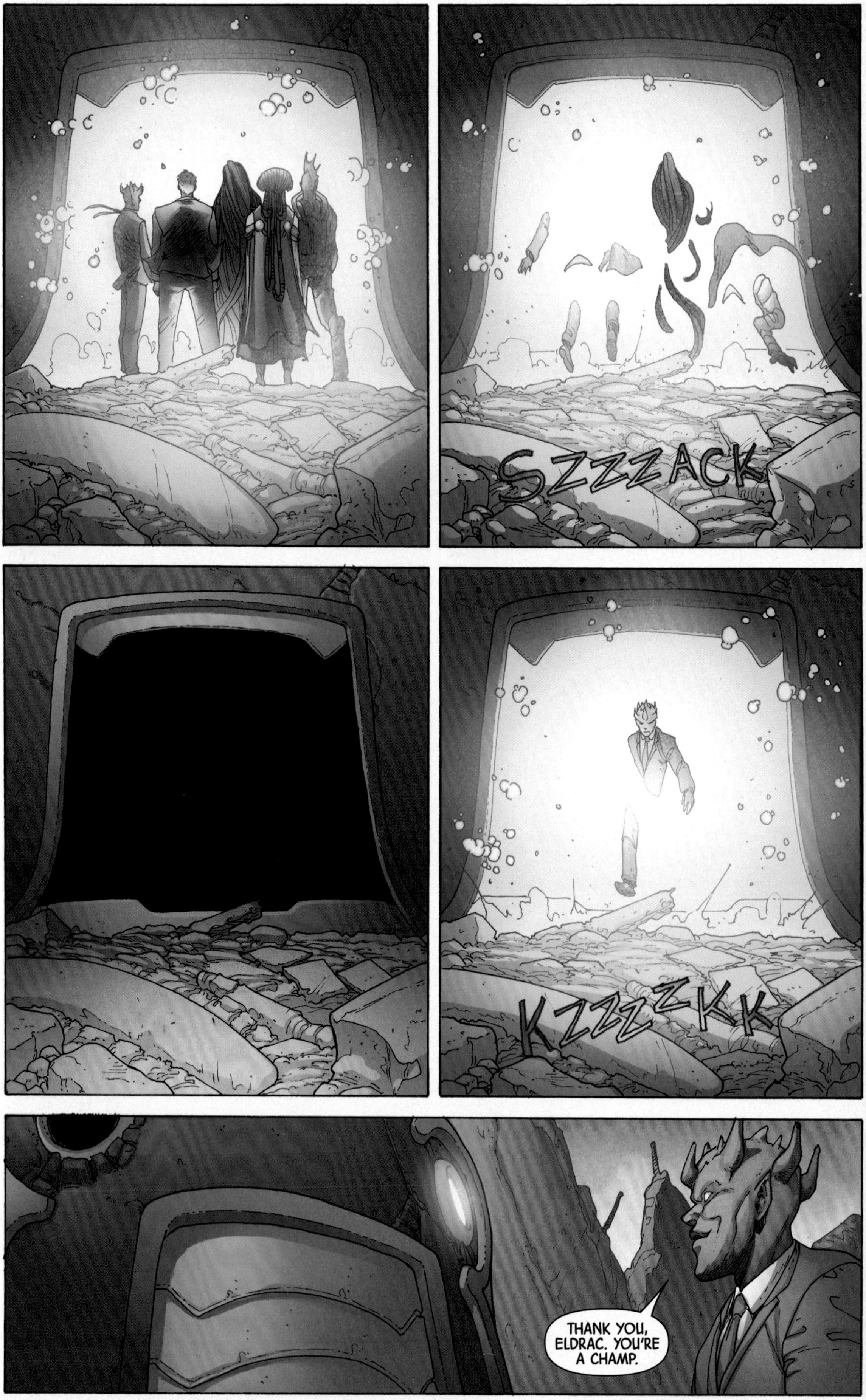
SZZZACK
KZZZZKK
THANK YOU, ELDRAC. YOU'RE A CHAMP.

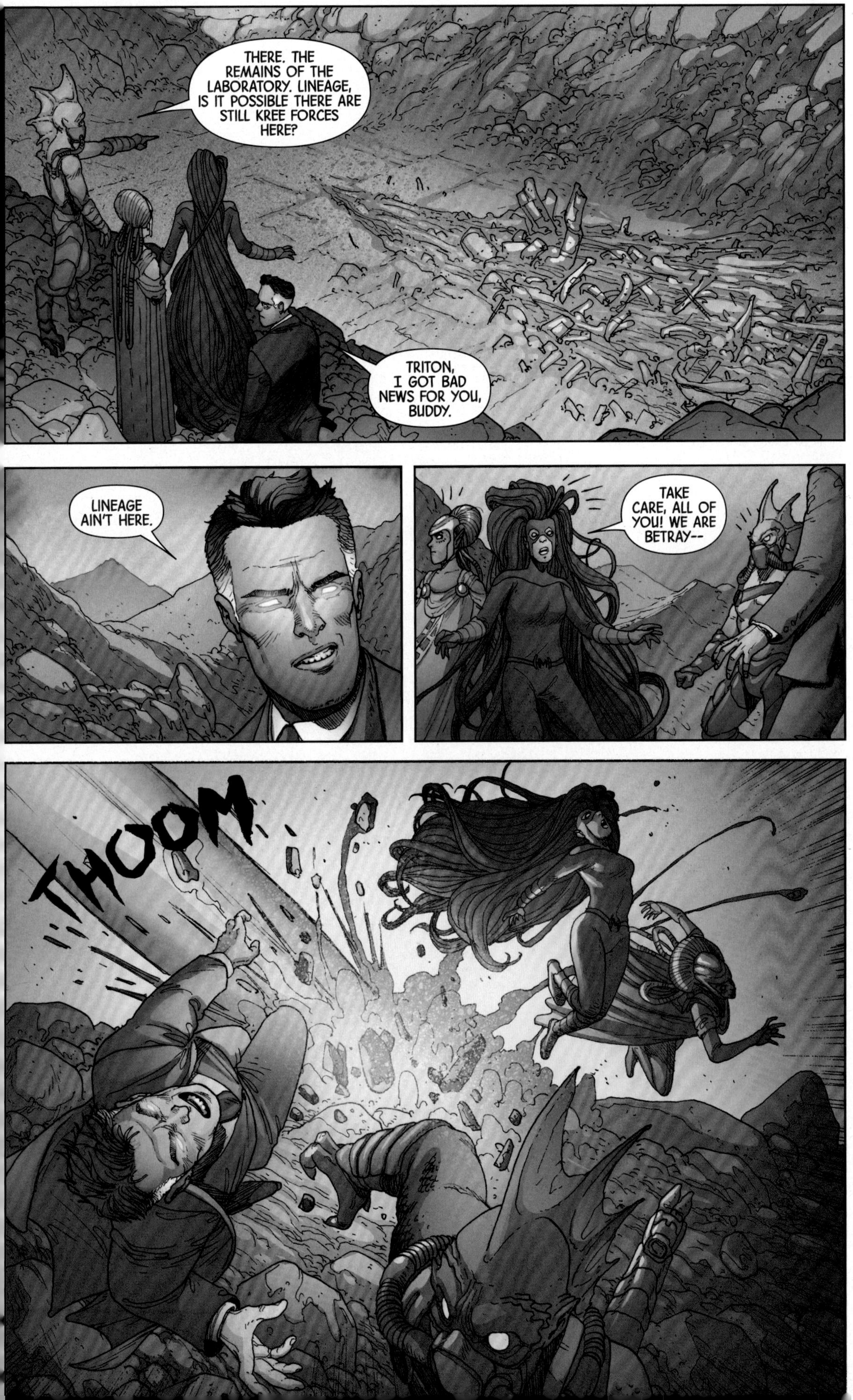
THERE. THE REMAINS OF THE LABORATORY. LINEAGE, IS IT POSSIBLE THERE ARE STILL KREE FORCES HERE?
TRITON, I GOT BAD NEWS FOR YOU, BUDDY.
LINEAGE AIN'T HERE.
TAKE CARE, ALL OF YOU! WE ARE BETRAY--
THOOM

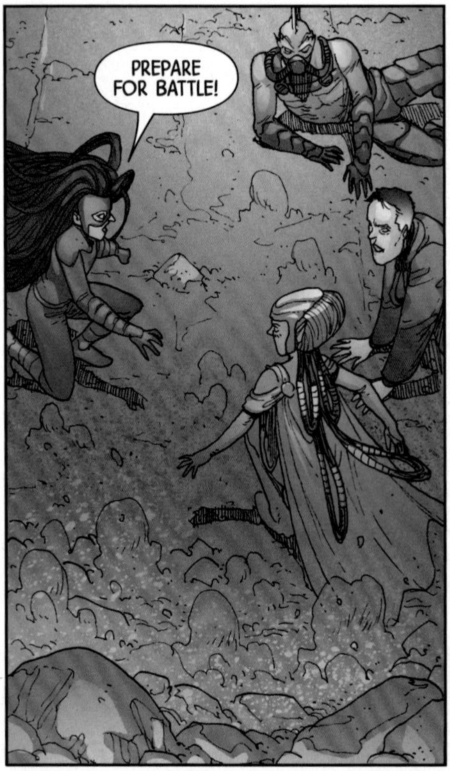
PREPARE FOR BATTLE!

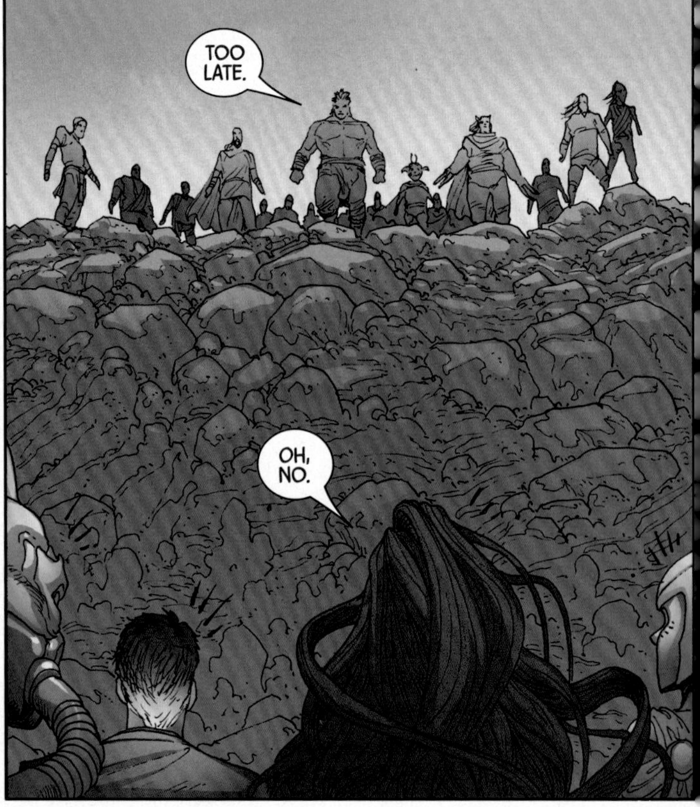
TOO LATE.
OH, NO.

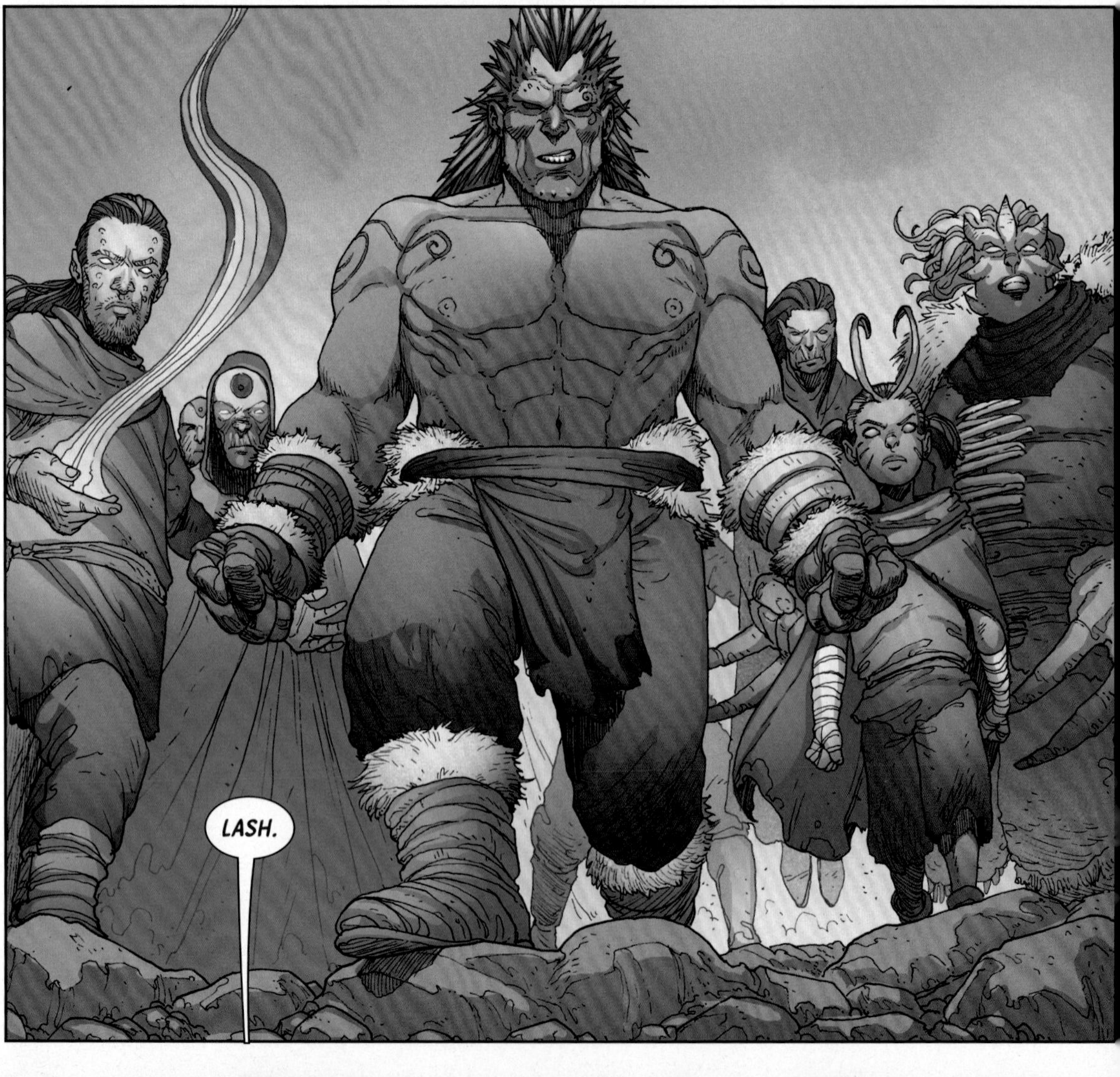
LASH.

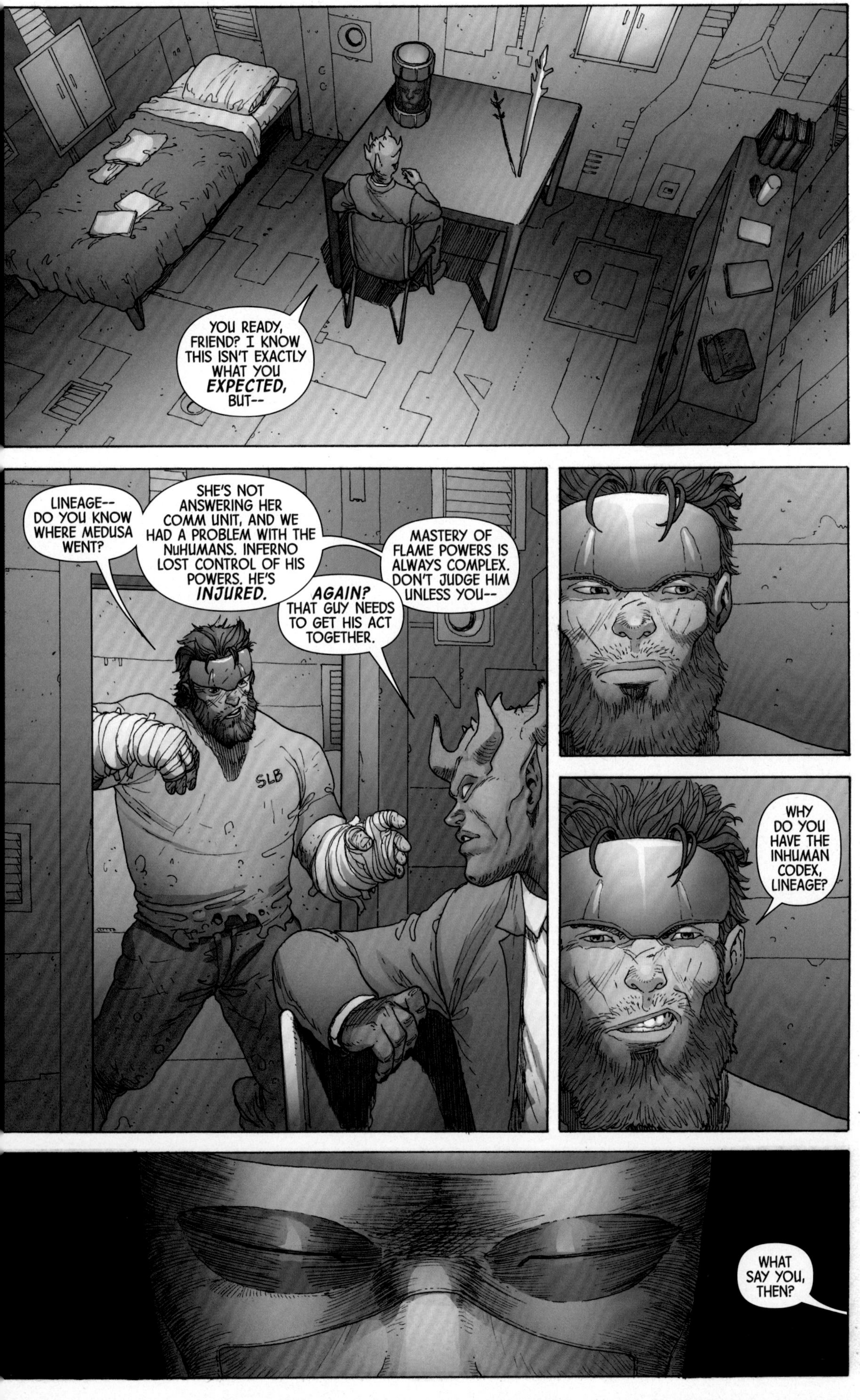

YOU READY, FRIEND? I KNOW THIS ISN'T EXACTLY WHAT YOU EXPECTED, BUT--
LINEAGE-- DO YOU KNOW WHERE MEDUSA WENT?
SHE'S NOT ANSWERING HER COMM UNIT, AND WE HAD A PROBLEM WITH THE NuHUMANS. INFERNO LOST CONTROL OF HIS POWERS. HE'S INJURED.
AGAIN? THAT GUY NEEDS TO GET HIS ACT TOGETHER.
MASTERY OF FLAME POWERS IS ALWAYS COMPLEX. DON'T JUDGE HIM UNLESS YOU--
SLB
WHY DO YOU HAVE THE INHUMAN CODEX, LINEAGE?
WHAT SAY YOU, THEN?

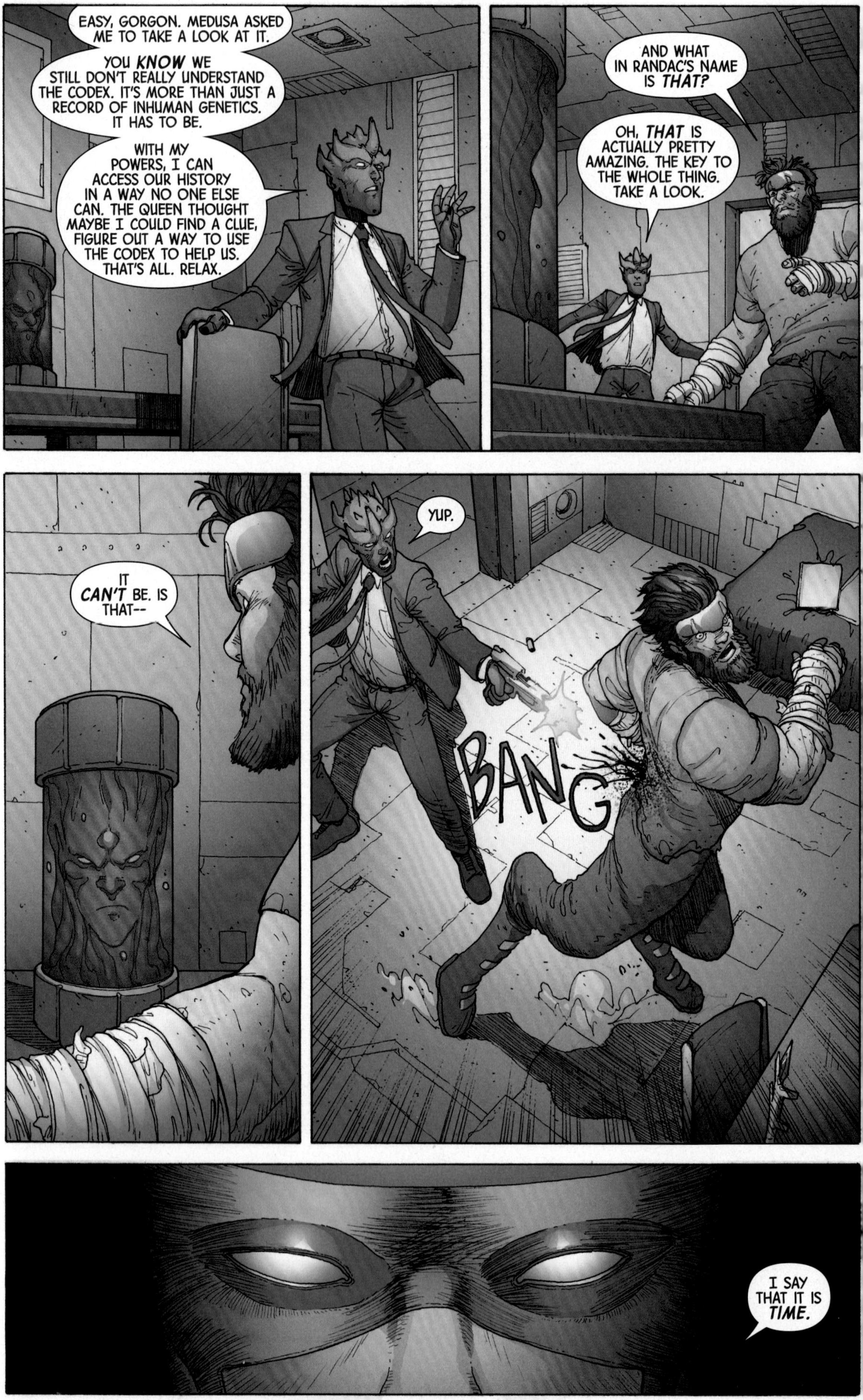
EASY, GORGON. MEDUSA ASKED ME TO TAKE A LOOK AT IT.
YOU *KNOW* WE STILL DON'T REALLY UNDERSTAND THE CODEX. IT'S MORE THAN JUST A RECORD OF INHUMAN GENETICS. IT HAS TO BE.
WITH MY POWERS, I CAN ACCESS OUR HISTORY IN A WAY NO ONE ELSE CAN. THE QUEEN THOUGHT MAYBE I COULD FIND A CLUE, FIGURE OUT A WAY TO USE THE CODEX TO HELP US. THAT'S ALL. RELAX.
AND WHAT IN RANDAC'S NAME IS *THAT?*
OH, *THAT* IS ACTUALLY PRETTY AMAZING. THE KEY TO THE WHOLE THING. TAKE A LOOK.
IT *CAN'T* BE. IS THAT--
YUP.
BANG
I SAY THAT IT IS *TIME.*

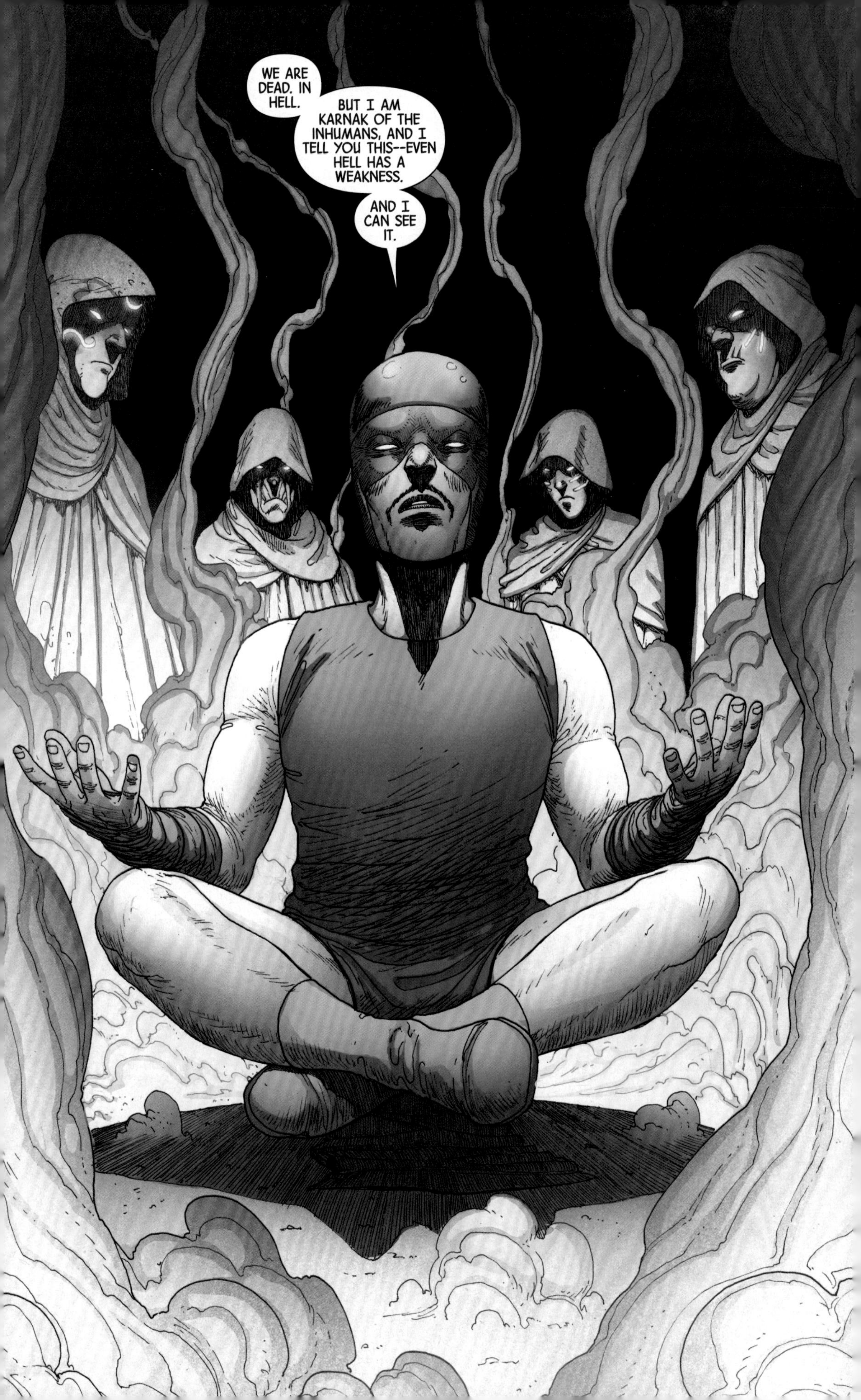
WE ARE DEAD. IN HELL.
BUT I AM KARNAK OF THE INHUMANS, AND I TELL YOU THIS--EVEN HELL HAS A WEAKNESS.
AND I CAN SEE IT.

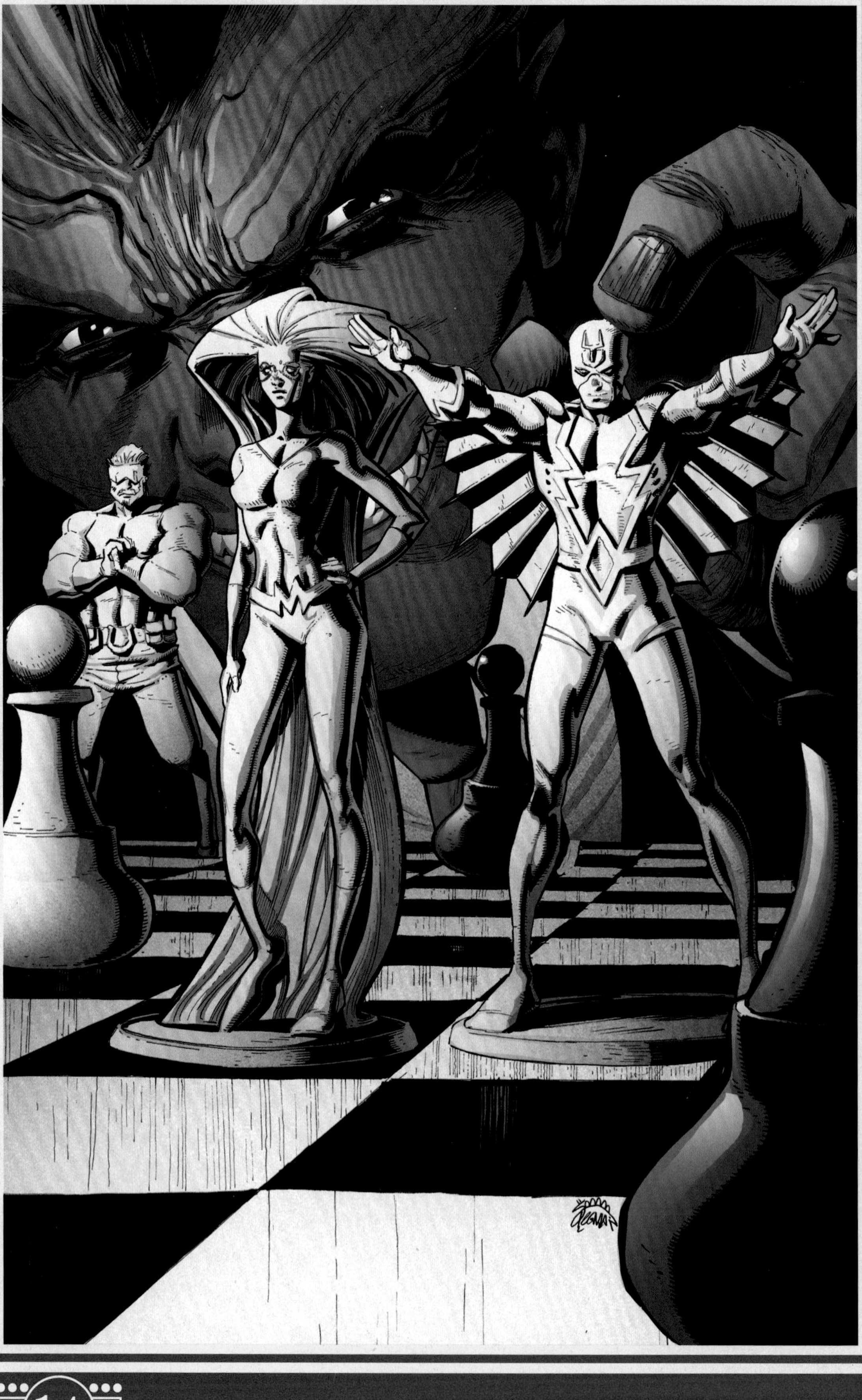

14 PART FOURTEEN: LINKAGES

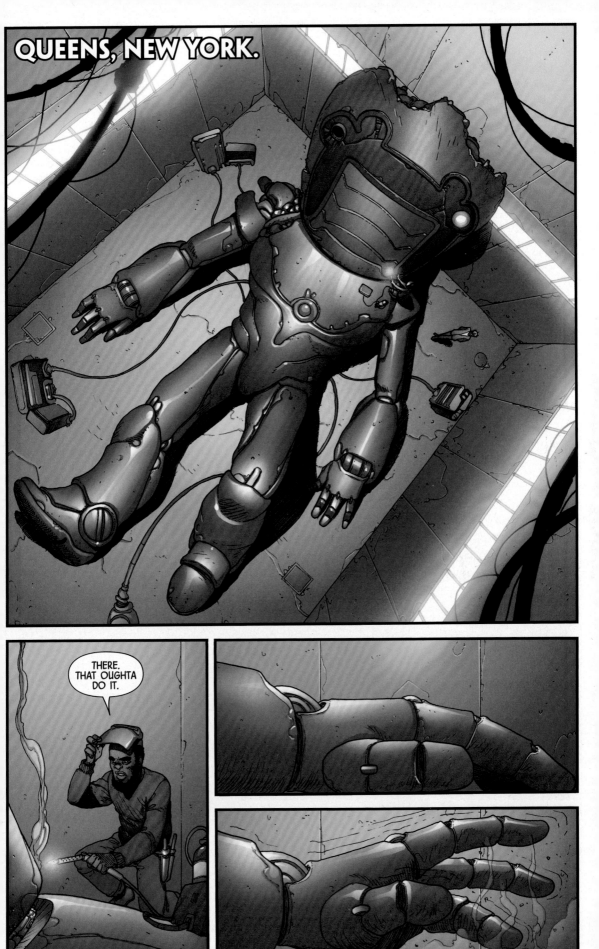

QUEENS, NEW YORK.

THERE.
THAT OUGHTA
DO IT.

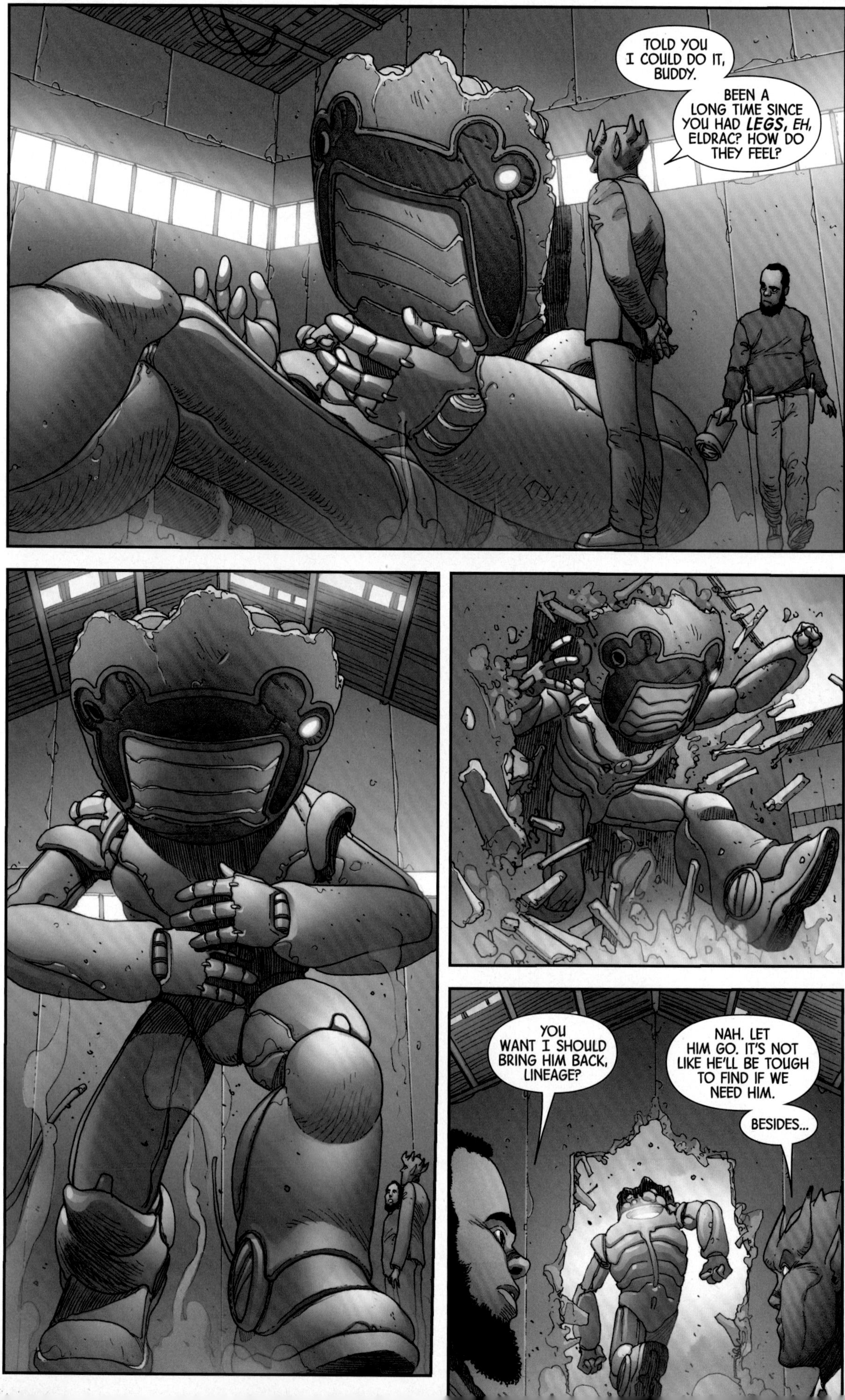
TOLD YOU I COULD DO IT, BUDDY.
BEEN A LONG TIME SINCE YOU HAD LEGS, EH, ELDRAC? HOW DO THEY FEEL?
YOU WANT I SHOULD BRING HIM BACK, LINEAGE?
NAH. LET HIM GO. IT'S NOT LIKE HE'LL BE TOUGH TO FIND IF WE NEED HIM.
BESIDES...

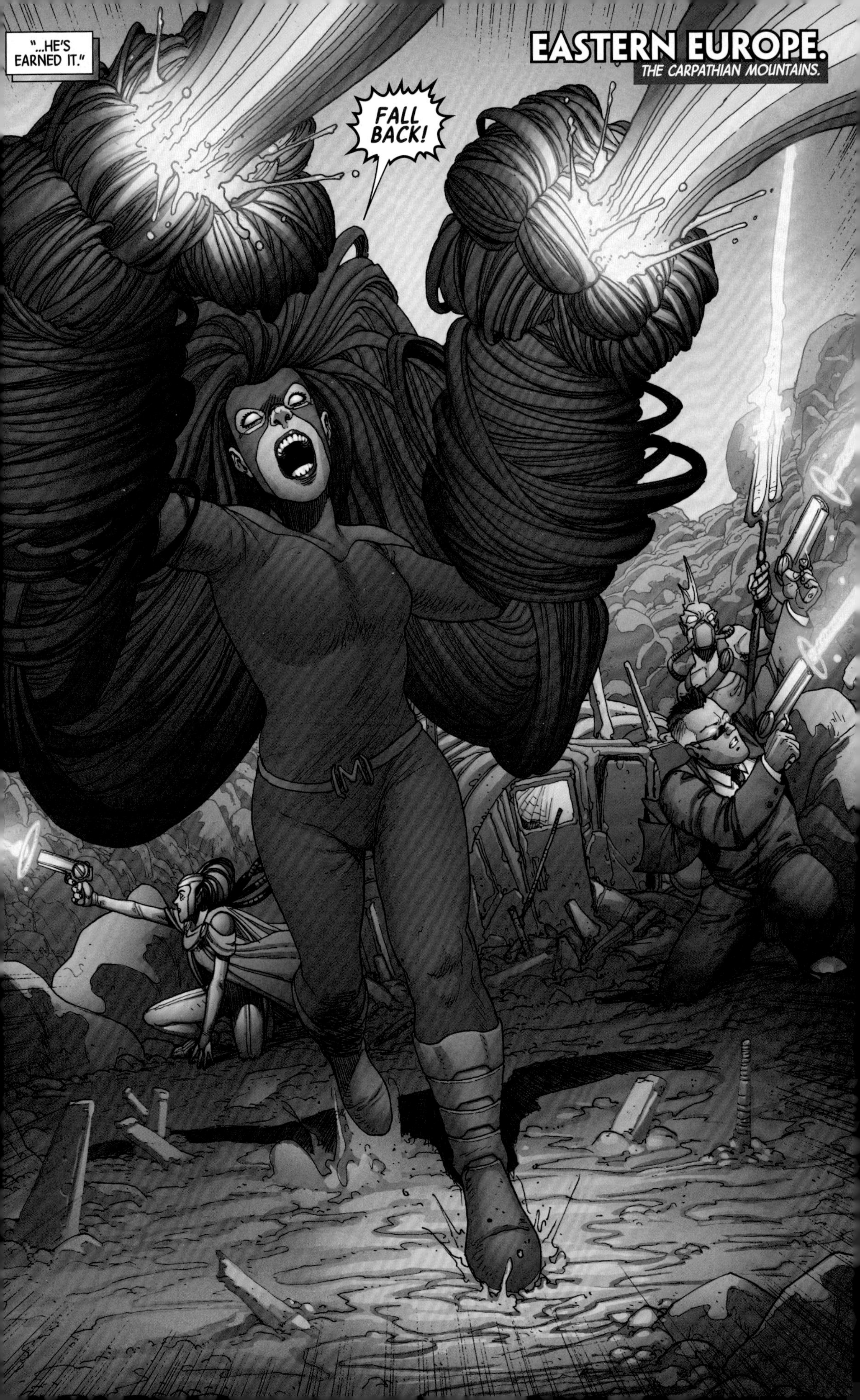
"...HE'S EARNED IT."
EASTERN EUROPE.
THE CARPATHIAN MOUNTAINS.
FALL BACK!

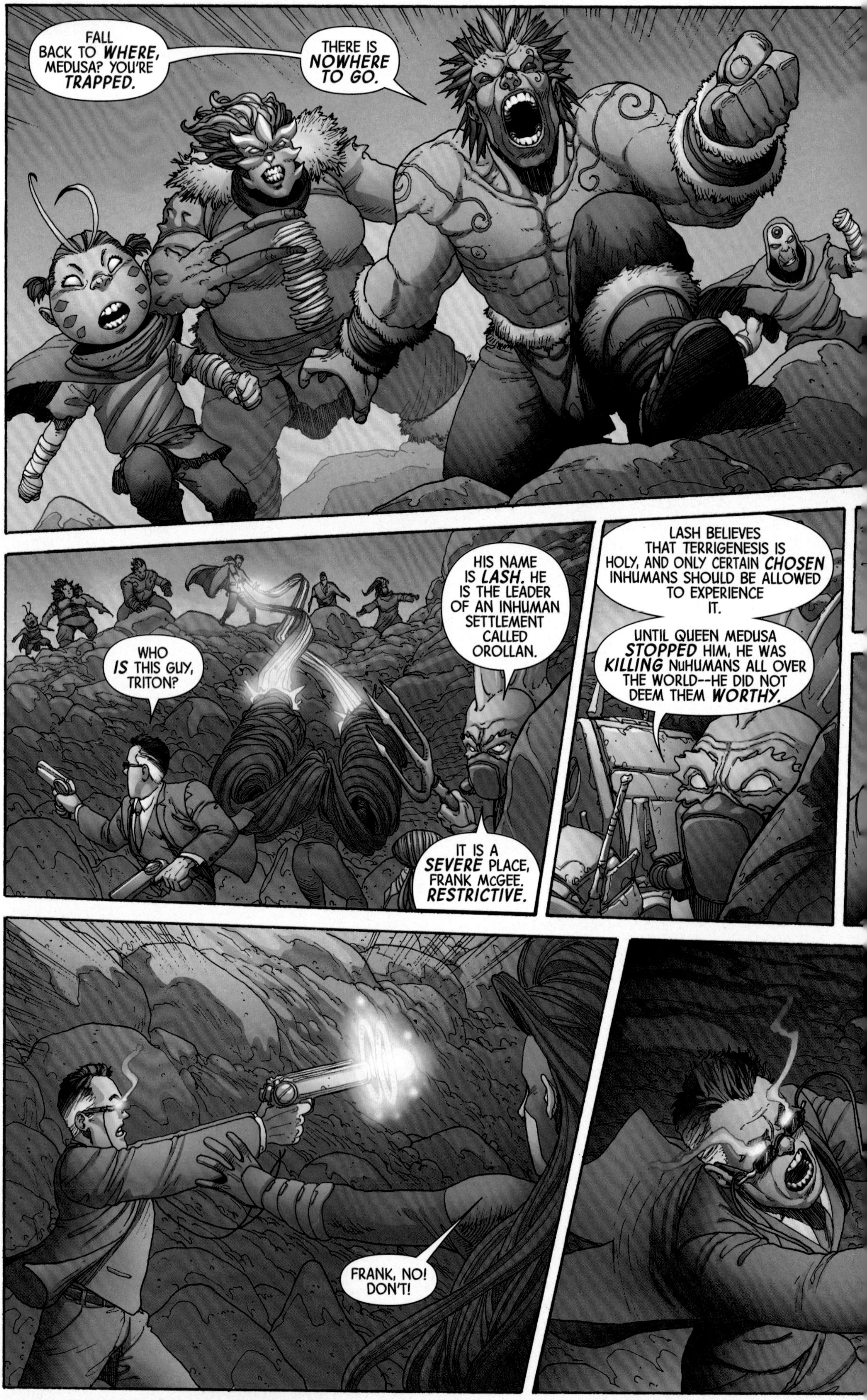
FALL BACK TO WHERE, MEDUSA? YOU'RE TRAPPED.
THERE IS NOWHERE TO GO.
WHO IS THIS GUY, TRITON?
HIS NAME IS LASH. HE IS THE LEADER OF AN INHUMAN SETTLEMENT CALLED OROLLAN.
IT IS A SEVERE PLACE, FRANK McGEE. RESTRICTIVE.
LASH BELIEVES THAT TERRIGENESIS IS HOLY, AND ONLY CERTAIN CHOSEN INHUMANS SHOULD BE ALLOWED TO EXPERIENCE IT.
UNTIL QUEEN MEDUSA STOPPED HIM, HE WAS KILLING NuHUMANS ALL OVER THE WORLD--HE DID NOT DEEM THEM WORTHY.
FRANK, NO! DON'T!

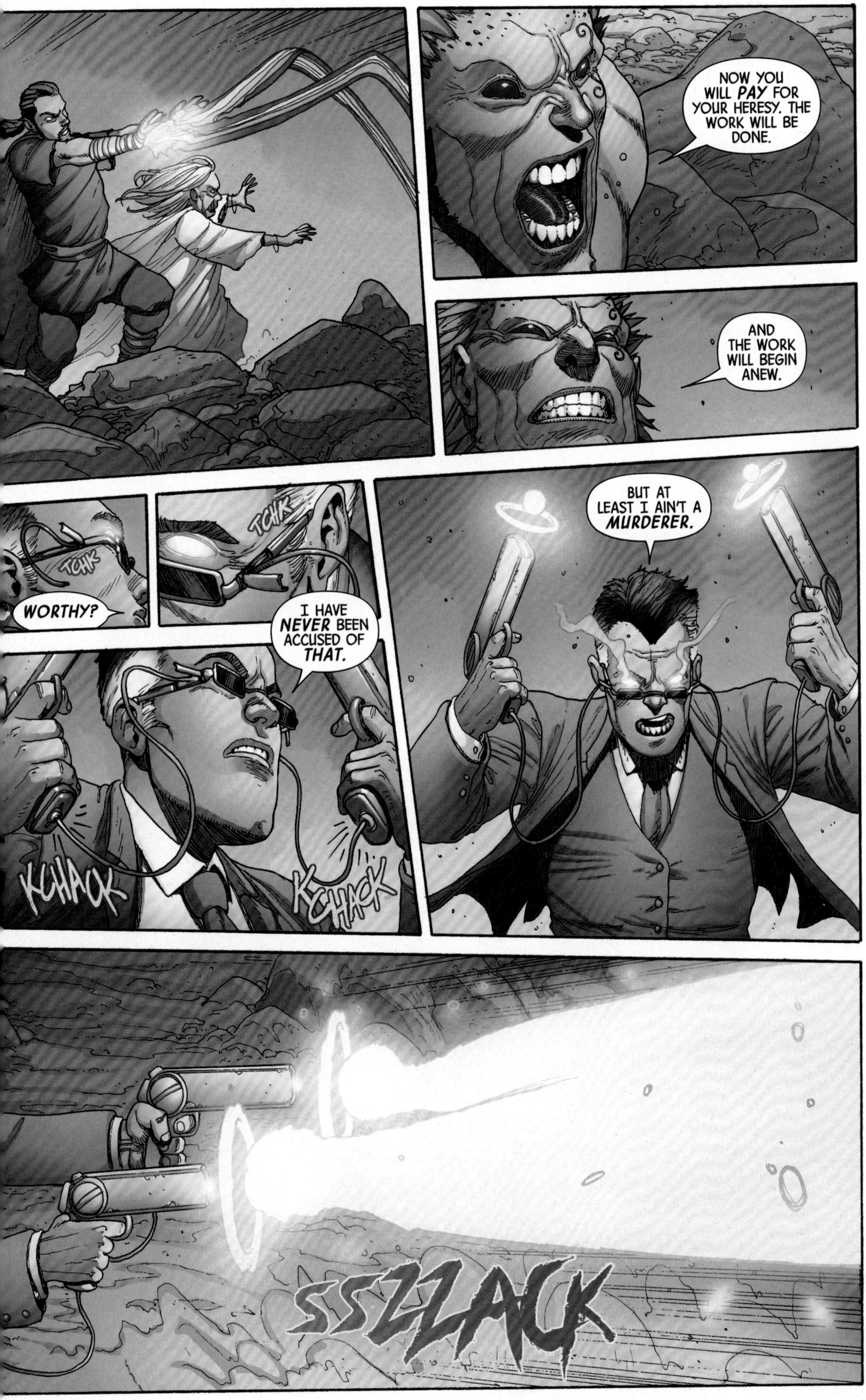
NOW YOU WILL PAY FOR YOUR HERESY. THE WORK WILL BE DONE.
AND THE WORK WILL BEGIN ANEW.
TCHK
WORTHY?
TCHK
I HAVE NEVER BEEN ACCUSED OF THAT.
KCHACK
KCHACK
BUT AT LEAST I AIN'T A MURDERER.
SSZZACK

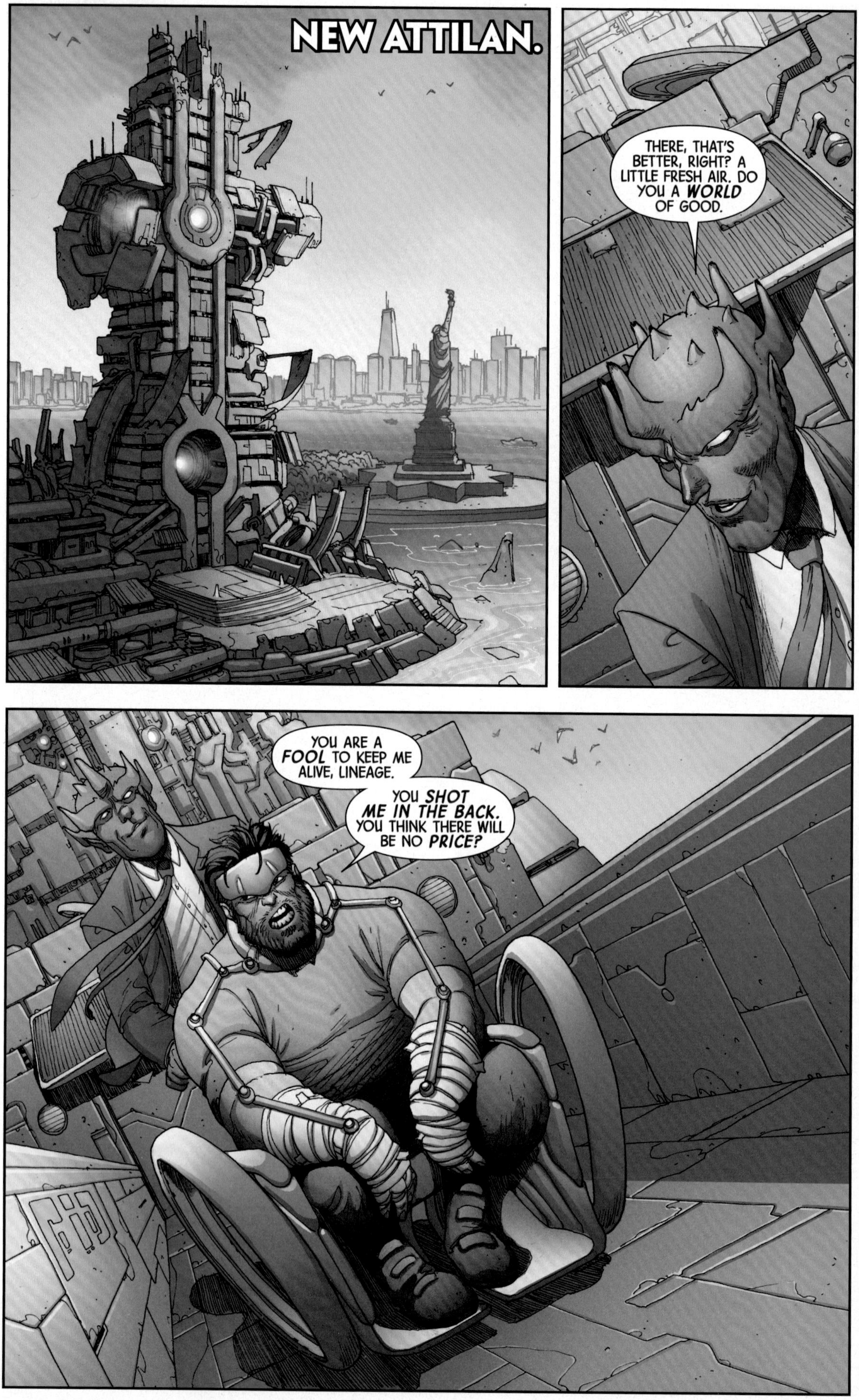
NEW ATTILAN.
THERE, THAT'S BETTER, RIGHT? A LITTLE FRESH AIR. DO YOU A WORLD OF GOOD.
YOU ARE A FOOL TO KEEP ME ALIVE, LINEAGE.
YOU SHOT ME IN THE BACK. YOU THINK THERE WILL BE NO PRICE?

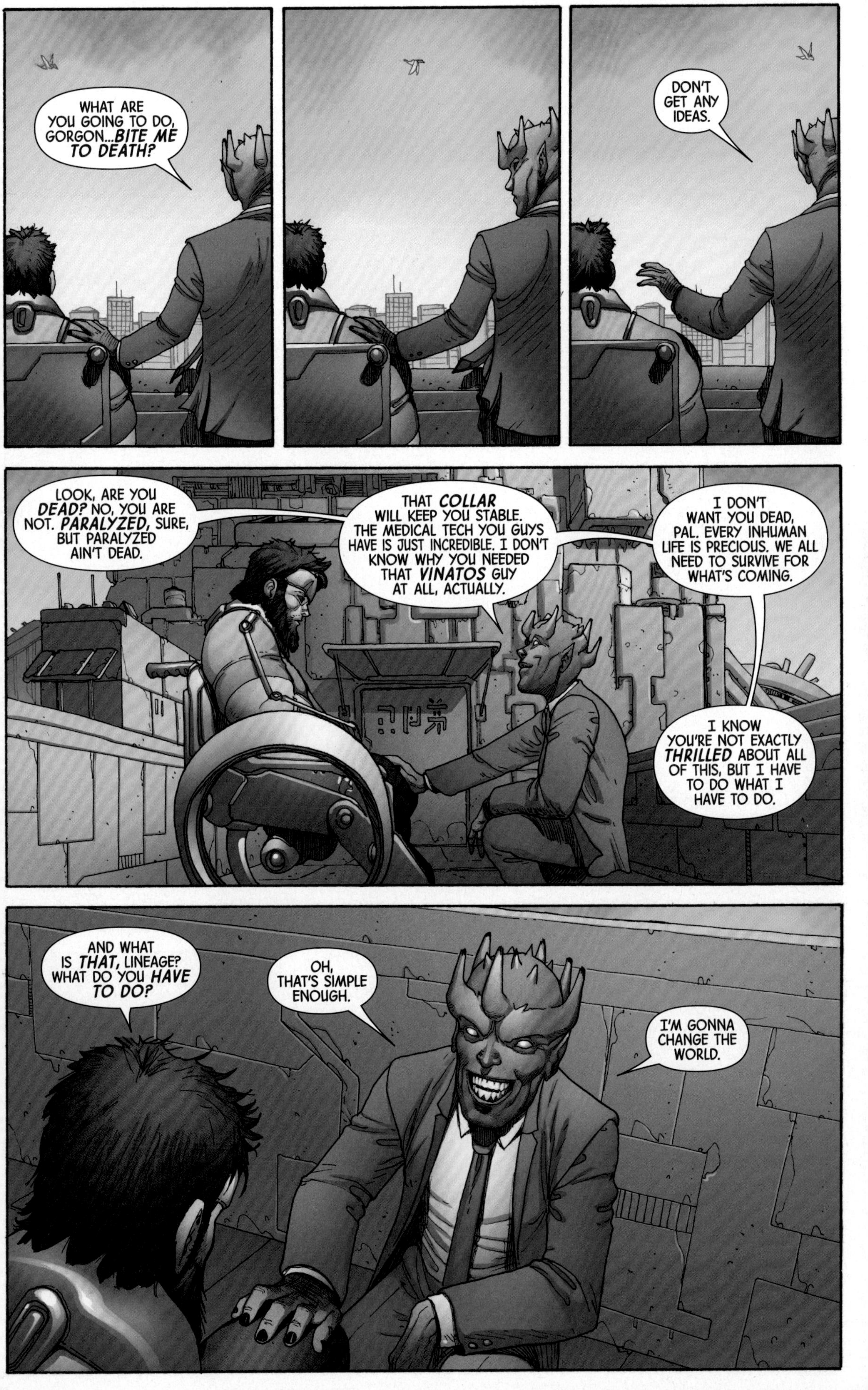
WHAT ARE YOU GOING TO DO, GORGON...BITE ME TO DEATH?
DON'T GET ANY IDEAS.
LOOK, ARE YOU DEAD? NO, YOU ARE NOT. PARALYZED, SURE, BUT PARALYZED AIN'T DEAD.
THAT COLLAR WILL KEEP YOU STABLE. THE MEDICAL TECH YOU GUYS HAVE IS JUST INCREDIBLE. I DON'T KNOW WHY YOU NEEDED THAT VINATOS GUY AT ALL, ACTUALLY.
I DON'T WANT YOU DEAD, PAL. EVERY INHUMAN LIFE IS PRECIOUS. WE ALL NEED TO SURVIVE FOR WHAT'S COMING.
I KNOW YOU'RE NOT EXACTLY THRILLED ABOUT ALL OF THIS, BUT I HAVE TO DO WHAT I HAVE TO DO.
AND WHAT IS THAT, LINEAGE? WHAT DO YOU HAVE TO DO?
OH, THAT'S SIMPLE ENOUGH.
I'M GONNA CHANGE THE WORLD.

AFTER LIFE.

THERE. THE PATH OUT OF HELL.

THIS IS NOTHING *NEW*, KARNAK. WE KNOW THE GATES MIGHT PROVIDE A WAY OUT.

BUT WE CANNOT *OPEN* THEM. THERE IS NO KEY. THERE IS NOT EVEN A LOCK.

AND WE CANNOT GET *CLOSE*, IN ANY CASE. OTHERS HAVE *TRIED*, AND THE GUARDS HAVE DESTROYED THEM UTTERLY.

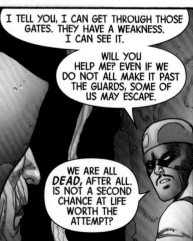

I TELL YOU, I CAN GET THROUGH THOSE GATES. THEY HAVE A WEAKNESS. I CAN SEE IT.

WILL YOU HELP ME? EVEN IF WE DO NOT ALL MAKE IT PAST THE GUARDS, SOME OF US MAY ESCAPE.

WE ARE ALL *DEAD*, AFTER ALL. IS NOT A SECOND CHANCE AT LIFE WORTH THE ATTEMPT?

ABSOLUTELY NOT.

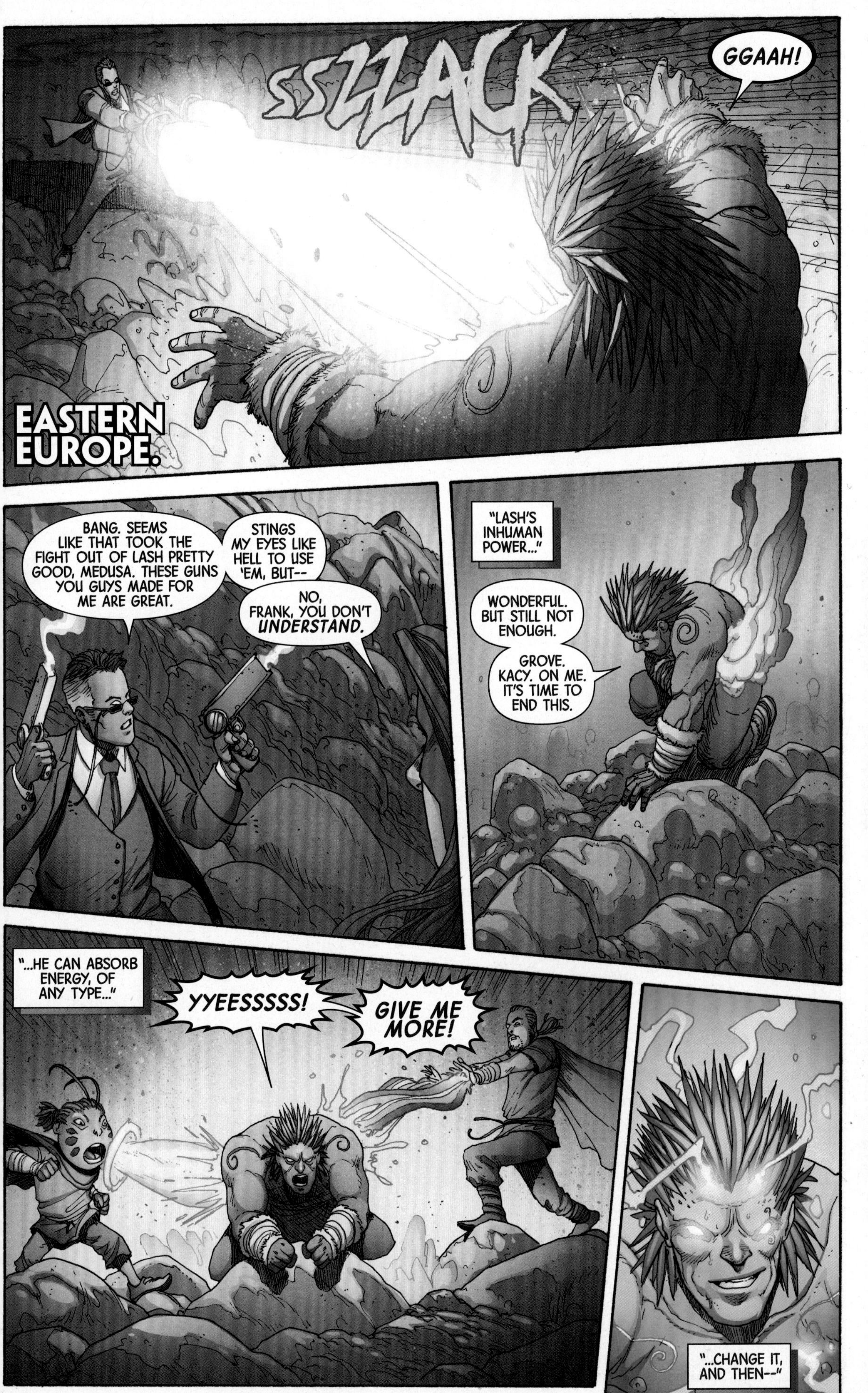
SSZZACK
GGAAH!
EASTERN EUROPE.
BANG. SEEMS LIKE THAT TOOK THE FIGHT OUT OF LASH PRETTY GOOD, MEDUSA. THESE GUNS YOU GUYS MADE FOR ME ARE GREAT.
STINGS MY EYES LIKE HELL TO USE 'EM, BUT--
NO, FRANK, YOU DON'T UNDERSTAND.
"LASH'S INHUMAN POWER..."
WONDERFUL. BUT STILL NOT ENOUGH.
GROVE. KACY. ON ME. IT'S TIME TO END THIS.
"...HE CAN ABSORB ENERGY, OF ANY TYPE..."
YYEESSSSS!
GIVE ME MORE!
"...CHANGE IT, AND THEN--"

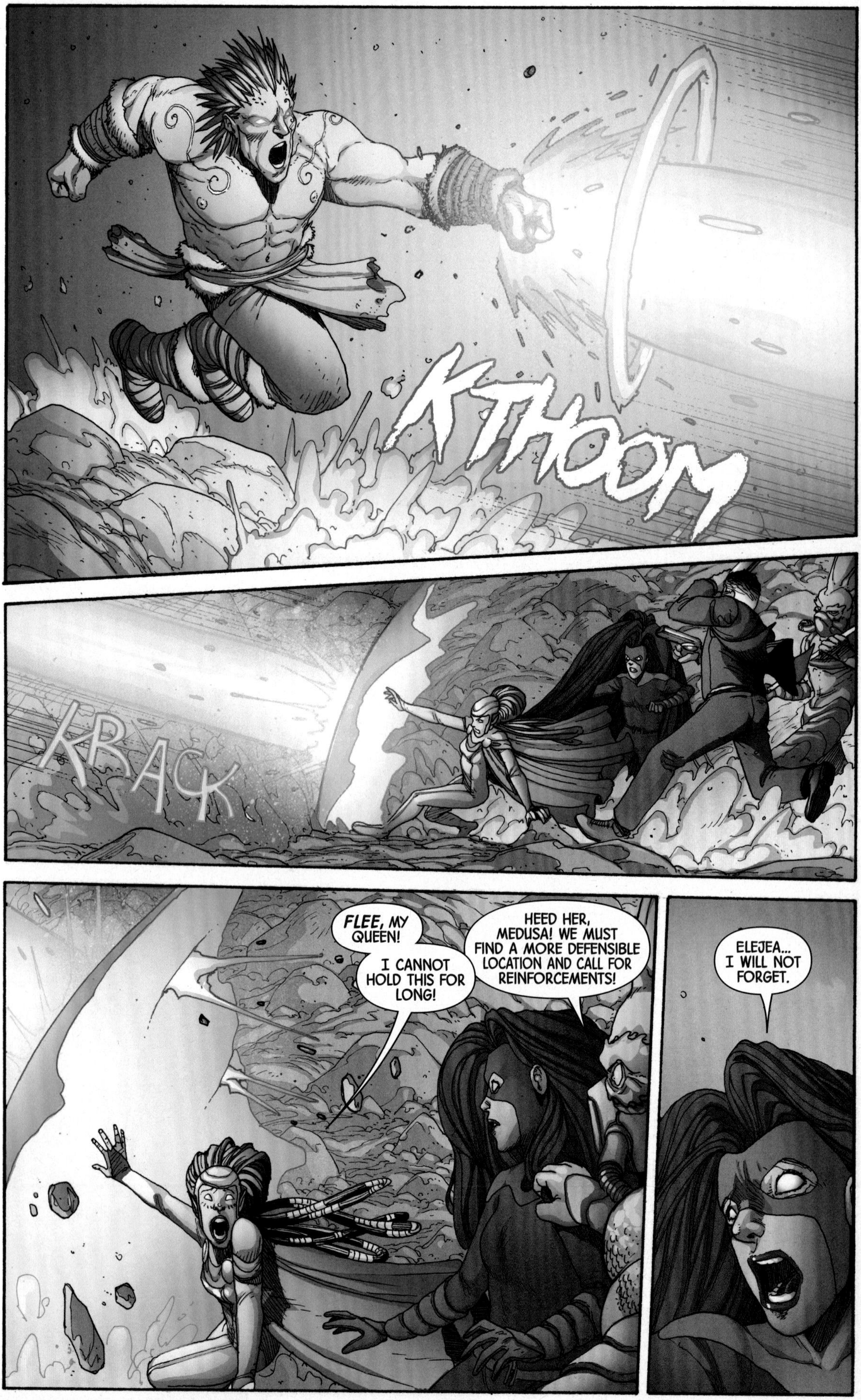
KTHOOM
KRACK
FLEE, MY QUEEN!
I CANNOT HOLD THIS FOR LONG!
HEED HER, MEDUSA! WE MUST FIND A MORE DEFENSIBLE LOCATION AND CALL FOR REINFORCEMENTS!
ELEJEA... I WILL NOT FORGET.

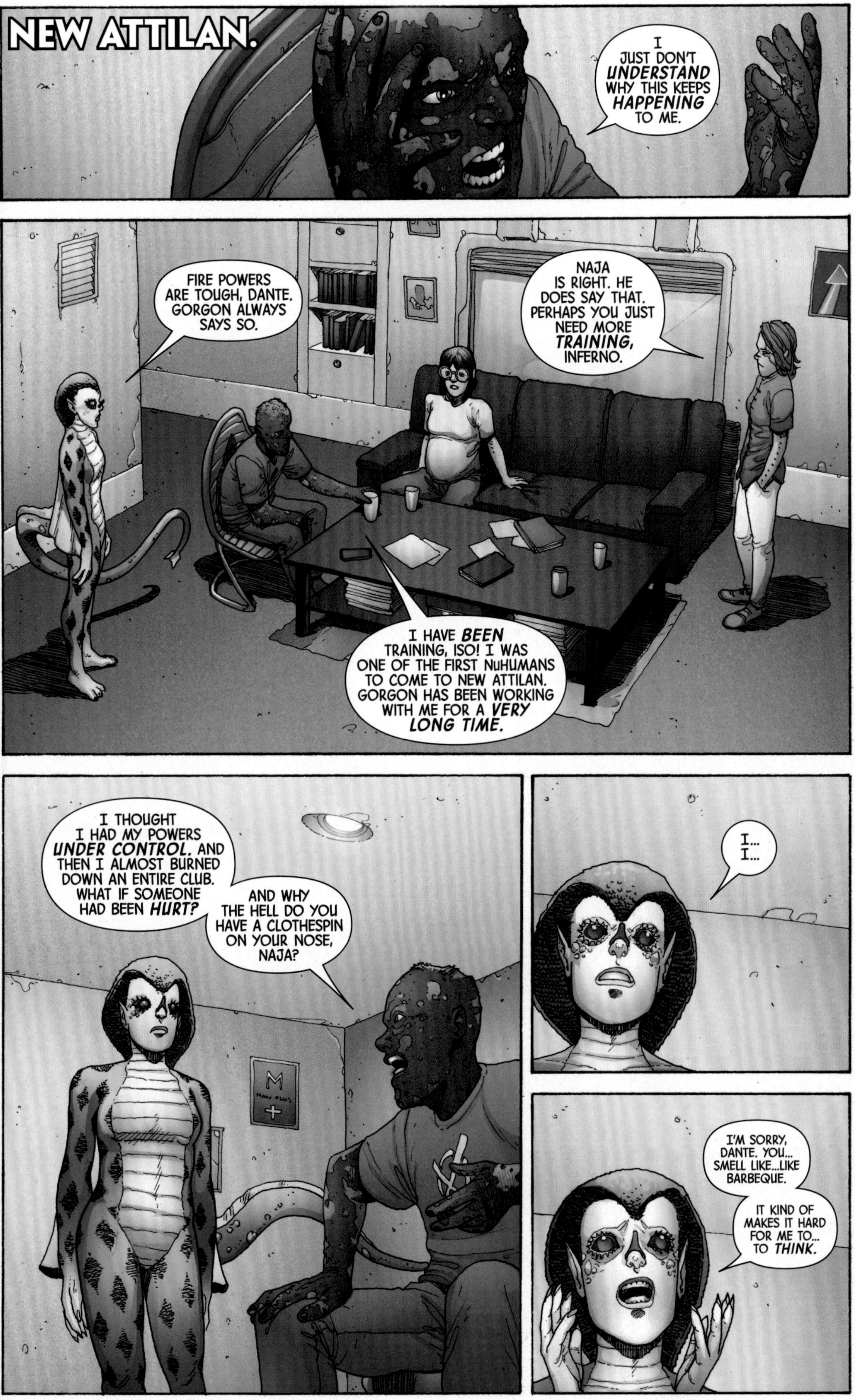
NEW ATTILAN.
I JUST DON'T UNDERSTAND WHY THIS KEEPS HAPPENING TO ME.
FIRE POWERS ARE TOUGH, DANTE. GORGON ALWAYS SAYS SO.
NAJA IS RIGHT. HE DOES SAY THAT. PERHAPS YOU JUST NEED MORE TRAINING, INFERNO.
I HAVE BEEN TRAINING, ISO! I WAS ONE OF THE FIRST NuHUMANS TO COME TO NEW ATTILAN. GORGON HAS BEEN WORKING WITH ME FOR A VERY LONG TIME.
I THOUGHT I HAD MY POWERS UNDER CONTROL. AND THEN I ALMOST BURNED DOWN AN ENTIRE CLUB. WHAT IF SOMEONE HAD BEEN HURT?
AND WHY THE HELL DO YOU HAVE A CLOTHESPIN ON YOUR NOSE, NAJA?
I... I...
I'M SORRY, DANTE. YOU... SMELL LIKE...LIKE BARBEQUE.
IT KIND OF MAKES IT HARD FOR ME TO... TO THINK.

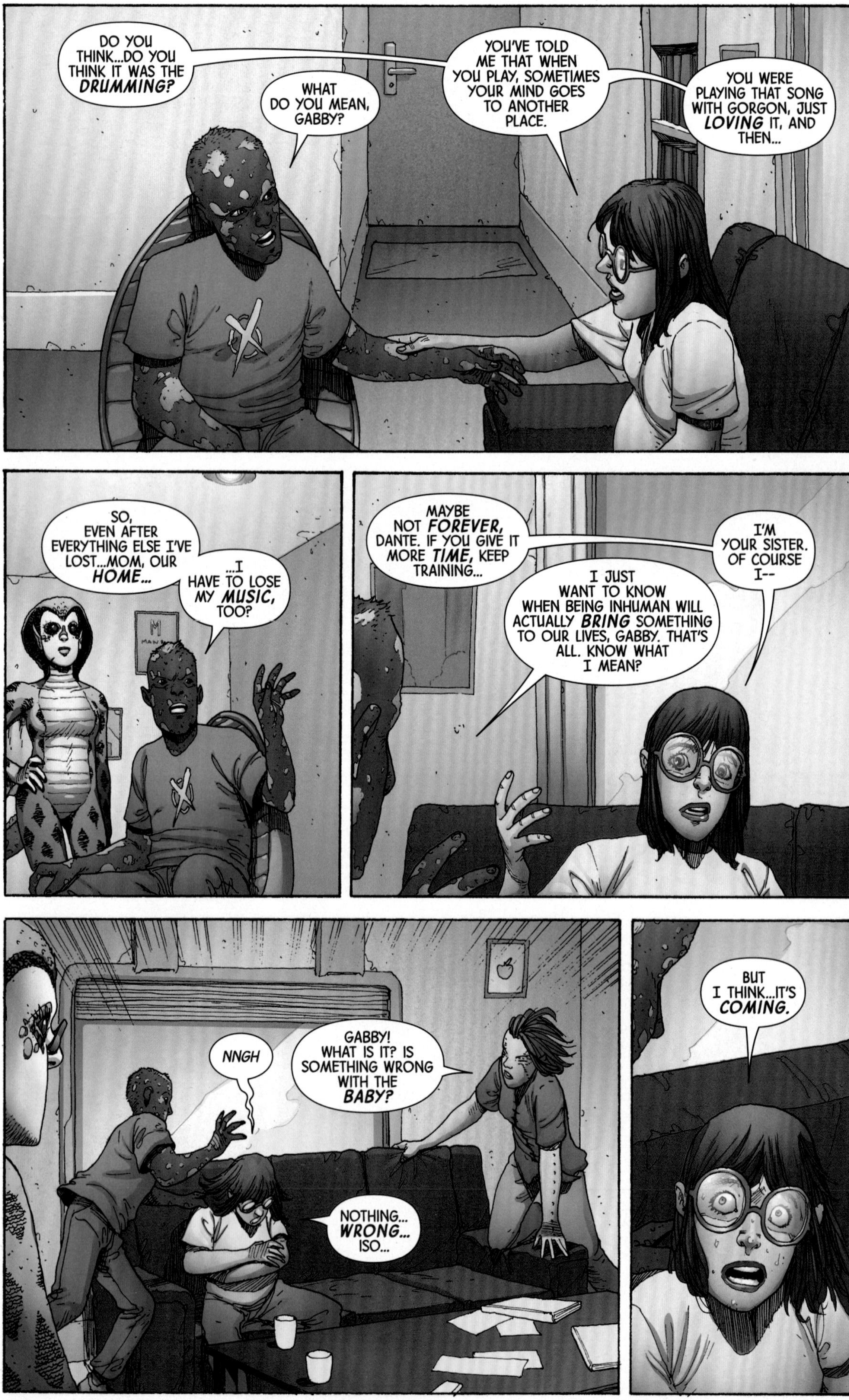
DO YOU THINK...DO YOU THINK IT WAS THE DRUMMING?
WHAT DO YOU MEAN, GABBY?
YOU'VE TOLD ME THAT WHEN YOU PLAY, SOMETIMES YOUR MIND GOES TO ANOTHER PLACE.
YOU WERE PLAYING THAT SONG WITH GORGON, JUST LOVING IT, AND THEN...
SO, EVEN AFTER EVERYTHING ELSE I'VE LOST...MOM, OUR HOME...
...I HAVE TO LOSE MY MUSIC, TOO?
MAYBE NOT FOREVER, DANTE. IF YOU GIVE IT MORE TIME, KEEP TRAINING...
I'M YOUR SISTER. OF COURSE I--
I JUST WANT TO KNOW WHEN BEING INHUMAN WILL ACTUALLY BRING SOMETHING TO OUR LIVES, GABBY. THAT'S ALL. KNOW WHAT I MEAN?
NNGH
GABBY! WHAT IS IT? IS SOMETHING WRONG WITH THE BABY?
NOTHING... WRONG... ISO...
BUT I THINK...IT'S COMING.

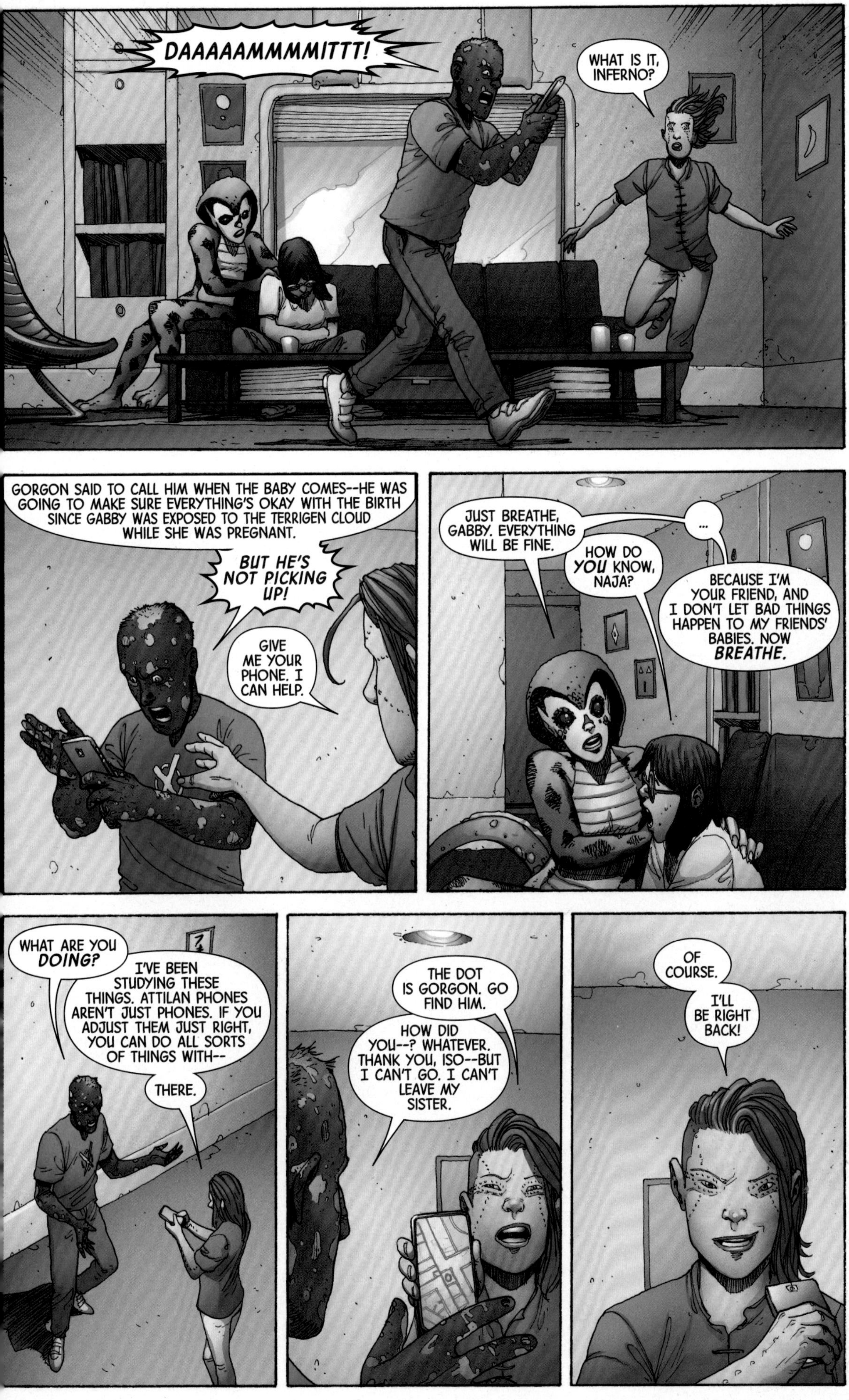

DAAAAAMMMMITTT!
WHAT IS IT, INFERNO?
GORGON SAID TO CALL HIM WHEN THE BABY COMES--HE WAS GOING TO MAKE SURE EVERYTHING'S OKAY WITH THE BIRTH SINCE GABBY WAS EXPOSED TO THE TERRIGEN CLOUD WHILE SHE WAS PREGNANT.
BUT HE'S NOT PICKING UP!
GIVE ME YOUR PHONE. I CAN HELP.
JUST BREATHE, GABBY. EVERYTHING WILL BE FINE.
HOW DO YOU KNOW, NAJA?
...
BECAUSE I'M YOUR FRIEND, AND I DON'T LET BAD THINGS HAPPEN TO MY FRIENDS' BABIES. NOW BREATHE.
WHAT ARE YOU DOING?
I'VE BEEN STUDYING THESE THINGS. ATTILAN PHONES AREN'T JUST PHONES. IF YOU ADJUST THEM JUST RIGHT, YOU CAN DO ALL SORTS OF THINGS WITH--
THERE.
THE DOT IS GORGON. GO FIND HIM.
HOW DID YOU--? WHATEVER. THANK YOU, ISO--BUT I CAN'T GO. I CAN'T LEAVE MY SISTER.
OF COURSE.
I'LL BE RIGHT BACK!

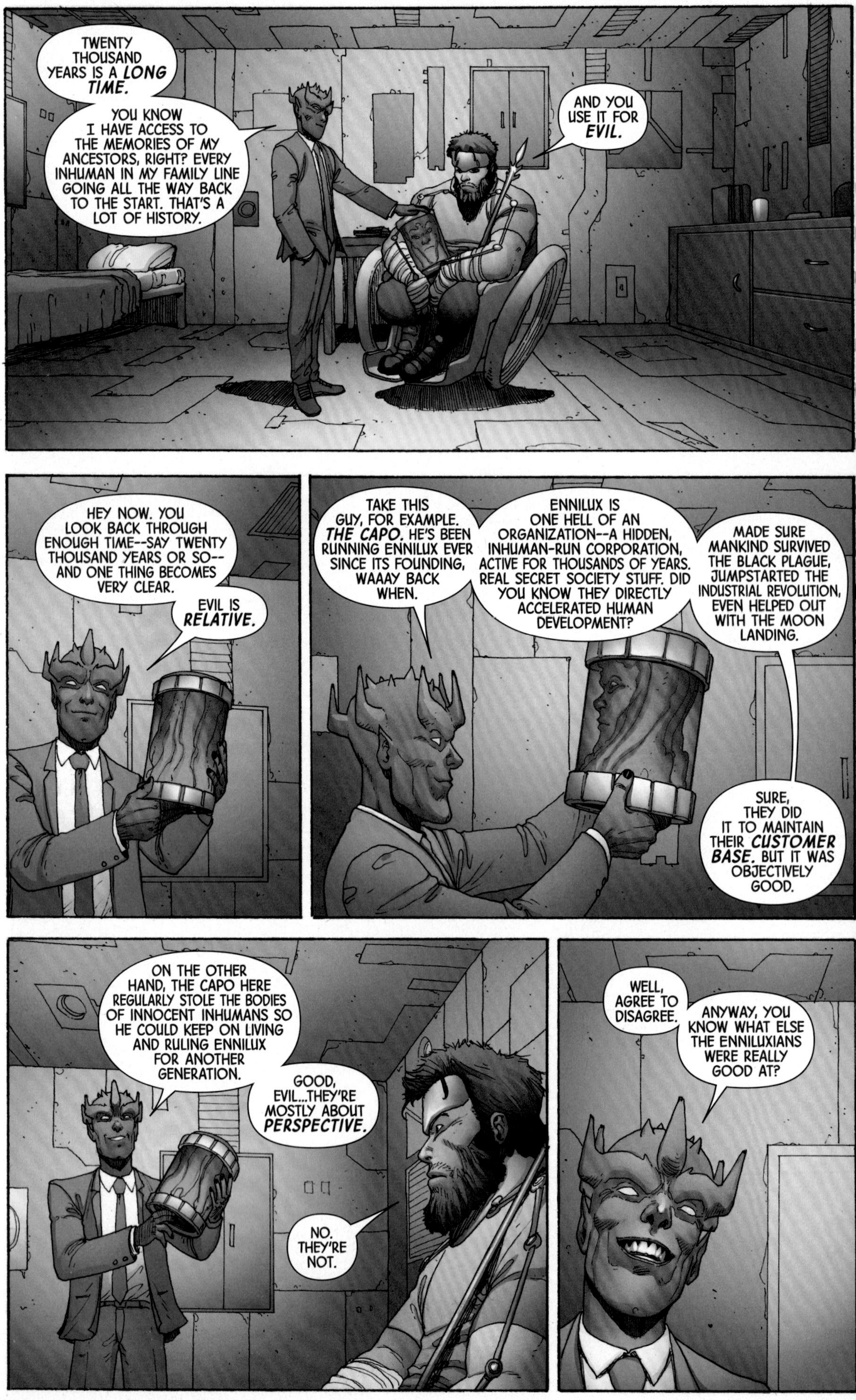
TWENTY THOUSAND YEARS IS A *LONG TIME.*
YOU KNOW I HAVE ACCESS TO THE MEMORIES OF MY ANCESTORS, RIGHT? EVERY INHUMAN IN MY FAMILY LINE GOING ALL THE WAY BACK TO THE START. THAT'S A LOT OF HISTORY.
AND YOU USE IT FOR *EVIL.*
HEY NOW. YOU LOOK BACK THROUGH ENOUGH TIME--SAY TWENTY THOUSAND YEARS OR SO--AND ONE THING BECOMES VERY CLEAR.
EVIL IS *RELATIVE.*
TAKE THIS GUY, FOR EXAMPLE. *THE CAPO.* HE'S BEEN RUNNING ENNILUX EVER SINCE ITS FOUNDING, WAAAY BACK WHEN.
ENNILUX IS ONE HELL OF AN ORGANIZATION--A HIDDEN, INHUMAN-RUN CORPORATION, ACTIVE FOR THOUSANDS OF YEARS. REAL SECRET SOCIETY STUFF. DID YOU KNOW THEY DIRECTLY ACCELERATED HUMAN DEVELOPMENT?
MADE SURE MANKIND SURVIVED THE BLACK PLAGUE, JUMPSTARTED THE INDUSTRIAL REVOLUTION, EVEN HELPED OUT WITH THE MOON LANDING.
SURE, THEY DID IT TO MAINTAIN THEIR *CUSTOMER BASE.* BUT IT WAS OBJECTIVELY GOOD.
ON THE OTHER HAND, THE CAPO HERE REGULARLY STOLE THE BODIES OF INNOCENT INHUMANS SO HE COULD KEEP ON LIVING AND RULING ENNILUX FOR ANOTHER GENERATION.
GOOD, EVIL...THEY'RE MOSTLY ABOUT *PERSPECTIVE.*
NO. THEY'RE NOT.
WELL, AGREE TO DISAGREE.
ANYWAY, YOU KNOW WHAT ELSE THE ENNILUXIANS WERE REALLY GOOD AT?

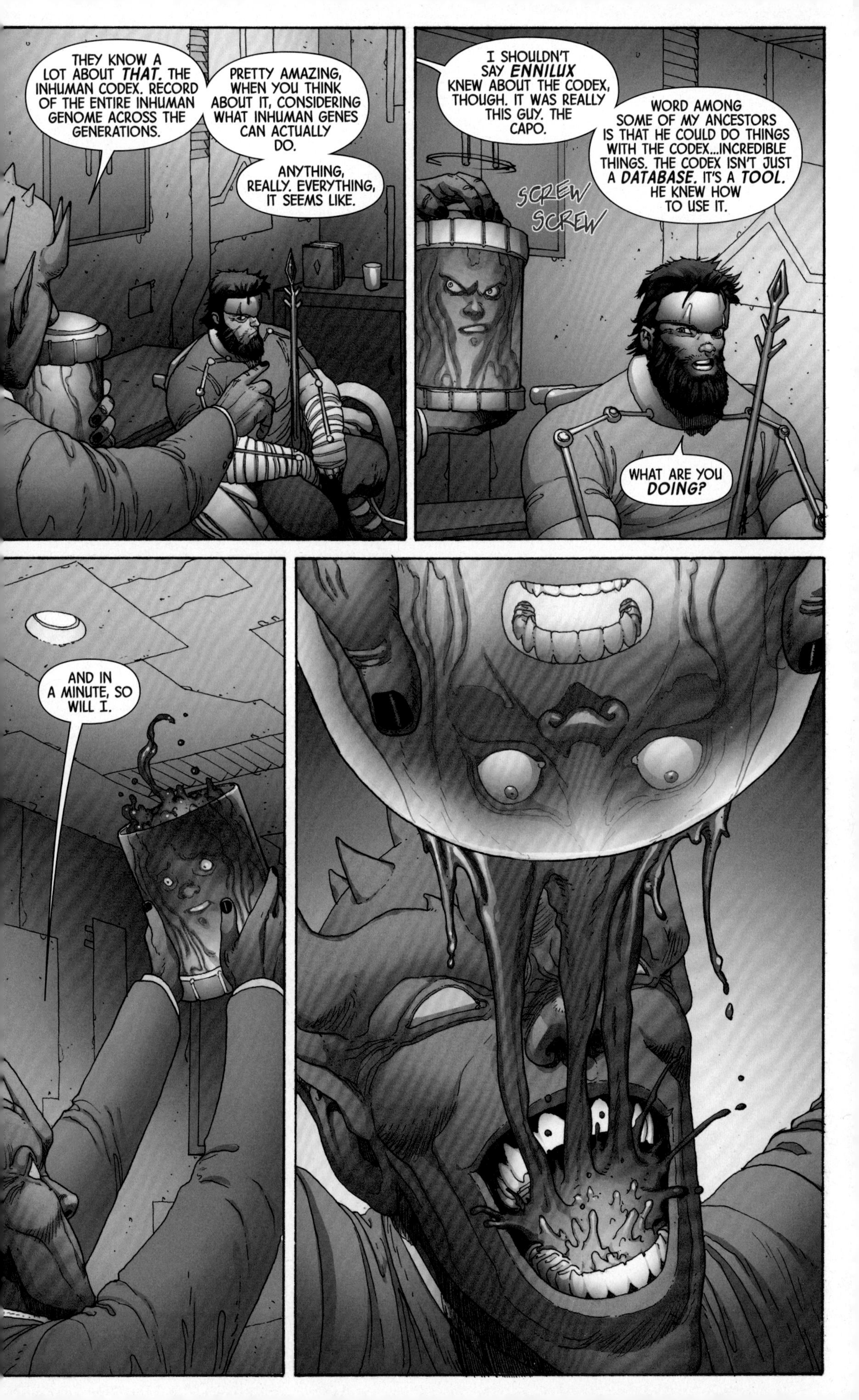
THEY KNOW A LOT ABOUT THAT. THE INHUMAN CODEX. RECORD OF THE ENTIRE INHUMAN GENOME ACROSS THE GENERATIONS.
PRETTY AMAZING, WHEN YOU THINK ABOUT IT, CONSIDERING WHAT INHUMAN GENES CAN ACTUALLY DO.
ANYTHING, REALLY. EVERYTHING, IT SEEMS LIKE.
I SHOULDN'T SAY ENNILUX KNEW ABOUT THE CODEX, THOUGH. IT WAS REALLY THIS GUY. THE CAPO.
SCREW SCREW
WORD AMONG SOME OF MY ANCESTORS IS THAT HE COULD DO THINGS WITH THE CODEX...INCREDIBLE THINGS. THE CODEX ISN'T JUST A DATABASE. IT'S A TOOL. HE KNEW HOW TO USE IT.
WHAT ARE YOU DOING?
AND IN A MINUTE, SO WILL I.

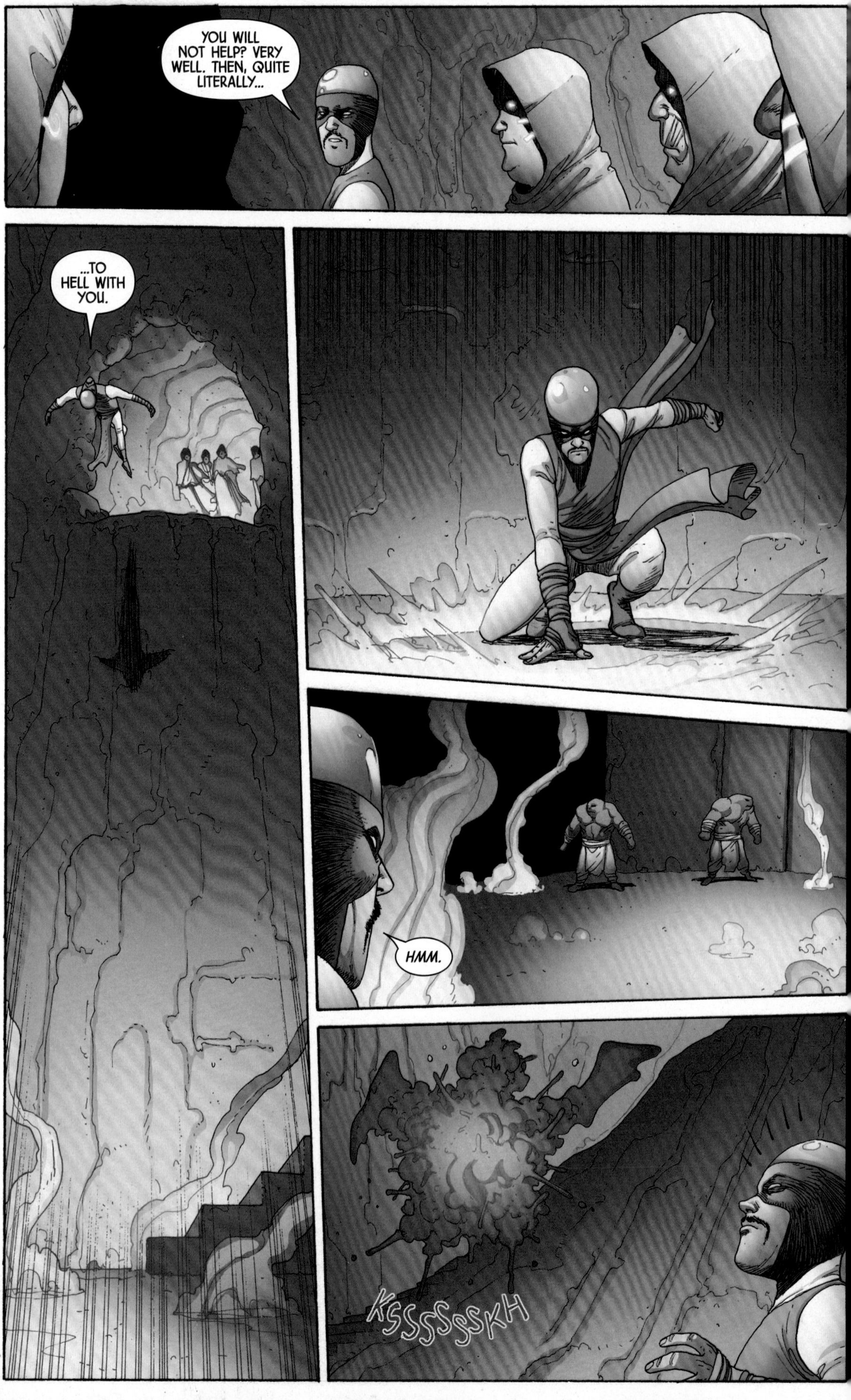
YOU WILL NOT HELP? VERY WELL. THEN, QUITE LITERALLY...
...TO HELL WITH YOU.
HMM.
KSSSSSSKH

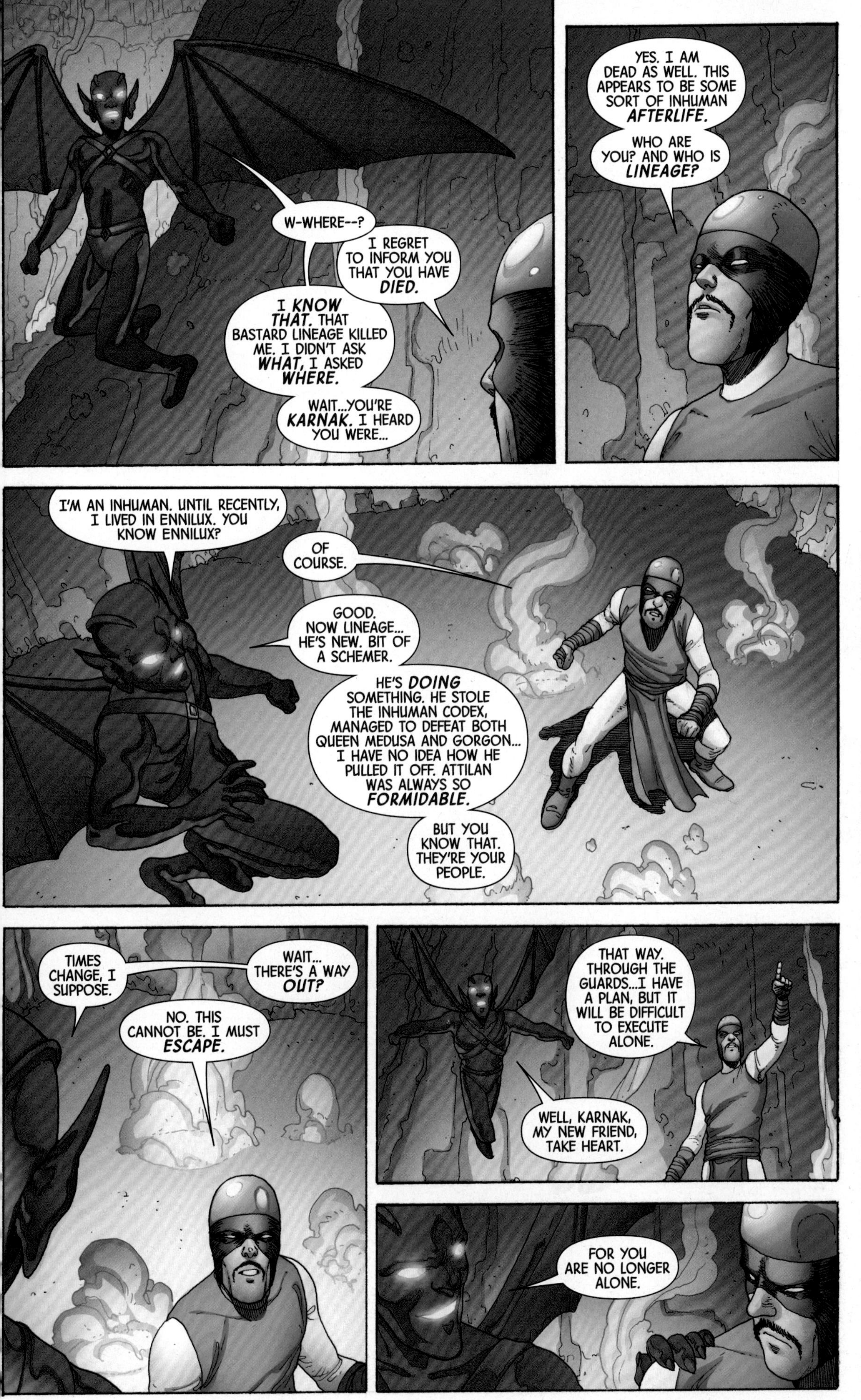
W-WHERE--?
I REGRET TO INFORM YOU THAT YOU HAVE DIED.
I KNOW THAT. THAT BASTARD LINEAGE KILLED ME. I DIDN'T ASK WHAT, I ASKED WHERE.
WAIT...YOU'RE KARNAK. I HEARD YOU WERE...
YES. I AM DEAD AS WELL. THIS APPEARS TO BE SOME SORT OF INHUMAN AFTERLIFE.
WHO ARE YOU? AND WHO IS LINEAGE?
I'M AN INHUMAN. UNTIL RECENTLY, I LIVED IN ENNILUX. YOU KNOW ENNILUX?
OF COURSE.
GOOD. NOW LINEAGE... HE'S NEW. BIT OF A SCHEMER.
HE'S DOING SOMETHING. HE STOLE THE INHUMAN CODEX, MANAGED TO DEFEAT BOTH QUEEN MEDUSA AND GORGON... I HAVE NO IDEA HOW HE PULLED IT OFF. ATTILAN WAS ALWAYS SO FORMIDABLE.
BUT YOU KNOW THAT. THEY'RE YOUR PEOPLE.
TIMES CHANGE, I SUPPOSE.
NO. THIS CANNOT BE. I MUST ESCAPE.
WAIT... THERE'S A WAY OUT?
THAT WAY. THROUGH THE GUARDS...I HAVE A PLAN, BUT IT WILL BE DIFFICULT TO EXECUTE ALONE.
WELL, KARNAK, MY NEW FRIEND, TAKE HEART.
FOR YOU ARE NO LONGER ALONE.

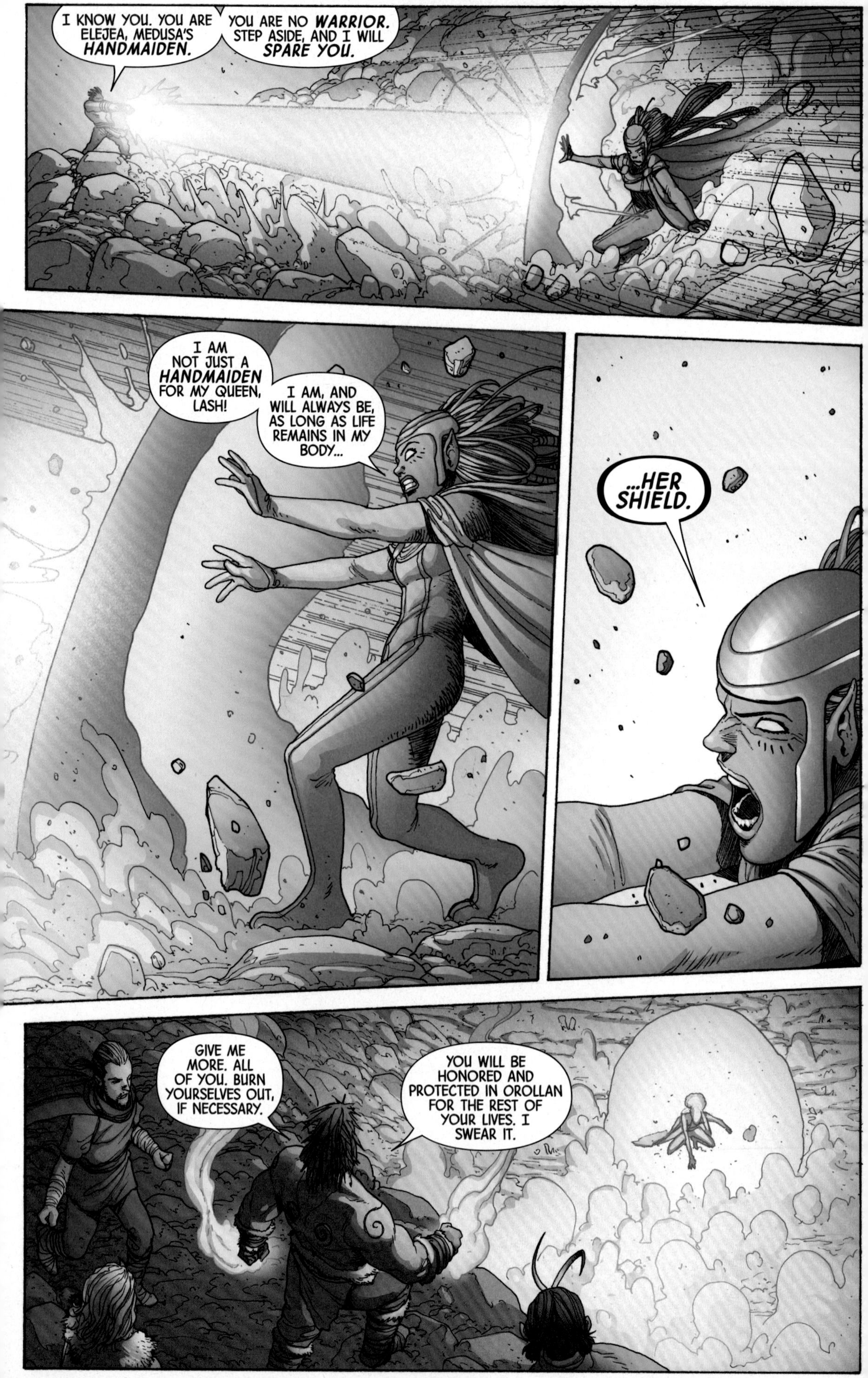
I KNOW YOU. YOU ARE ELEJEA, MEDUSA'S HANDMAIDEN.
YOU ARE NO WARRIOR. STEP ASIDE, AND I WILL SPARE YOU.
I AM NOT JUST A HANDMAIDEN FOR MY QUEEN, LASH!
I AM, AND WILL ALWAYS BE, AS LONG AS LIFE REMAINS IN MY BODY...
...HER SHIELD.
GIVE ME MORE. ALL OF YOU. BURN YOURSELVES OUT, IF NECESSARY.
YOU WILL BE HONORED AND PROTECTED IN OROLLAN FOR THE REST OF YOUR LIVES. I SWEAR IT.

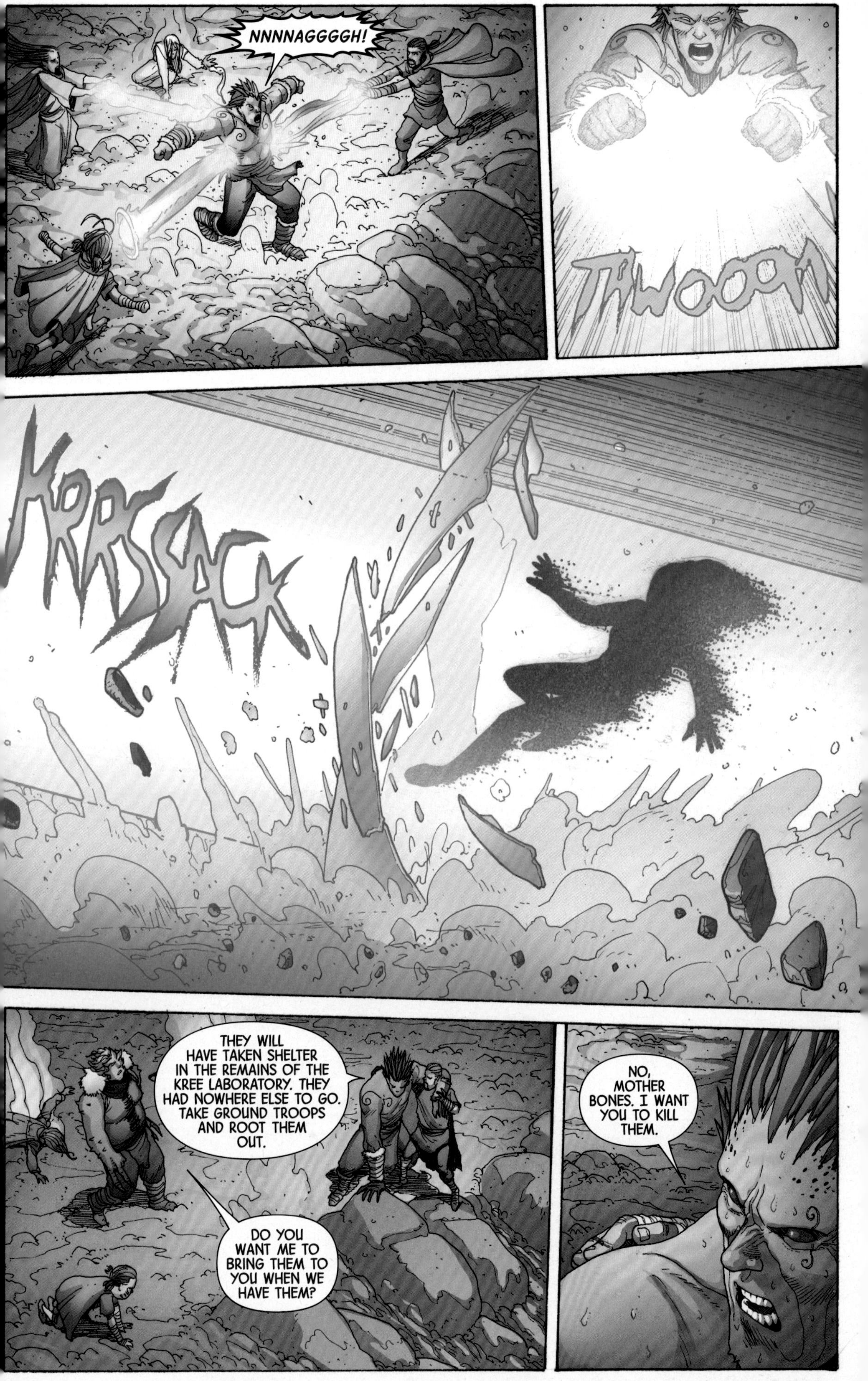
NNNNAGGGGH!
TAWOOOM
KRASACK
THEY WILL HAVE TAKEN SHELTER IN THE REMAINS OF THE KREE LABORATORY. THEY HAD NOWHERE ELSE TO GO. TAKE GROUND TROOPS AND ROOT THEM OUT.
DO YOU WANT ME TO BRING THEM TO YOU WHEN WE HAVE THEM?
NO, MOTHER BONES. I WANT YOU TO KILL THEM.

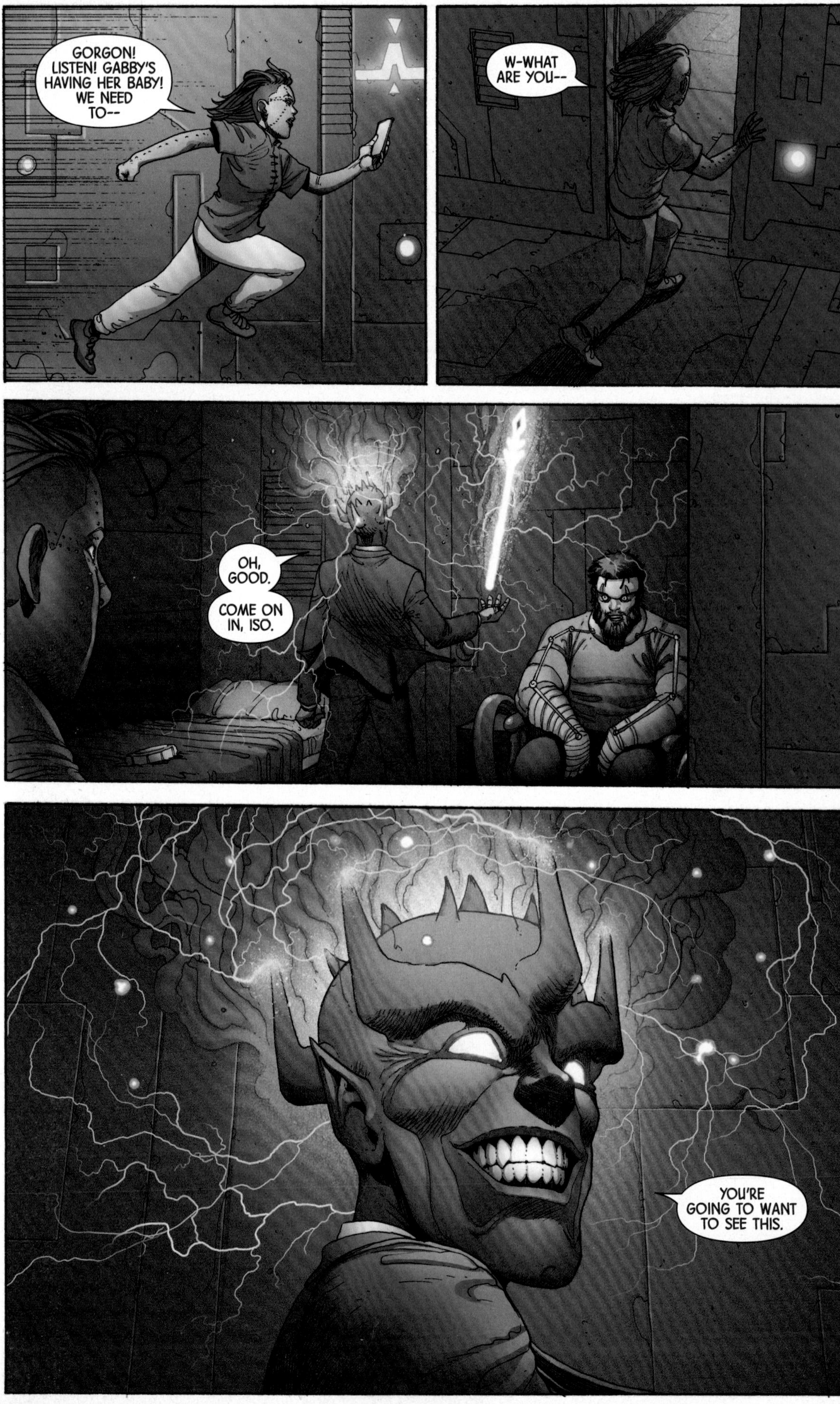
GORGON! LISTEN! GABBY'S HAVING HER BABY! WE NEED TO--
W-WHAT ARE YOU--
OH, GOOD.
COME ON IN, ISO.
YOU'RE GOING TO WANT TO SEE THIS.

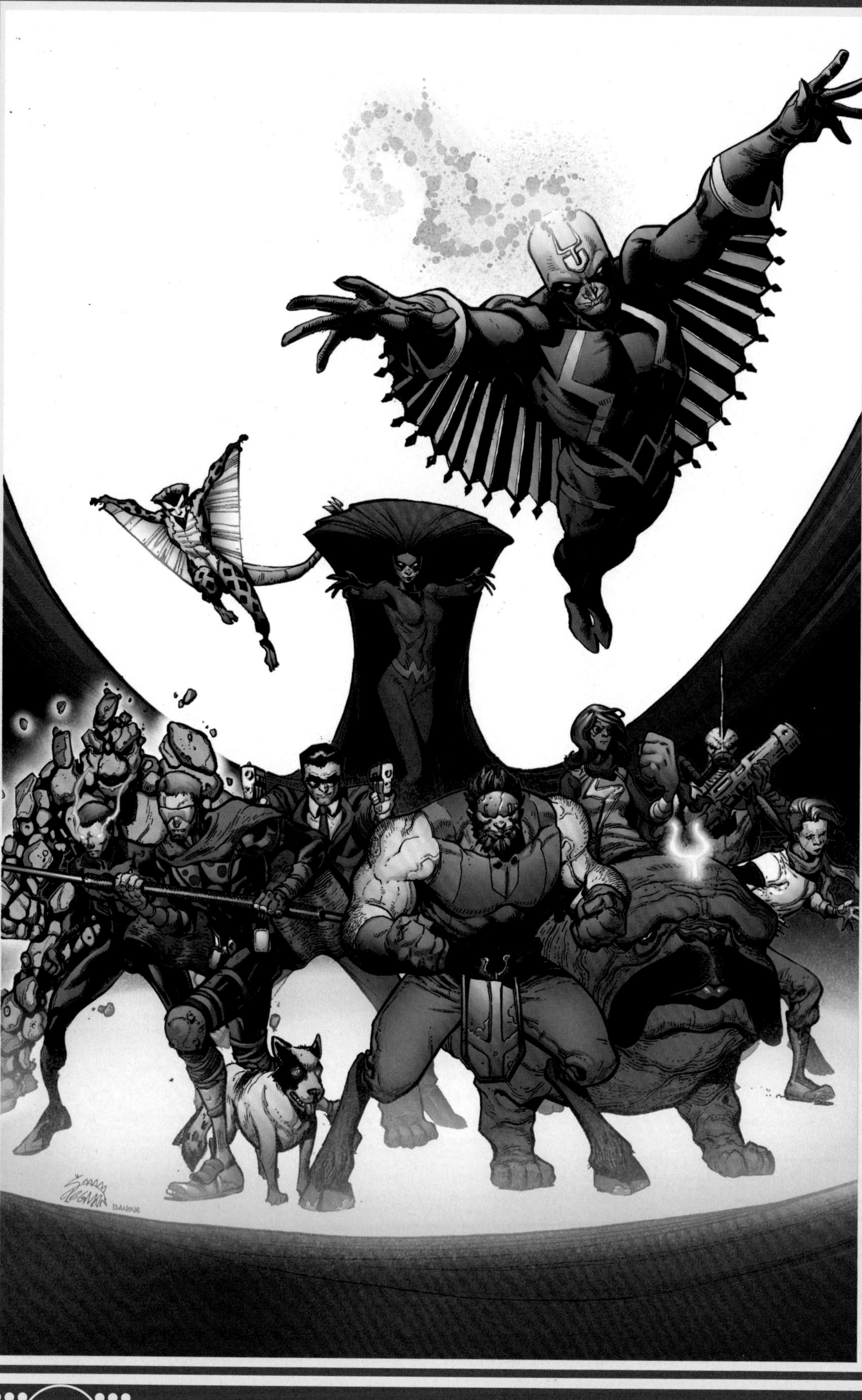

ANNUAL 1

PART FIFTEEN: LEGACY

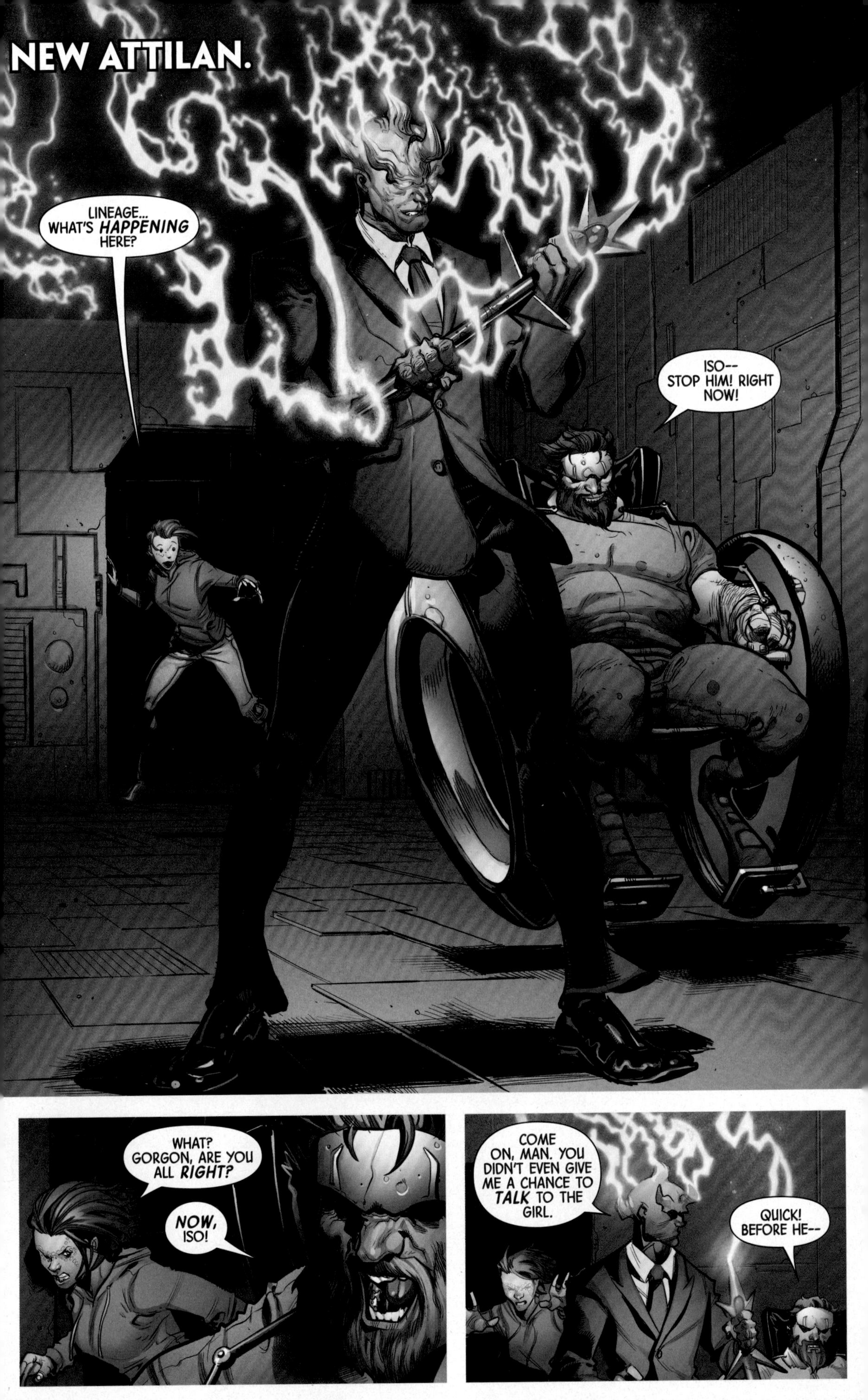
NEW ATTILAN.
LINEAGE... WHAT'S HAPPENING HERE?
ISO-- STOP HIM! RIGHT NOW!
WHAT? GORGON, ARE YOU ALL RIGHT?
NOW, ISO!
COME ON, MAN. YOU DIDN'T EVEN GIVE ME A CHANCE TO TALK TO THE GIRL.
QUICK! BEFORE HE--

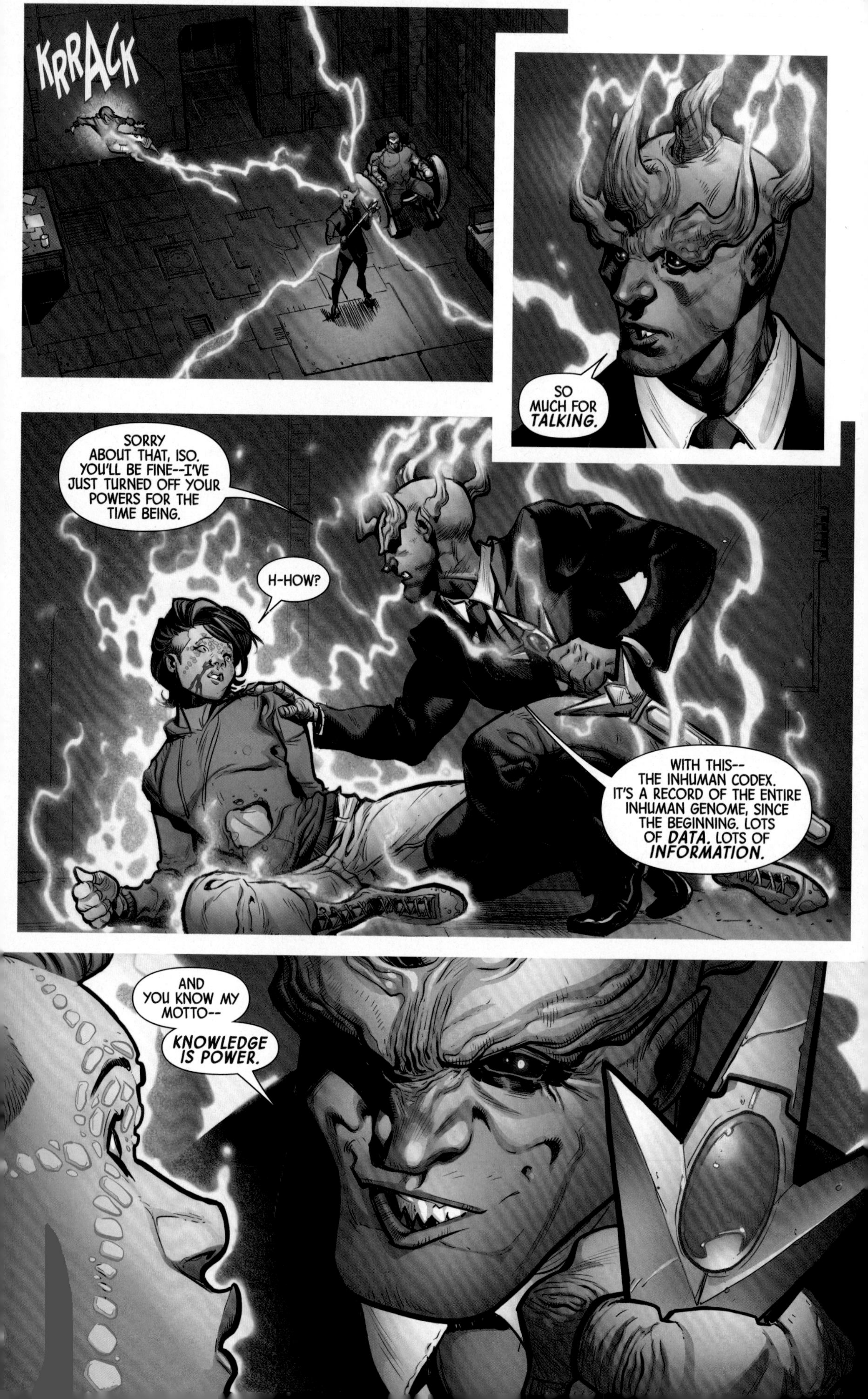
KRRACK
SO MUCH FOR TALKING.
SORRY ABOUT THAT, ISO. YOU'LL BE FINE--I'VE JUST TURNED OFF YOUR POWERS FOR THE TIME BEING.
H-HOW?
WITH THIS-- THE INHUMAN CODEX. IT'S A RECORD OF THE ENTIRE INHUMAN GENOME, SINCE THE BEGINNING. LOTS OF DATA. LOTS OF INFORMATION.
AND YOU KNOW MY MOTTO--
KNOWLEDGE IS POWER.

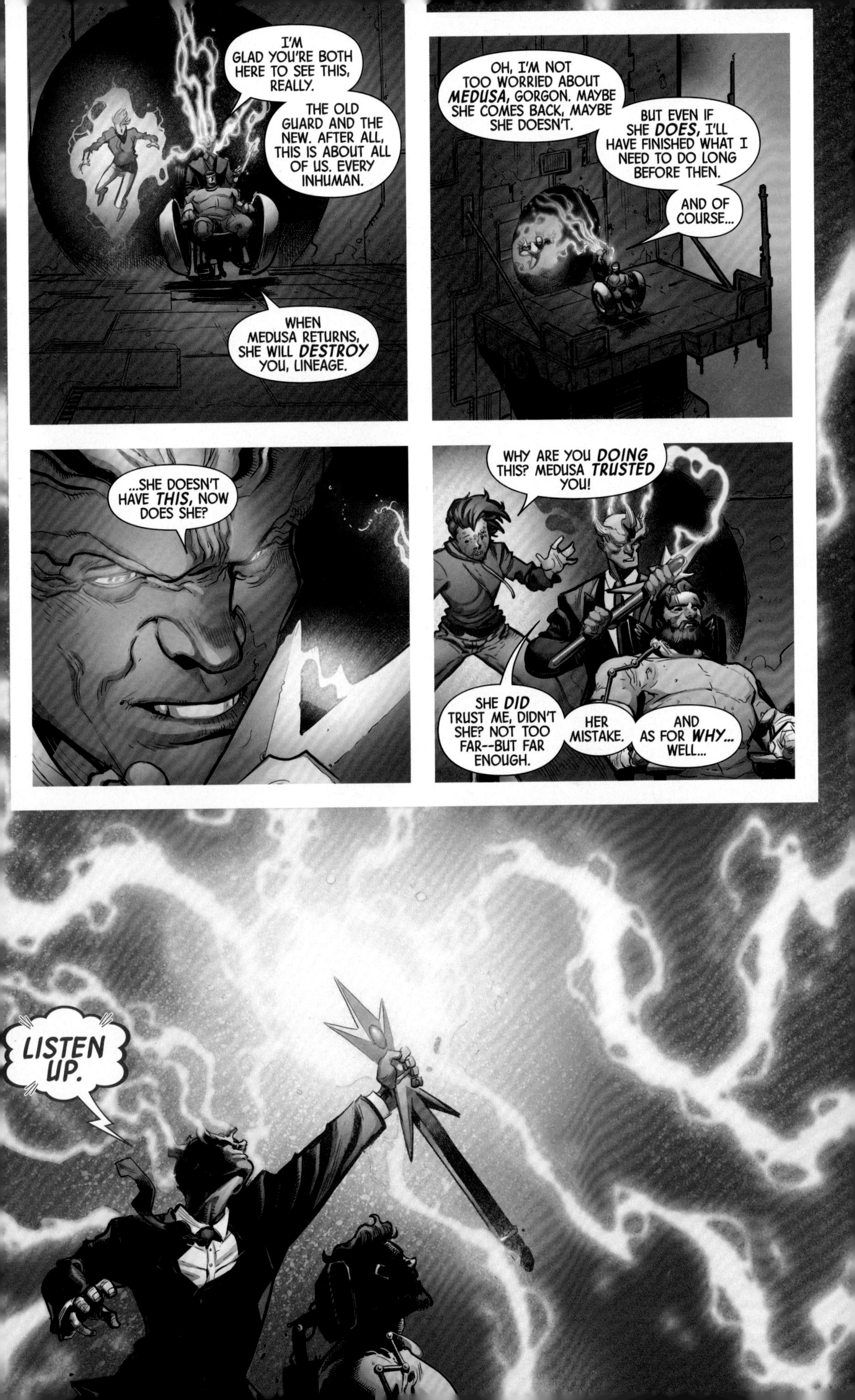
I'M GLAD YOU'RE BOTH HERE TO SEE THIS, REALLY.
THE OLD GUARD AND THE NEW. AFTER ALL, THIS IS ABOUT ALL OF US. EVERY INHUMAN.
WHEN MEDUSA RETURNS, SHE WILL DESTROY YOU, LINEAGE.
OH, I'M NOT TOO WORRIED ABOUT MEDUSA, GORGON. MAYBE SHE COMES BACK, MAYBE SHE DOESN'T.
BUT EVEN IF SHE DOES, I'LL HAVE FINISHED WHAT I NEED TO DO LONG BEFORE THEN.
AND OF COURSE...
...SHE DOESN'T HAVE THIS, NOW DOES SHE?
WHY ARE YOU DOING THIS? MEDUSA TRUSTED YOU!
SHE DID TRUST ME, DIDN'T SHE? NOT TOO FAR--BUT FAR ENOUGH.
HER MISTAKE.
AND AS FOR WHY... WELL...
LISTEN UP.

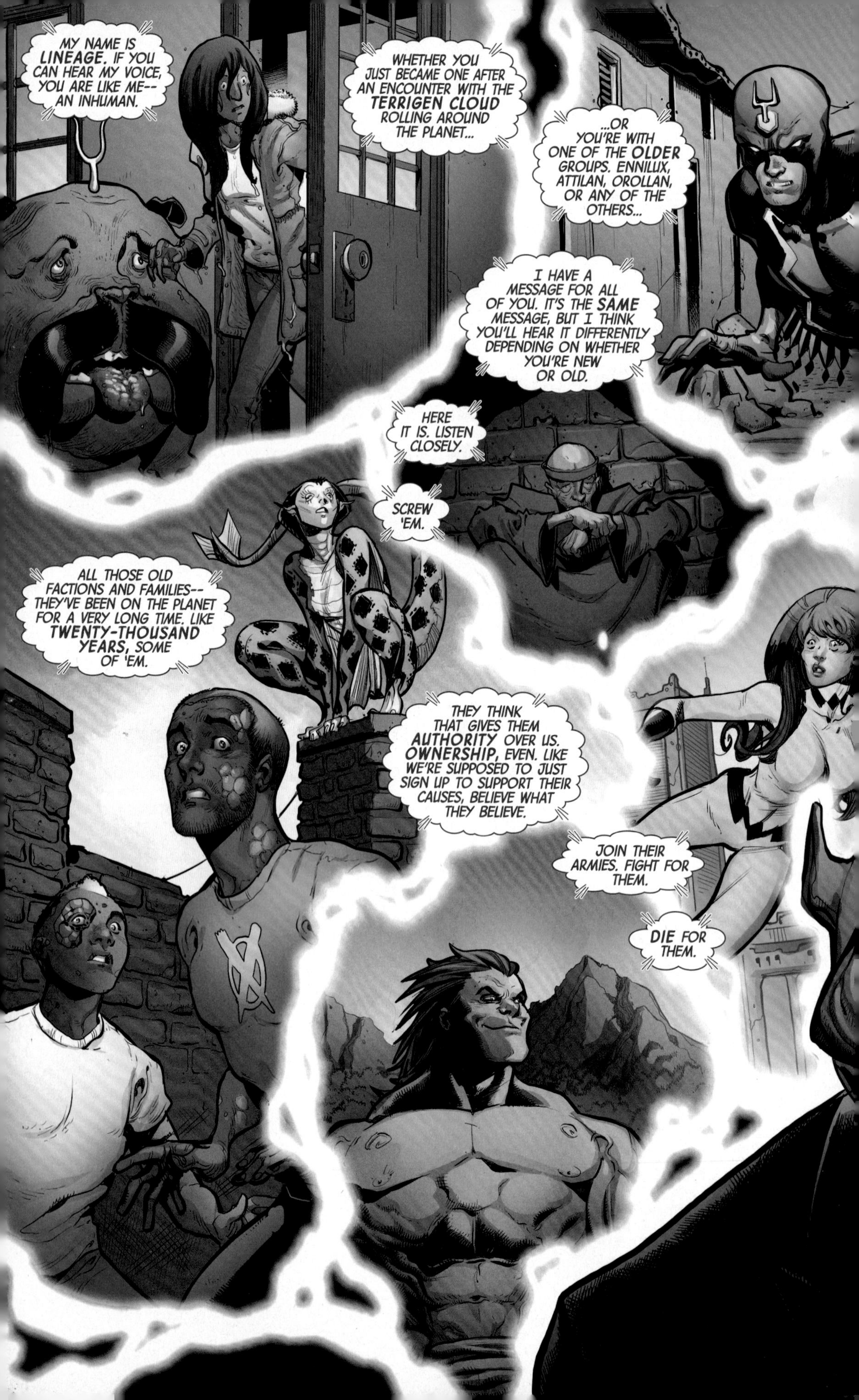
MY NAME IS LINEAGE. IF YOU CAN HEAR MY VOICE, YOU ARE LIKE ME-- AN INHUMAN.
WHETHER YOU JUST BECAME ONE AFTER AN ENCOUNTER WITH THE TERRIGEN CLOUD ROLLING AROUND THE PLANET...
...OR YOU'RE WITH ONE OF THE OLDER GROUPS. ENNILUX, ATTILAN, OROLLAN, OR ANY OF THE OTHERS...
I HAVE A MESSAGE FOR ALL OF YOU. IT'S THE SAME MESSAGE, BUT I THINK YOU'LL HEAR IT DIFFERENTLY DEPENDING ON WHETHER YOU'RE NEW OR OLD.
HERE IT IS. LISTEN CLOSELY.
SCREW 'EM.
ALL THOSE OLD FACTIONS AND FAMILIES-- THEY'VE BEEN ON THE PLANET FOR A VERY LONG TIME. LIKE TWENTY-THOUSAND YEARS, SOME OF 'EM.
THEY THINK THAT GIVES THEM AUTHORITY OVER US. OWNERSHIP, EVEN. LIKE WE'RE SUPPOSED TO JUST SIGN UP TO SUPPORT THEIR CAUSES, BELIEVE WHAT THEY BELIEVE.
JOIN THEIR ARMIES. FIGHT FOR THEM.
DIE FOR THEM.

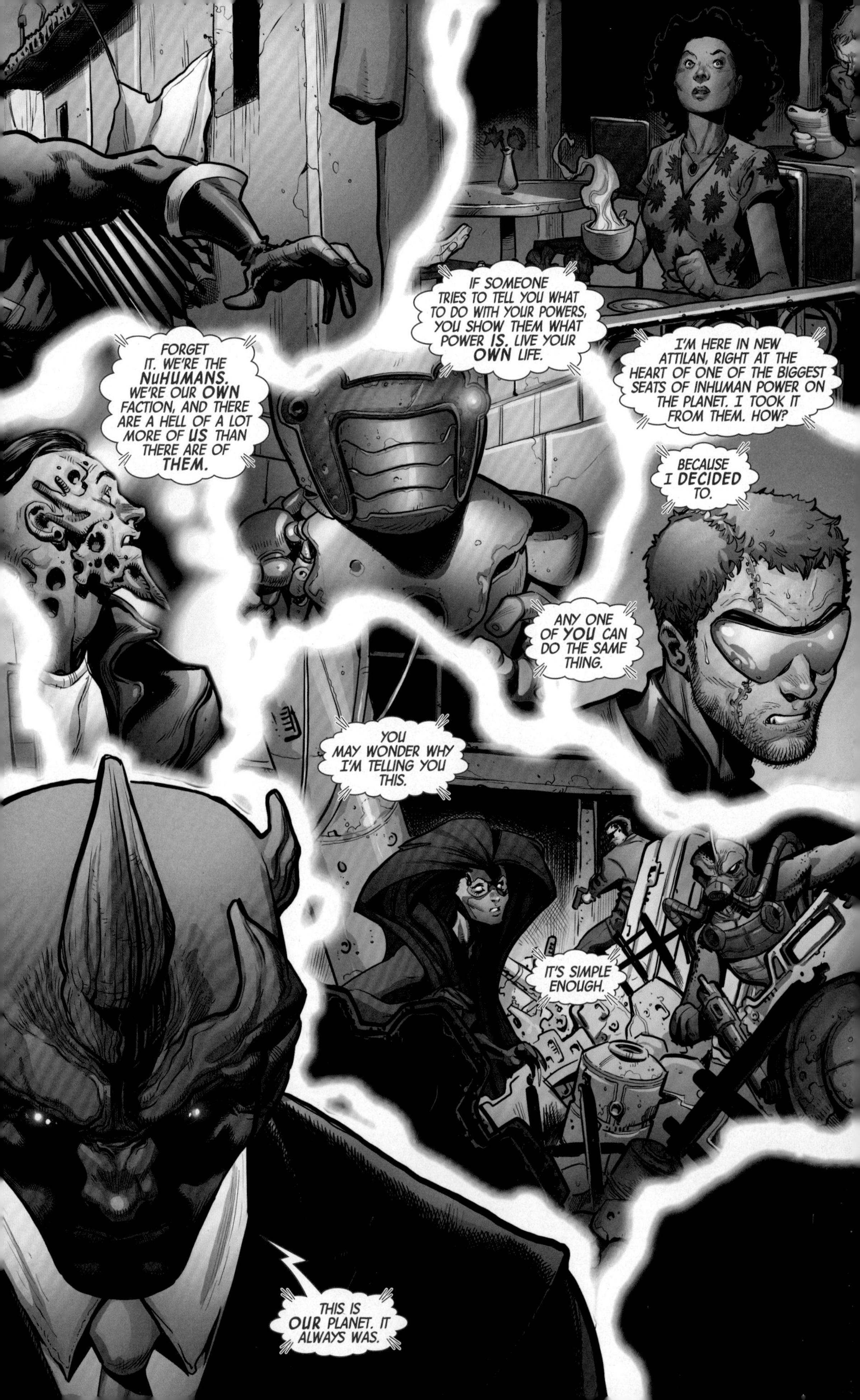
IF SOMEONE TRIES TO TELL YOU WHAT TO DO WITH YOUR POWERS, YOU SHOW THEM WHAT POWER IS. LIVE YOUR OWN LIFE.
FORGET IT. WE'RE THE NuHUMANS. WE'RE OUR OWN FACTION, AND THERE ARE A HELL OF A LOT MORE OF US THAN THERE ARE OF THEM.
I'M HERE IN NEW ATTILAN, RIGHT AT THE HEART OF ONE OF THE BIGGEST SEATS OF INHUMAN POWER ON THE PLANET. I TOOK IT FROM THEM. HOW?
BECAUSE I DECIDED TO.
ANY ONE OF YOU CAN DO THE SAME THING.
YOU MAY WONDER WHY I'M TELLING YOU THIS.
IT'S SIMPLE ENOUGH.
THIS IS OUR PLANET. IT ALWAYS WAS.

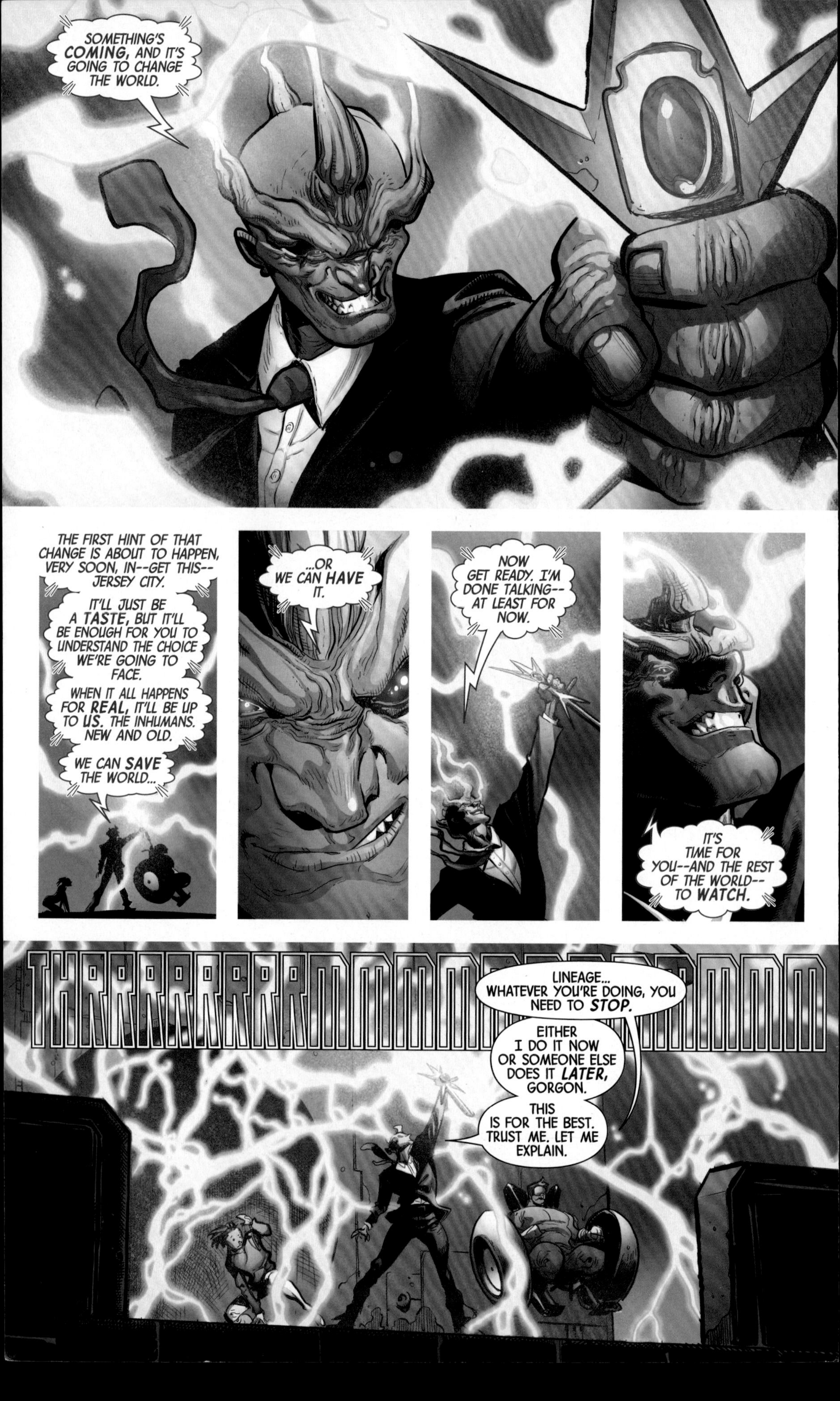
SOMETHING'S COMING, AND IT'S GOING TO CHANGE THE WORLD.
THE FIRST HINT OF THAT CHANGE IS ABOUT TO HAPPEN, VERY SOON, IN--GET THIS--JERSEY CITY.
IT'LL JUST BE A TASTE, BUT IT'LL BE ENOUGH FOR YOU TO UNDERSTAND THE CHOICE WE'RE GOING TO FACE.
WHEN IT ALL HAPPENS FOR REAL, IT'LL BE UP TO US. THE INHUMANS. NEW AND OLD.
WE CAN SAVE THE WORLD...
...OR WE CAN HAVE IT.
NOW GET READY. I'M DONE TALKING--AT LEAST FOR NOW.
IT'S TIME FOR YOU--AND THE REST OF THE WORLD--TO WATCH.
THRRRRRRRRRMMMMMMMMMMMMMM
LINEAGE... WHATEVER YOU'RE DOING, YOU NEED TO STOP.
EITHER I DO IT NOW OR SOMEONE ELSE DOES IT LATER, GORGON.
THIS IS FOR THE BEST. TRUST ME. LET ME EXPLAIN.

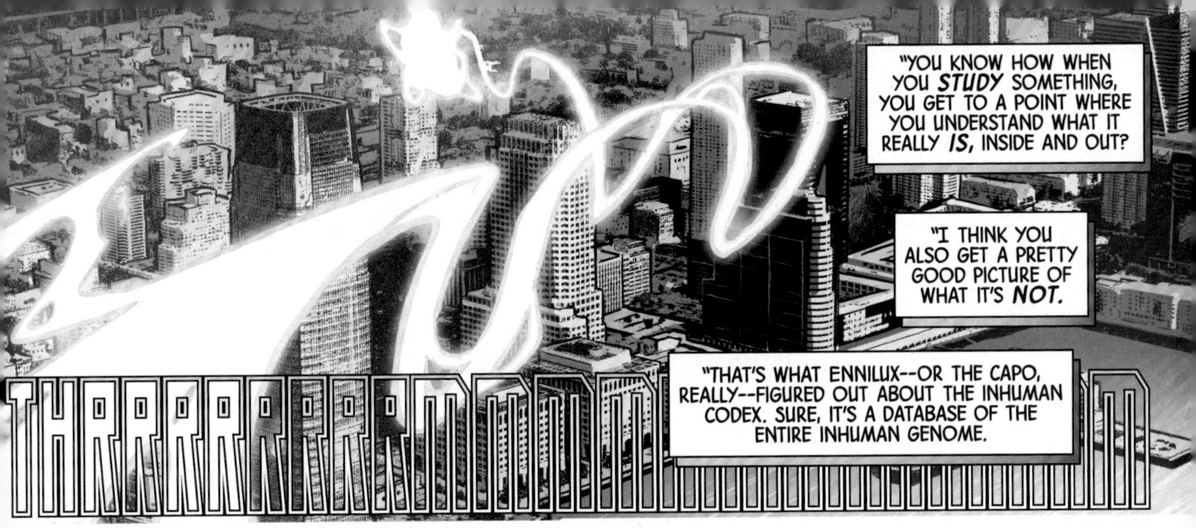
"YOU KNOW HOW WHEN YOU STUDY SOMETHING, YOU GET TO A POINT WHERE YOU UNDERSTAND WHAT IT REALLY IS, INSIDE AND OUT?
"I THINK YOU ALSO GET A PRETTY GOOD PICTURE OF WHAT IT'S NOT.
THRRRRRRRRRMMMMMMMMMMMMMMMMMMMMMMMMMMMM
"THAT'S WHAT ENNILUX--OR THE CAPO, REALLY--FIGURED OUT ABOUT THE INHUMAN CODEX. SURE, IT'S A DATABASE OF THE ENTIRE INHUMAN GENOME.

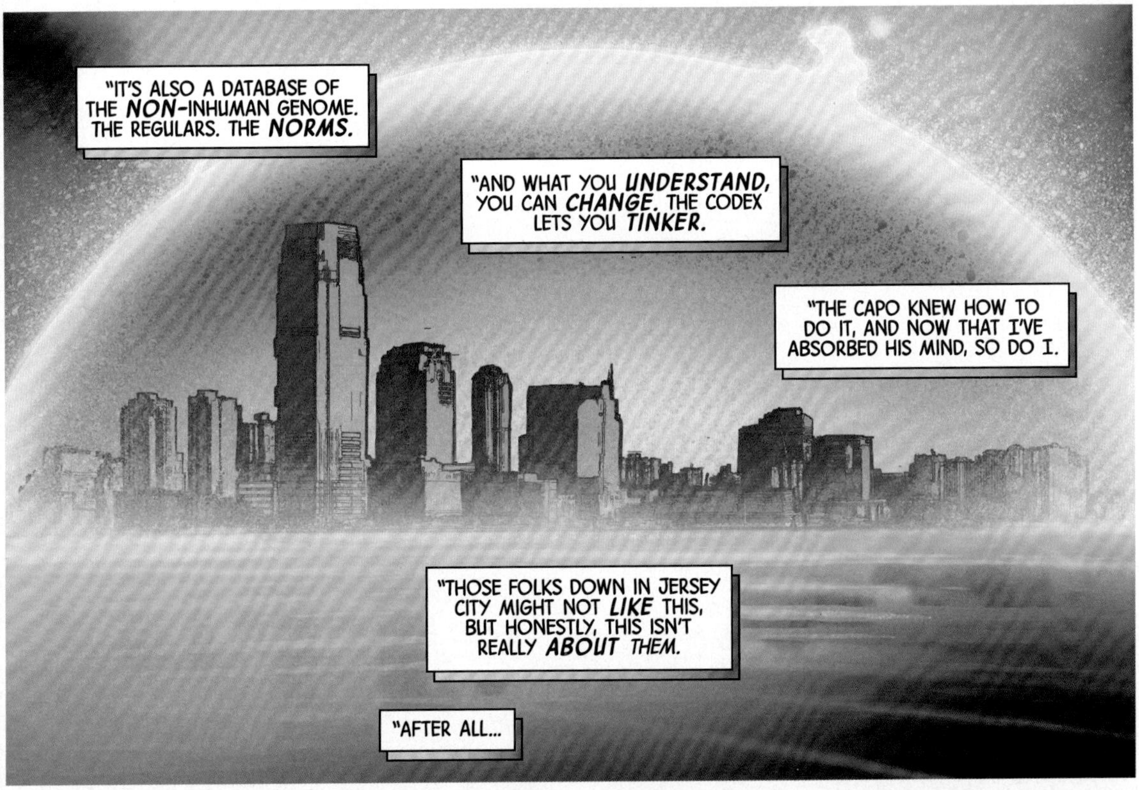
"IT'S ALSO A DATABASE OF THE NON-INHUMAN GENOME. THE REGULARS. THE NORMS.
"AND WHAT YOU UNDERSTAND, YOU CAN CHANGE. THE CODEX LETS YOU TINKER.
"THE CAPO KNEW HOW TO DO IT, AND NOW THAT I'VE ABSORBED HIS MIND, SO DO I.
"THOSE FOLKS DOWN IN JERSEY CITY MIGHT NOT LIKE THIS, BUT HONESTLY, THIS ISN'T REALLY ABOUT THEM.
"AFTER ALL...

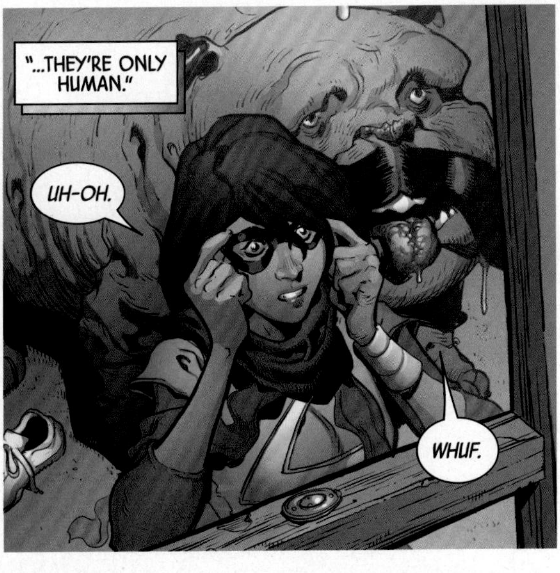
"...THEY'RE ONLY HUMAN."
UH-OH.
WHUF.

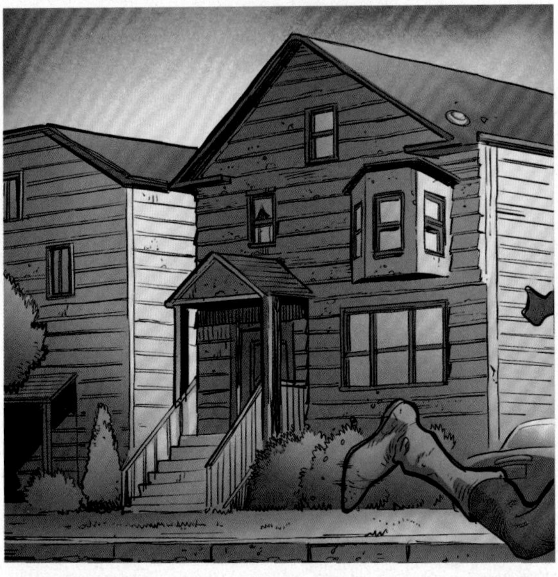

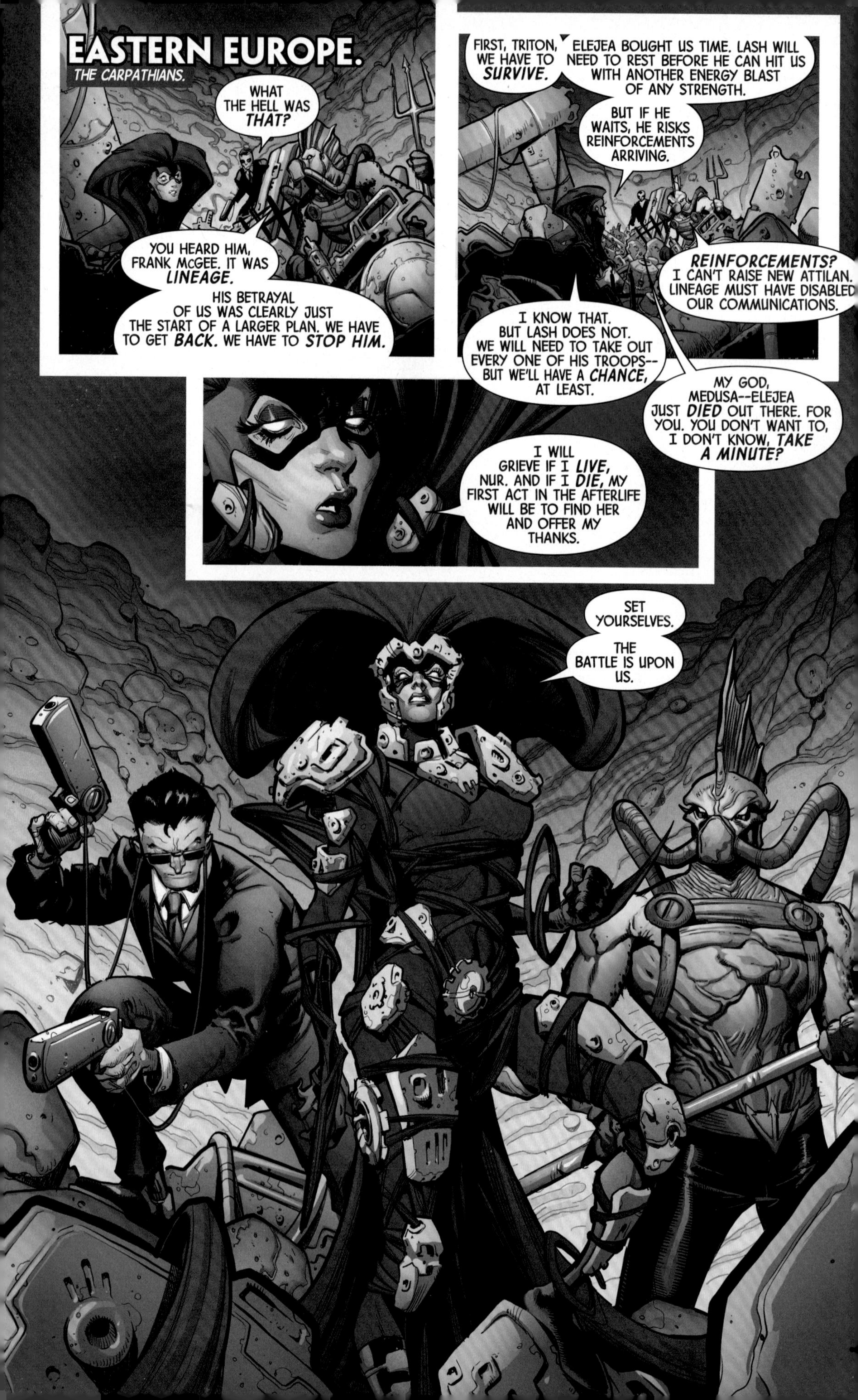
EASTERN EUROPE.
THE CARPATHIANS.
WHAT THE HELL WAS THAT?
YOU HEARD HIM, FRANK McGEE. IT WAS LINEAGE.
HIS BETRAYAL OF US WAS CLEARLY JUST THE START OF A LARGER PLAN. WE HAVE TO GET BACK. WE HAVE TO STOP HIM.
FIRST, TRITON, WE HAVE TO SURVIVE.
ELEJEA BOUGHT US TIME. LASH WILL NEED TO REST BEFORE HE CAN HIT US WITH ANOTHER ENERGY BLAST OF ANY STRENGTH.
BUT IF HE WAITS, HE RISKS REINFORCEMENTS ARRIVING.
REINFORCEMENTS? I CAN'T RAISE NEW ATTILAN. LINEAGE MUST HAVE DISABLED OUR COMMUNICATIONS.
I KNOW THAT. BUT LASH DOES NOT. WE WILL NEED TO TAKE OUT EVERY ONE OF HIS TROOPS-- BUT WE'LL HAVE A CHANCE, AT LEAST.
MY GOD, MEDUSA--ELEJEA JUST DIED OUT THERE. FOR YOU. YOU DON'T WANT TO, I DON'T KNOW, TAKE A MINUTE?
I WILL GRIEVE IF I LIVE, NUR. AND IF I DIE, MY FIRST ACT IN THE AFTERLIFE WILL BE TO FIND HER AND OFFER MY THANKS.
SET YOURSELVES.
THE BATTLE IS UPON US.

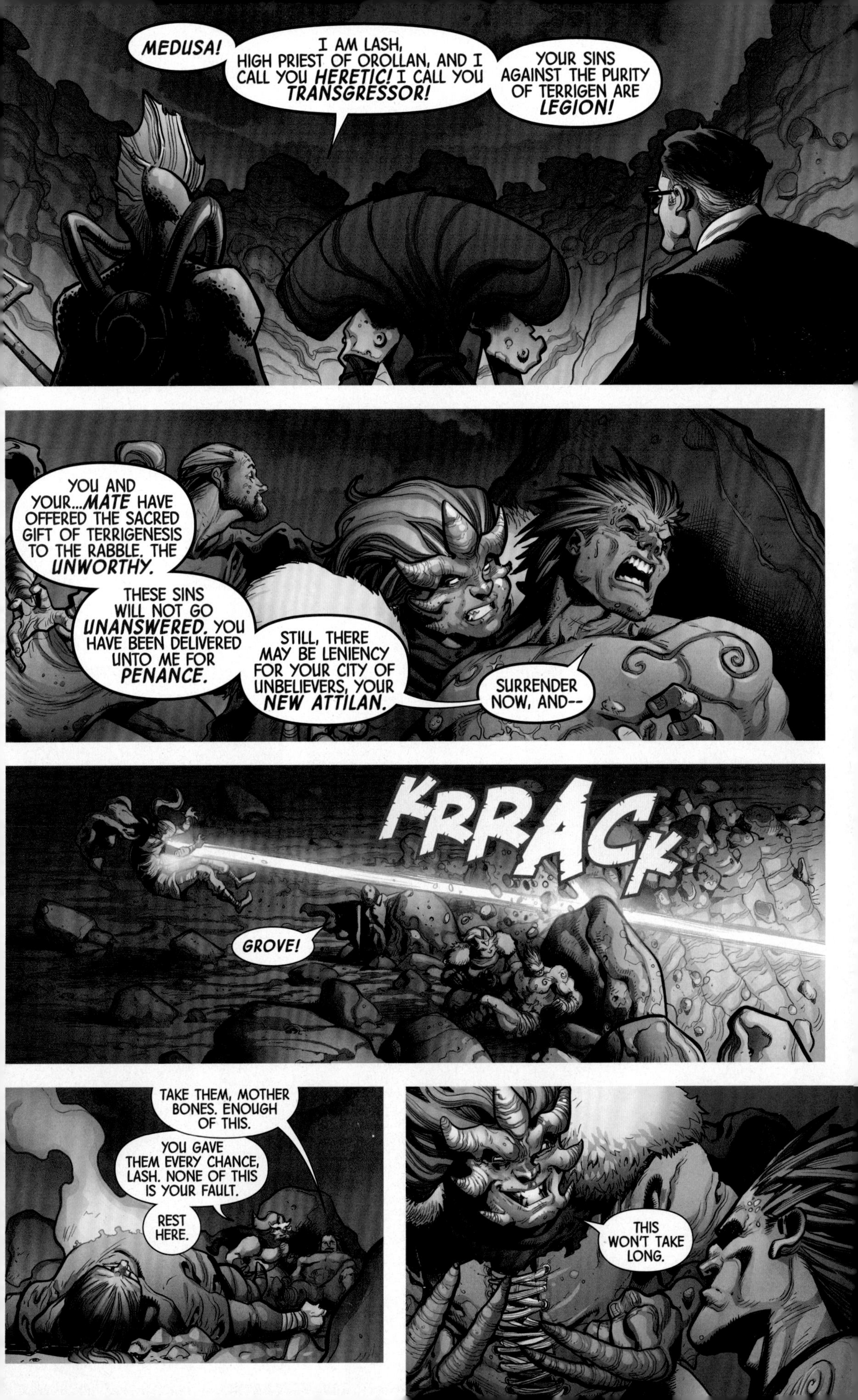
MEDUSA!
I AM LASH, HIGH PRIEST OF OROLLAN, AND I CALL YOU HERETIC! I CALL YOU TRANSGRESSOR!
YOUR SINS AGAINST THE PURITY OF TERRIGEN ARE LEGION!
YOU AND YOUR...MATE HAVE OFFERED THE SACRED GIFT OF TERRIGENESIS TO THE RABBLE. THE UNWORTHY.
THESE SINS WILL NOT GO UNANSWERED. YOU HAVE BEEN DELIVERED UNTO ME FOR PENANCE.
STILL, THERE MAY BE LENIENCY FOR YOUR CITY OF UNBELIEVERS, YOUR NEW ATTILAN.
SURRENDER NOW, AND--
KRRACK
GROVE!
TAKE THEM, MOTHER BONES. ENOUGH OF THIS.
YOU GAVE THEM EVERY CHANCE, LASH. NONE OF THIS IS YOUR FAULT.
REST HERE.
THIS WON'T TAKE LONG.

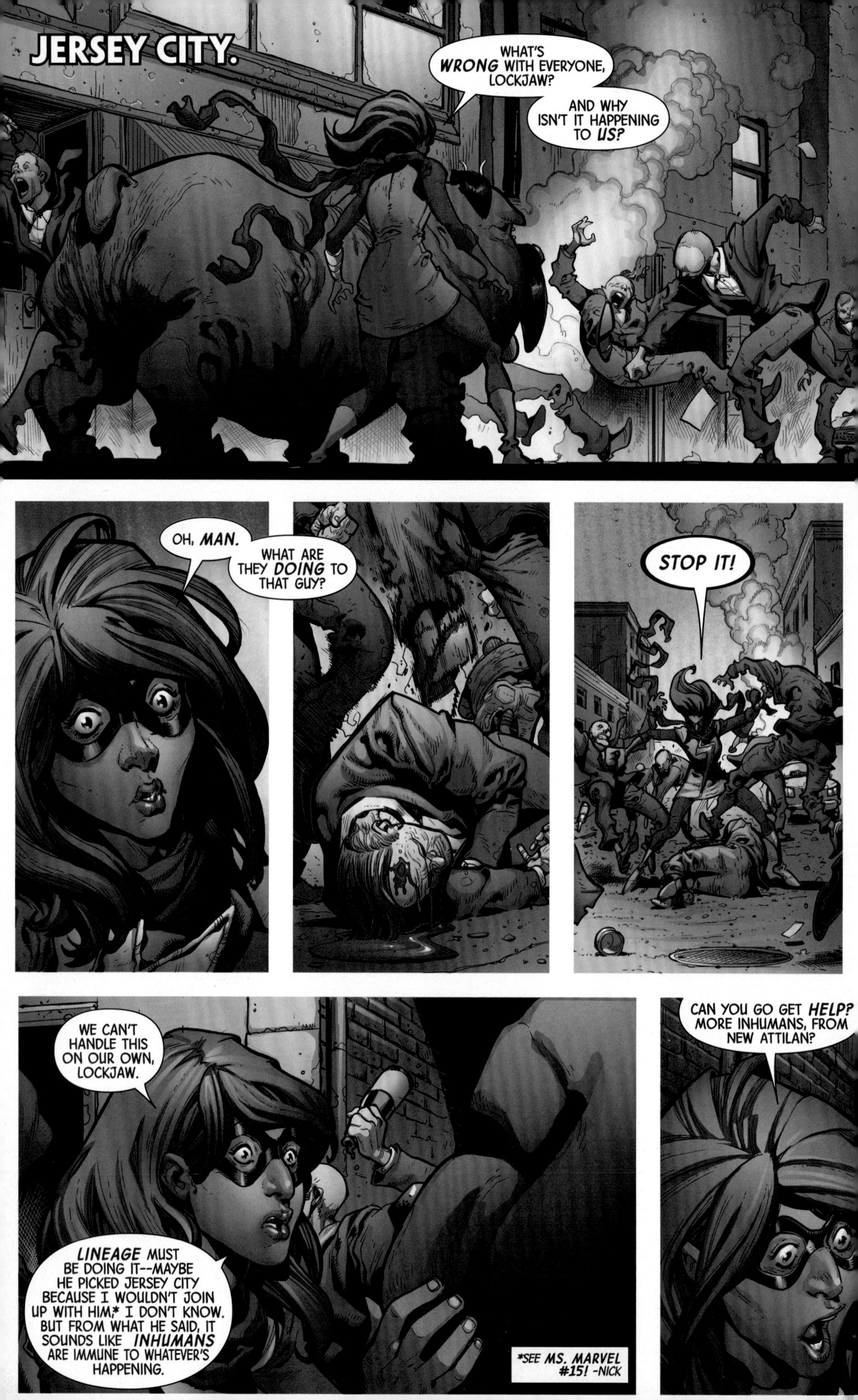
JERSEY CITY.
WHAT'S WRONG WITH EVERYONE, LOCKJAW?
AND WHY ISN'T IT HAPPENING TO US?
OH, MAN.
WHAT ARE THEY DOING TO THAT GUY?
STOP IT!
WE CAN'T HANDLE THIS ON OUR OWN, LOCKJAW.
LINEAGE MUST BE DOING IT--MAYBE HE PICKED JERSEY CITY BECAUSE I WOULDN'T JOIN UP WITH HIM,* I DON'T KNOW. BUT FROM WHAT HE SAID, IT SOUNDS LIKE INHUMANS ARE IMMUNE TO WHATEVER'S HAPPENING.
*SEE MS. MARVEL #15! -NICK
CAN YOU GO GET HELP? MORE INHUMANS, FROM NEW ATTILAN?

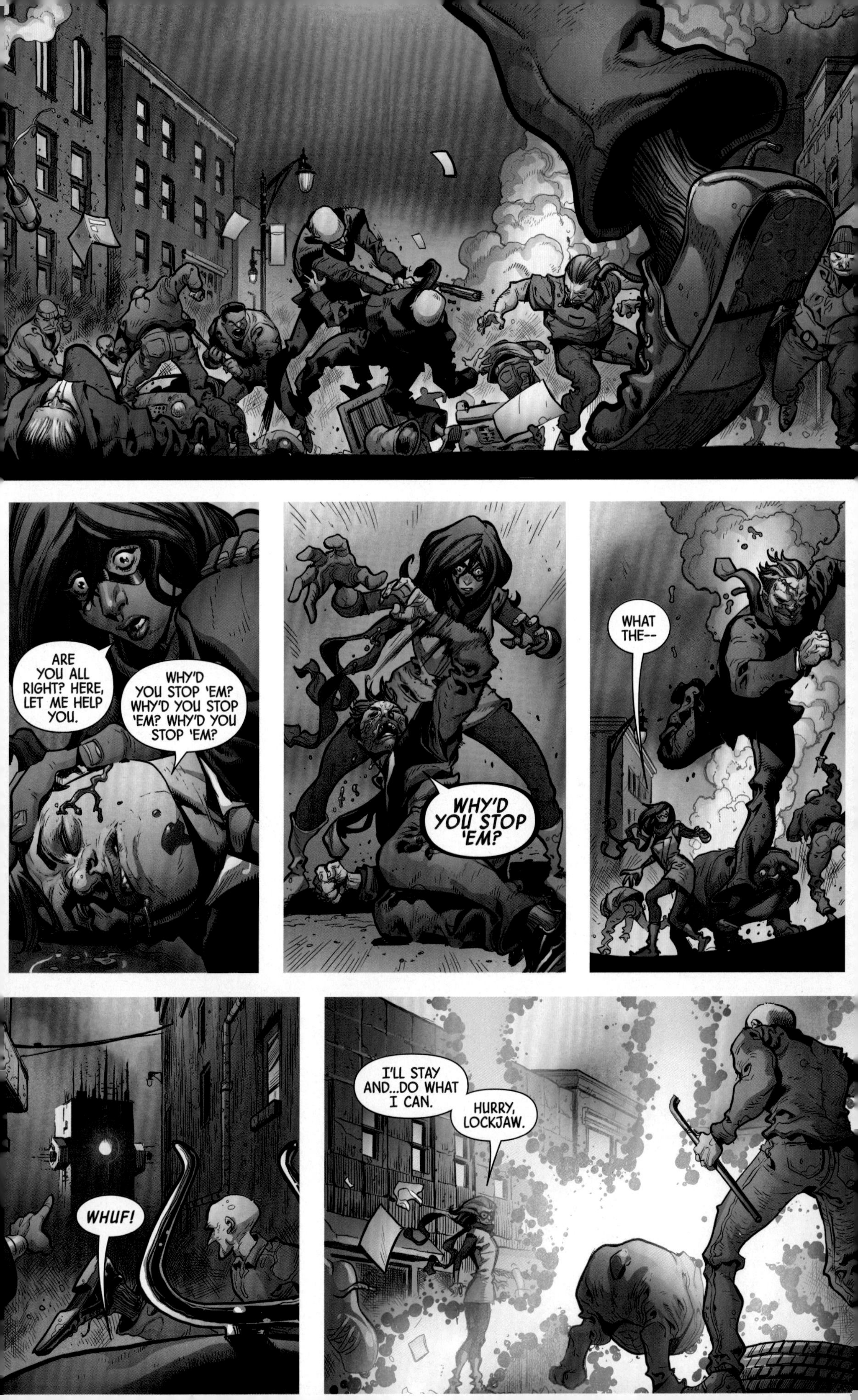
ARE YOU ALL RIGHT? HERE, LET ME HELP YOU.
WHY'D YOU STOP 'EM? WHY'D YOU STOP 'EM? WHY'D YOU STOP 'EM?
WHY'D YOU STOP 'EM?
WHAT THE--
WHUF!
I'LL STAY AND...DO WHAT I CAN.
HURRY, LOCKJAW.

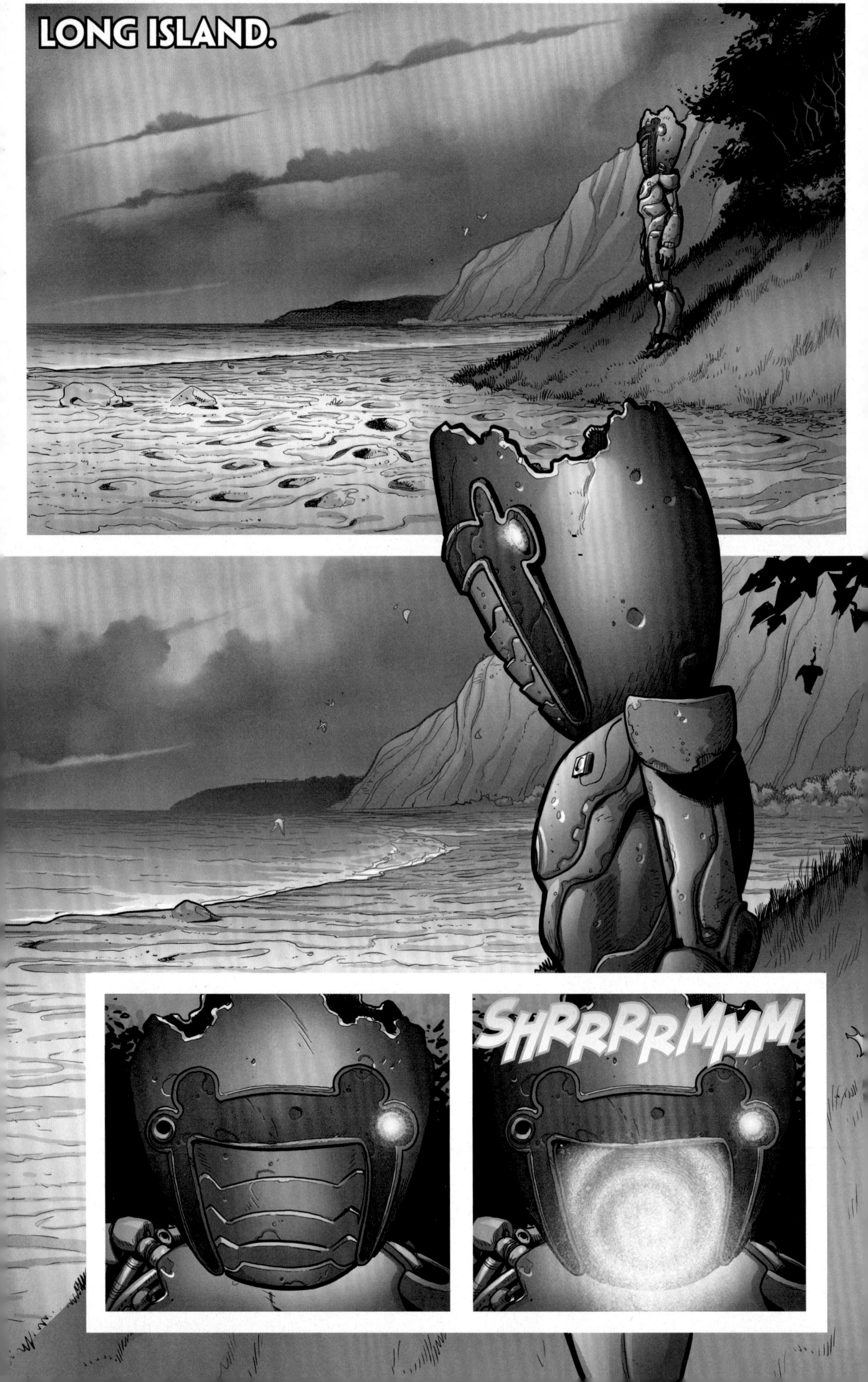
LONG ISLAND.
SHRRRRMMM

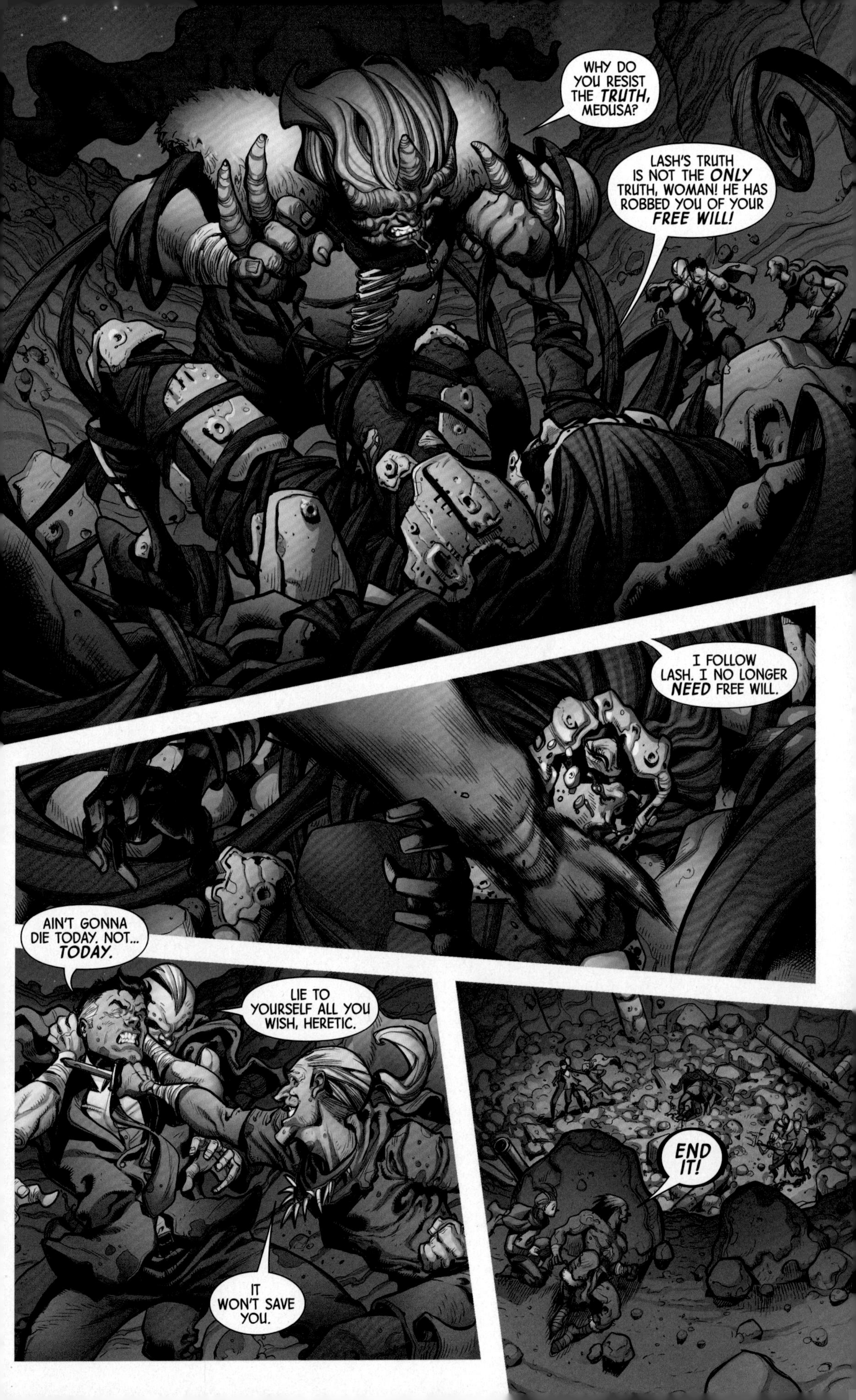
WHY DO YOU RESIST THE TRUTH, MEDUSA?
LASH'S TRUTH IS NOT THE ONLY TRUTH, WOMAN! HE HAS ROBBED YOU OF YOUR FREE WILL!
I FOLLOW LASH. I NO LONGER NEED FREE WILL.
AIN'T GONNA DIE TODAY. NOT... TODAY.
LIE TO YOURSELF ALL YOU WISH, HERETIC.
IT WON'T SAVE YOU.
END IT!

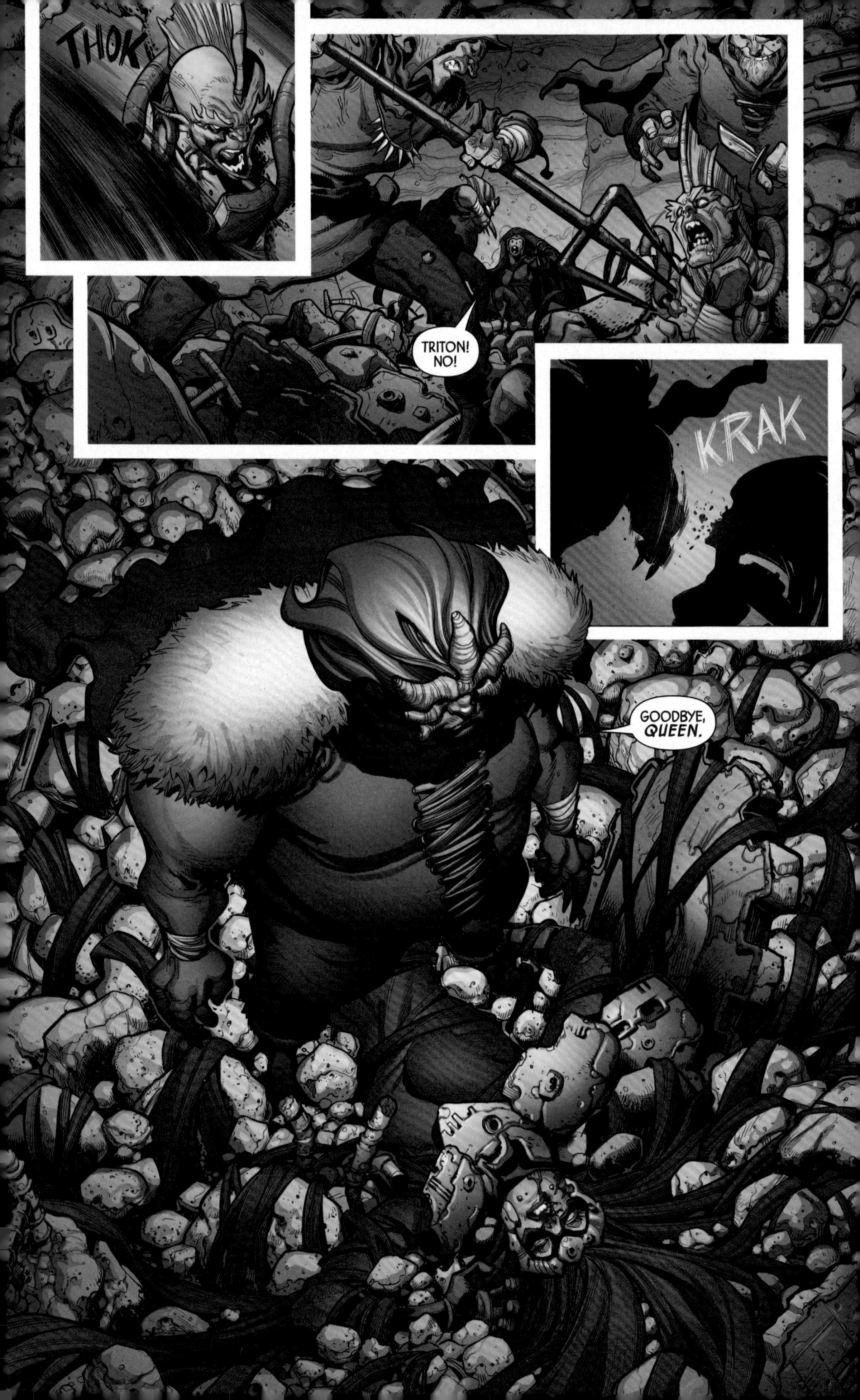
THOK
TRITON! NO!
KRAK
GOODBYE, QUEEN.

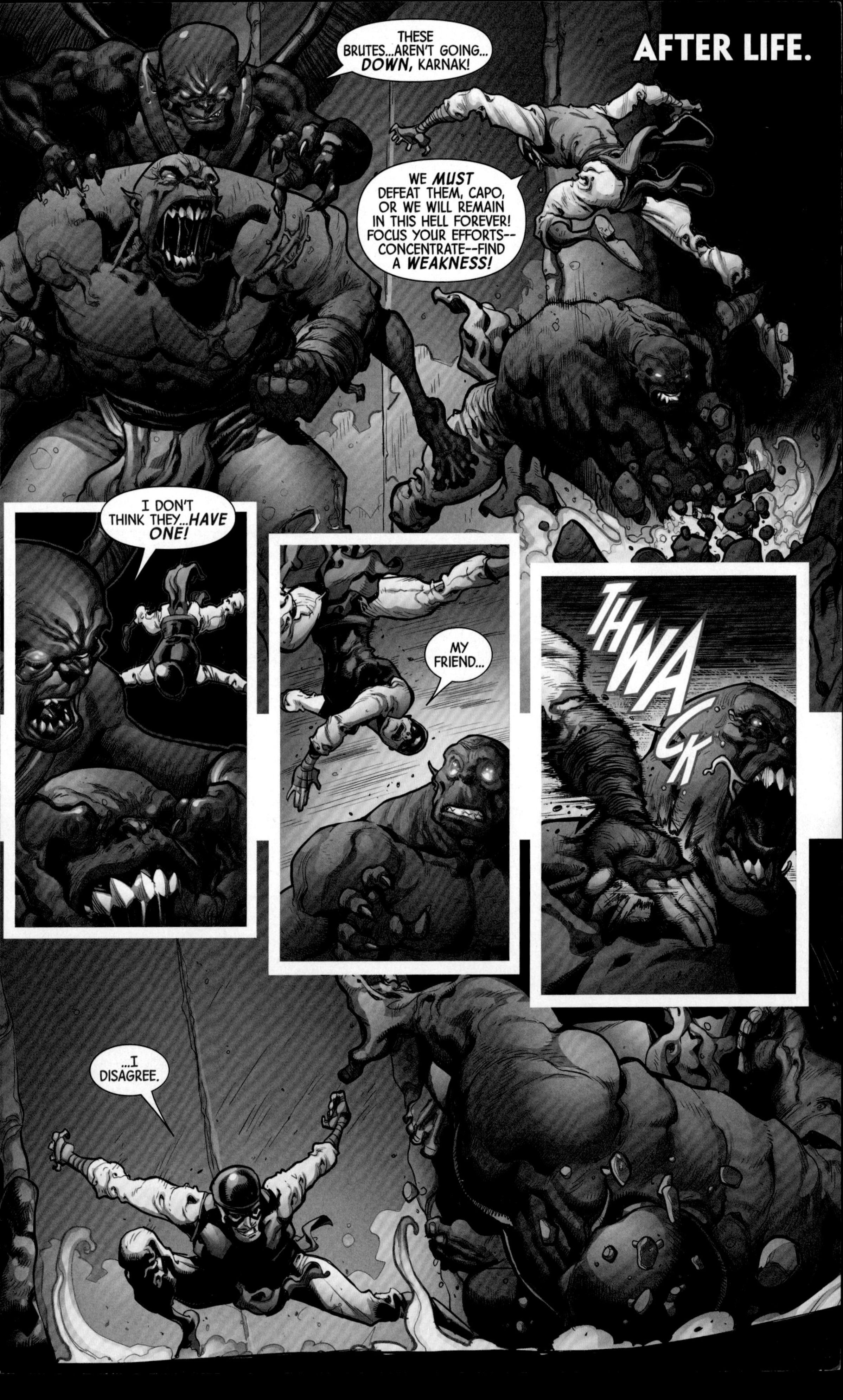
AFTER LIFE.
THESE BRUTES...AREN'T GOING... DOWN, KARNAK!
WE MUST DEFEAT THEM, CAPO, OR WE WILL REMAIN IN THIS HELL FOREVER! FOCUS YOUR EFFORTS--CONCENTRATE--FIND A WEAKNESS!
I DON'T THINK THEY...HAVE ONE!
MY FRIEND...
THWACK
...I DISAGREE.

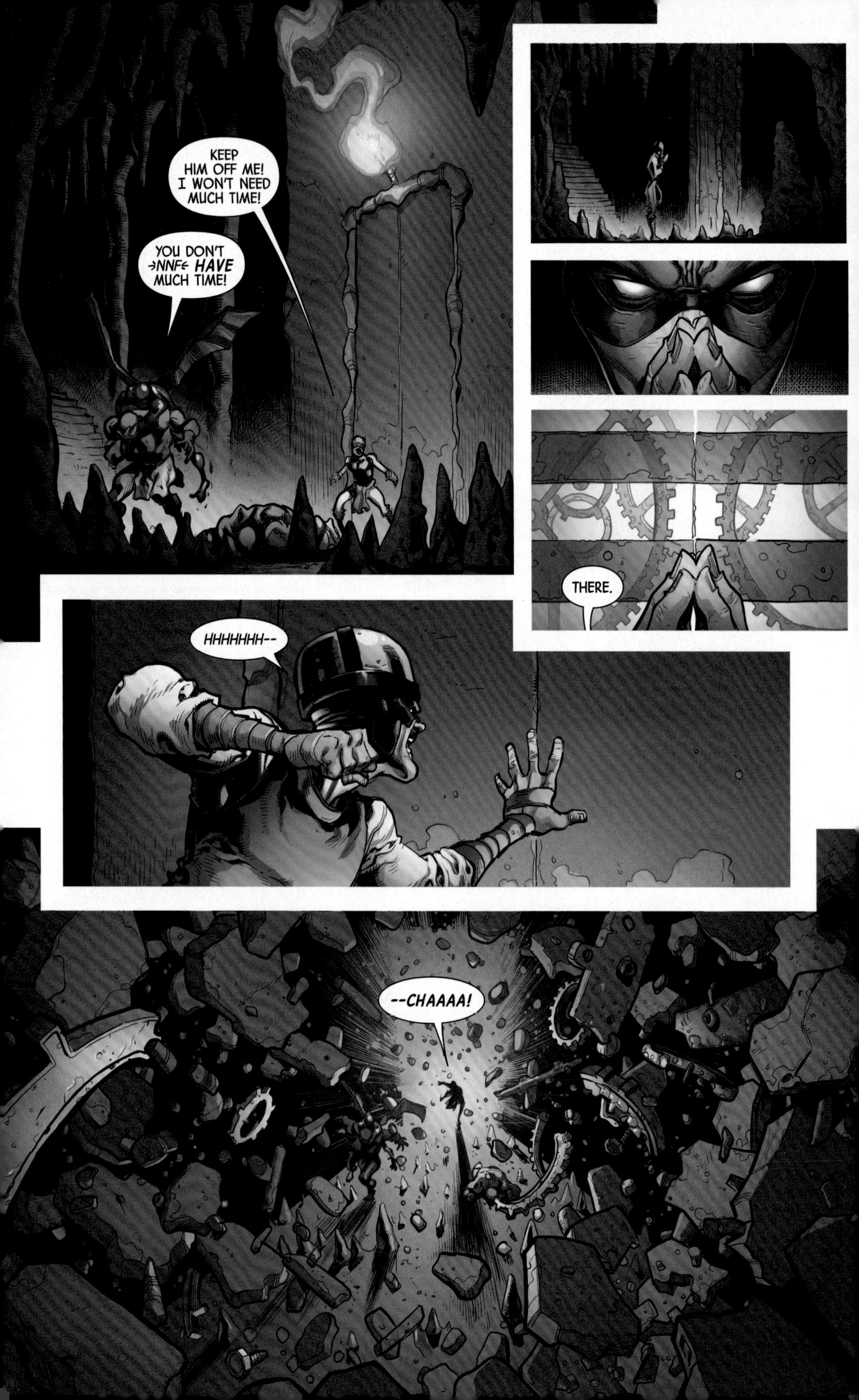
KEEP HIM OFF ME! I WON'T NEED MUCH TIME!
YOU DON'T →NNF← HAVE MUCH TIME!
THERE.
HHHHHHH--
--CHAAAA!

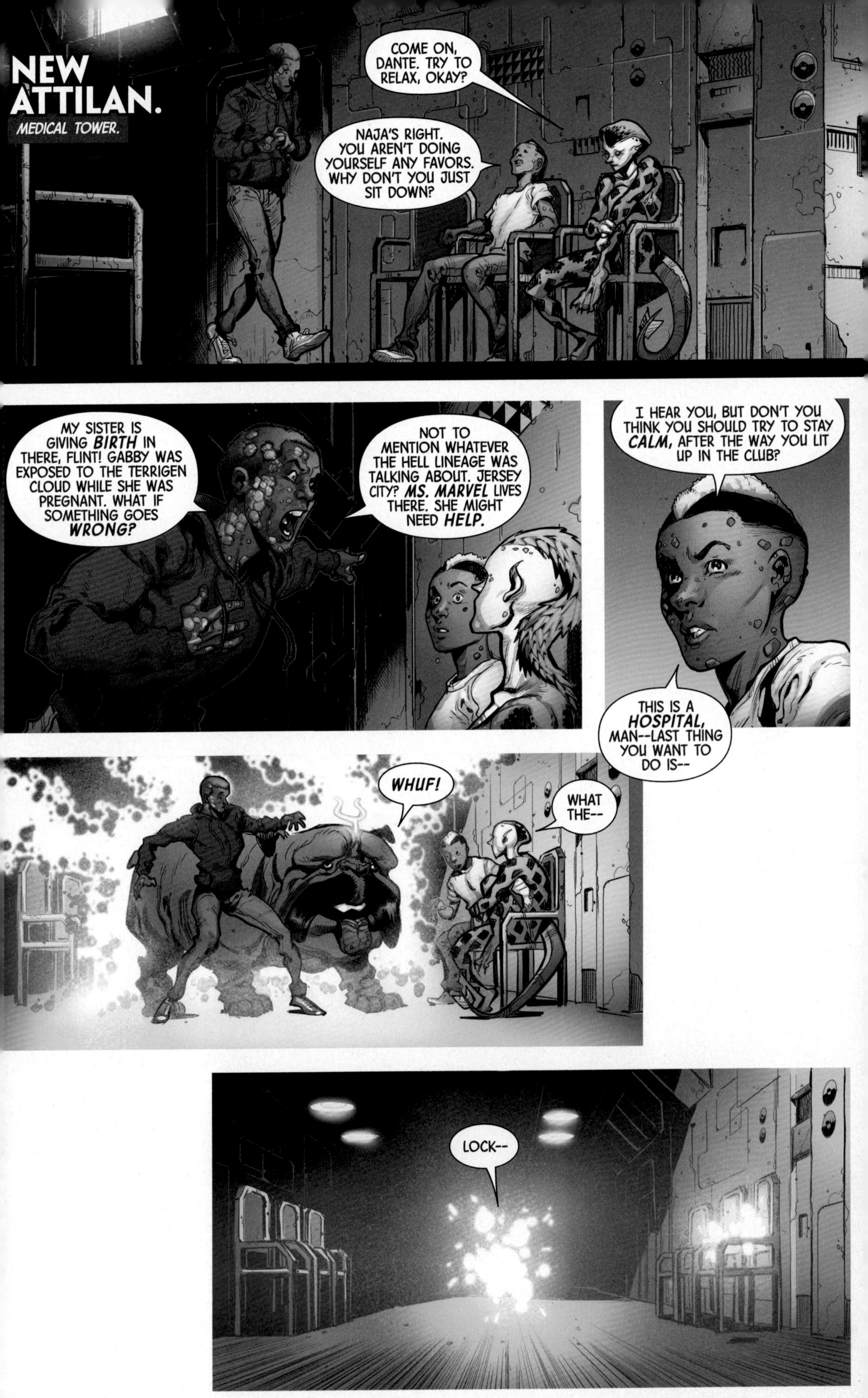
NEW ATTILAN.
MEDICAL TOWER.
COME ON, DANTE. TRY TO RELAX, OKAY?
NAJA'S RIGHT. YOU AREN'T DOING YOURSELF ANY FAVORS. WHY DON'T YOU JUST SIT DOWN?
MY SISTER IS GIVING BIRTH IN THERE, FLINT! GABBY WAS EXPOSED TO THE TERRIGEN CLOUD WHILE SHE WAS PREGNANT. WHAT IF SOMETHING GOES WRONG?
NOT TO MENTION WHATEVER THE HELL LINEAGE WAS TALKING ABOUT. JERSEY CITY? MS. MARVEL LIVES THERE. SHE MIGHT NEED HELP.
I HEAR YOU, BUT DON'T YOU THINK YOU SHOULD TRY TO STAY CALM, AFTER THE WAY YOU LIT UP IN THE CLUB?
THIS IS A HOSPITAL, MAN--LAST THING YOU WANT TO DO IS--
WHUF!
WHAT THE--
LOCK--

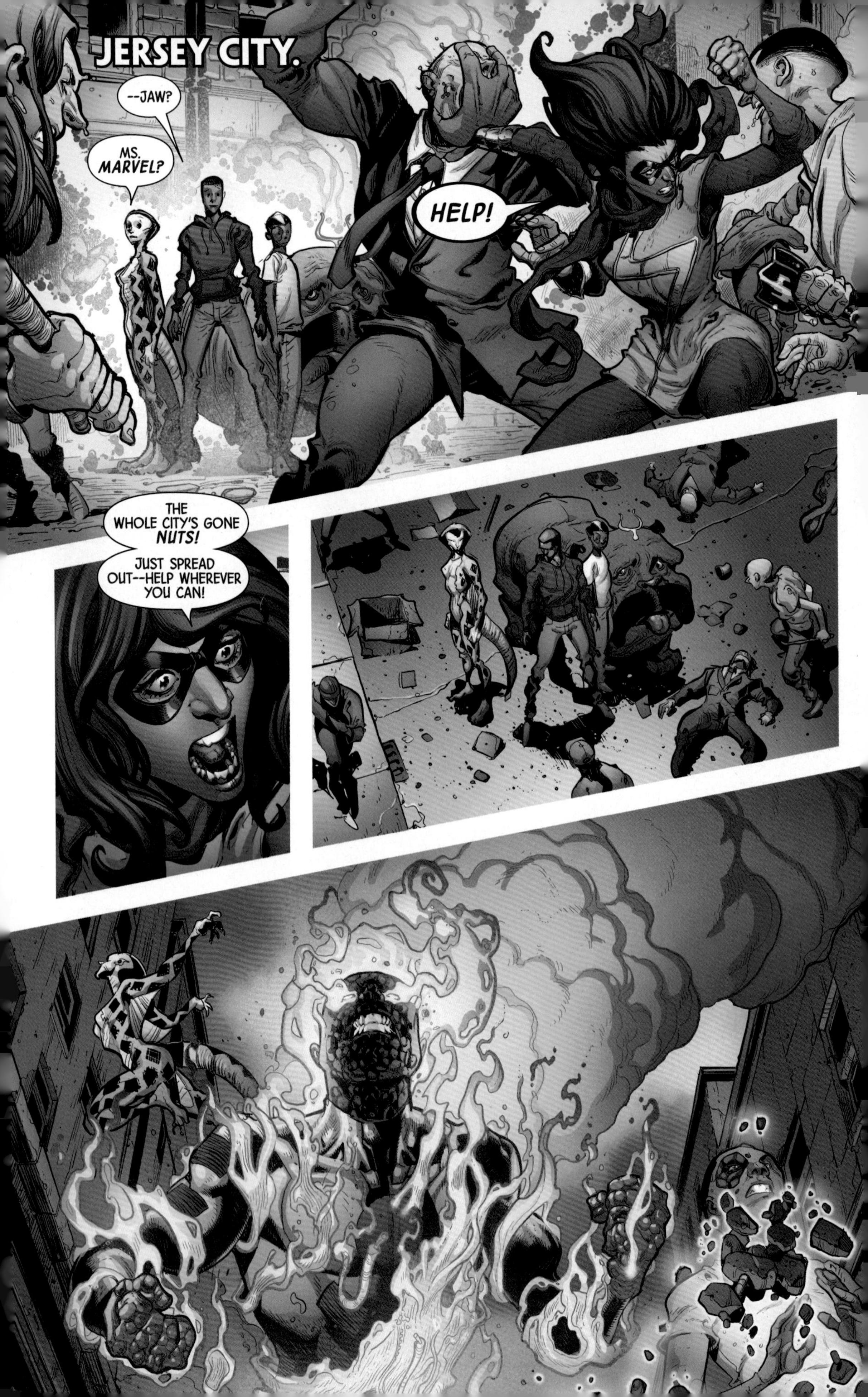
JERSEY CITY.
MS. MARVEL?
--JAW?
HELP!
THE WHOLE CITY'S GONE NUTS!
JUST SPREAD OUT--HELP WHEREVER YOU CAN!

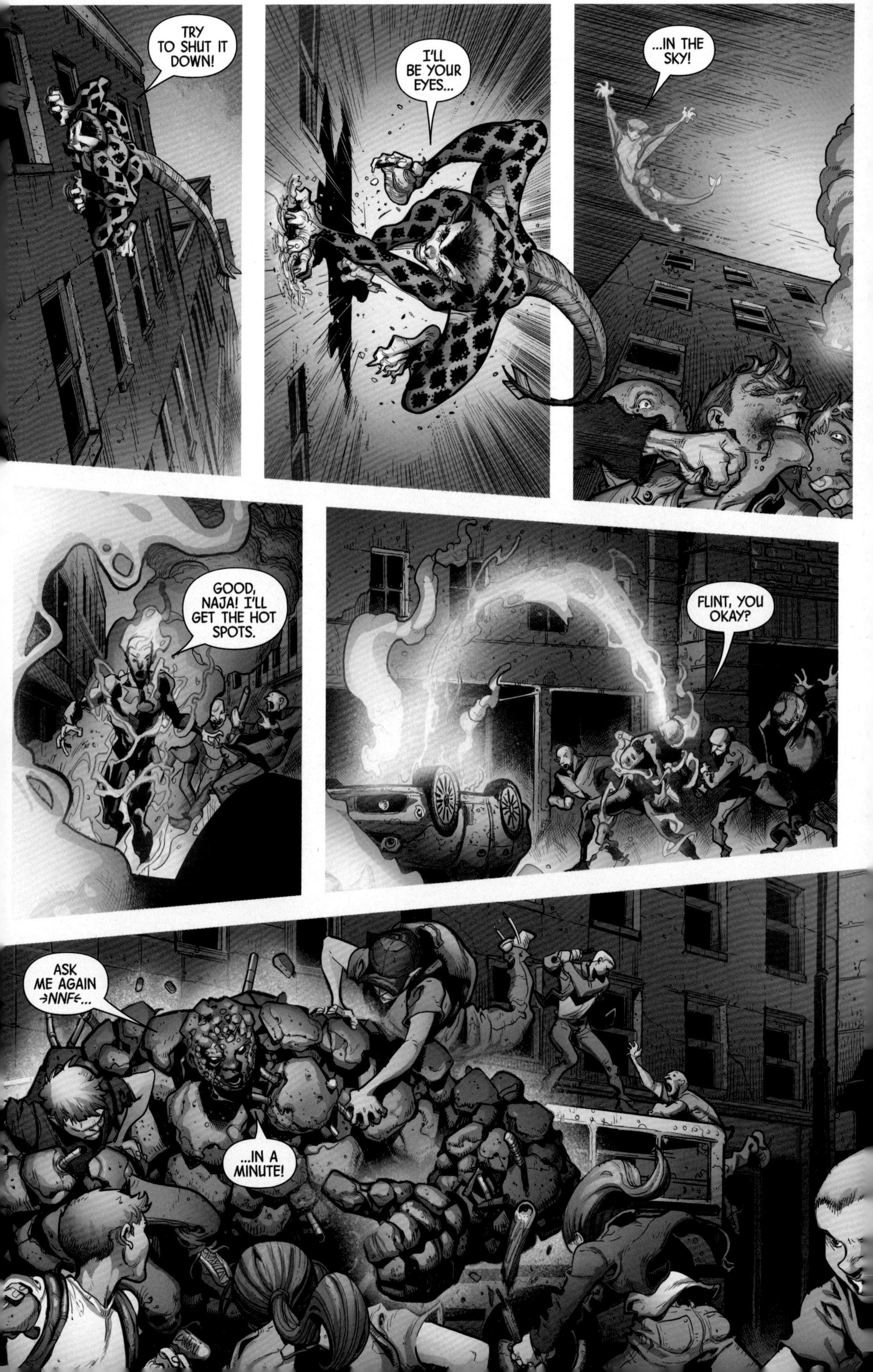
TRY TO SHUT IT DOWN!
I'LL BE YOUR EYES...
...IN THE SKY!
GOOD, NAJA! I'LL GET THE HOT SPOTS.
FLINT, YOU OKAY?
ASK ME AGAIN →NNF←...
...IN A MINUTE!

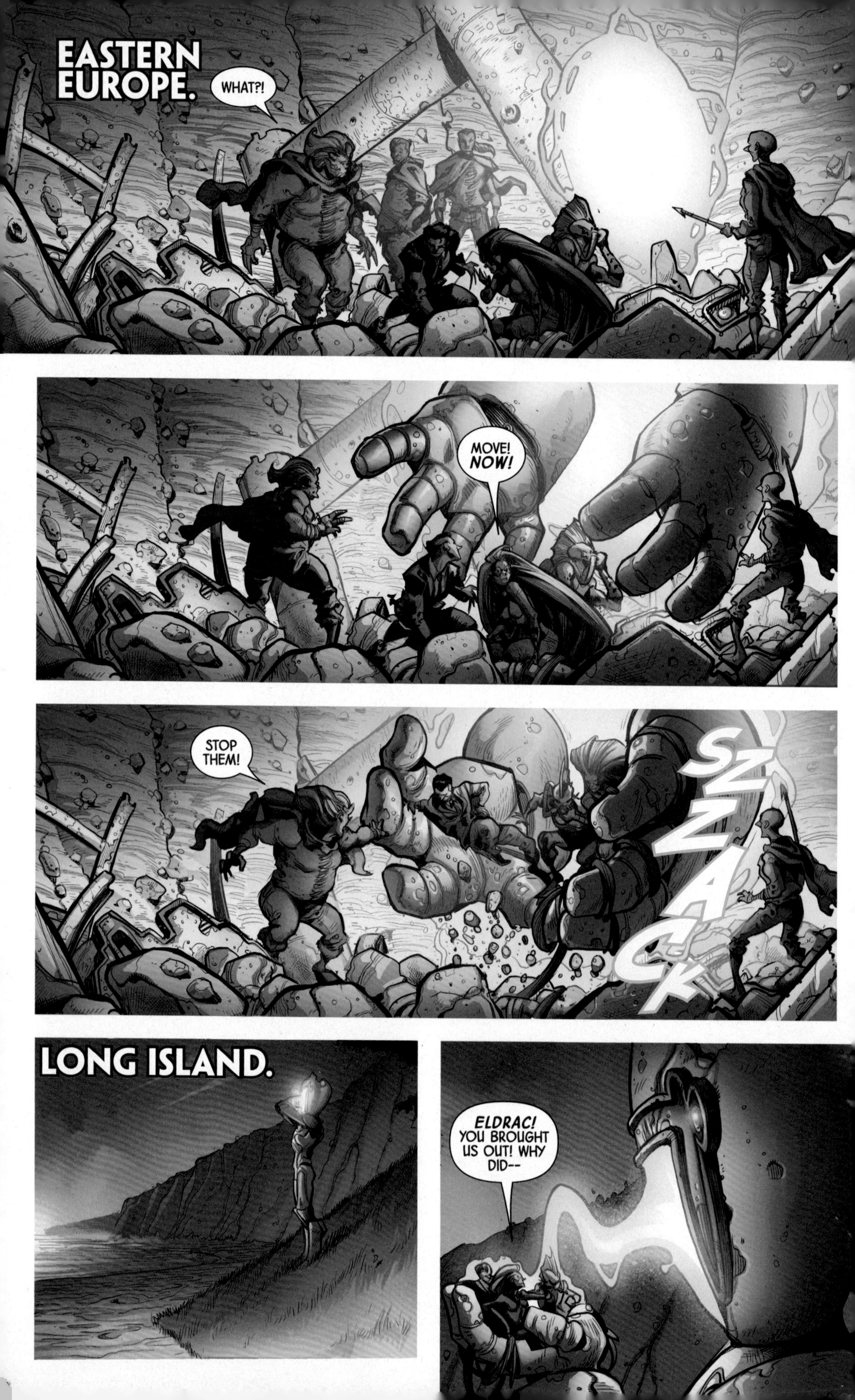
EASTERN EUROPE.
WHAT?!
MOVE! NOW!
STOP THEM!
SZZACK
LONG ISLAND.
ELDRAC! YOU BROUGHT US OUT! WHY DID--

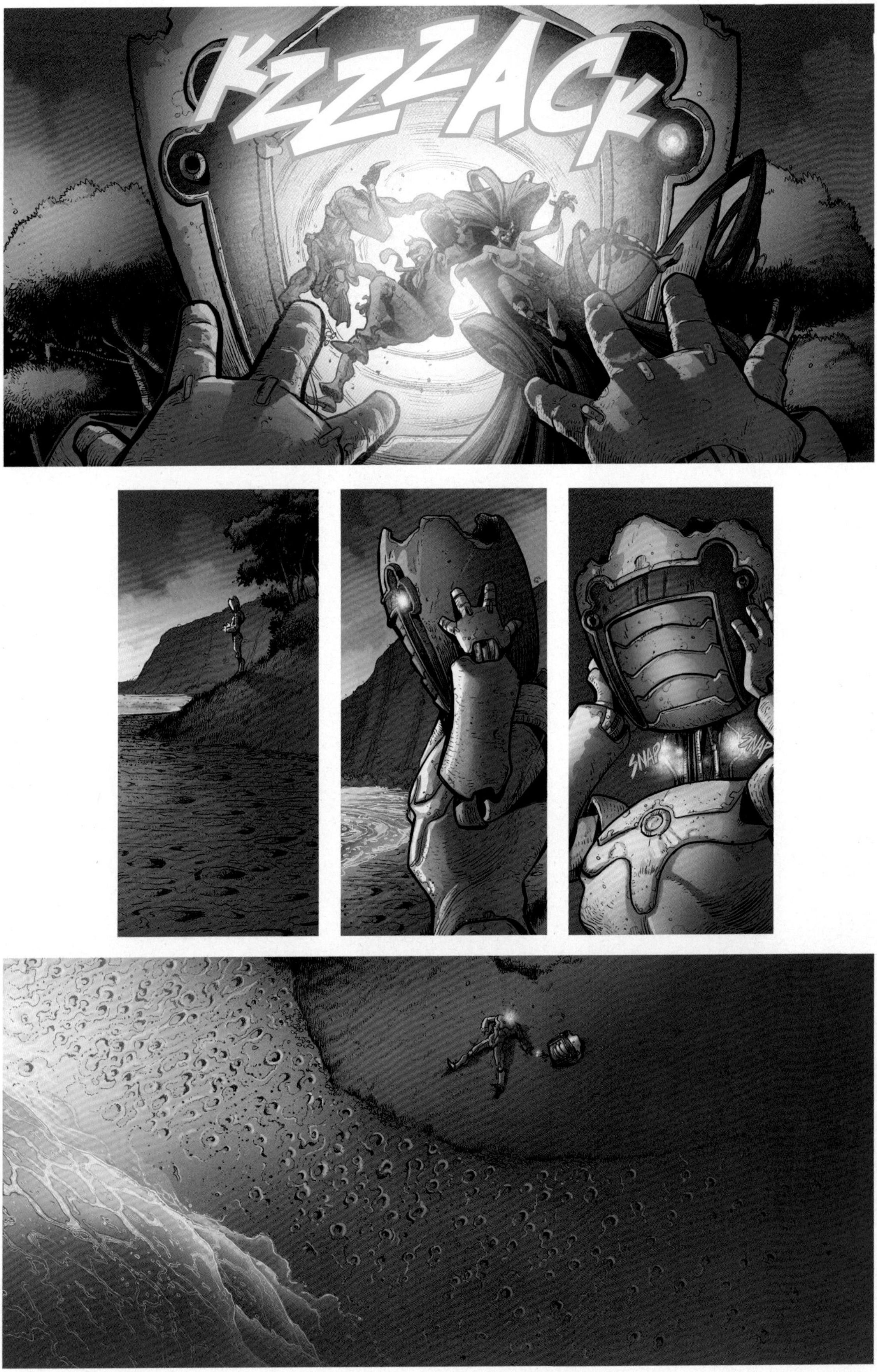
KZZZACK
SNAP
SNAP

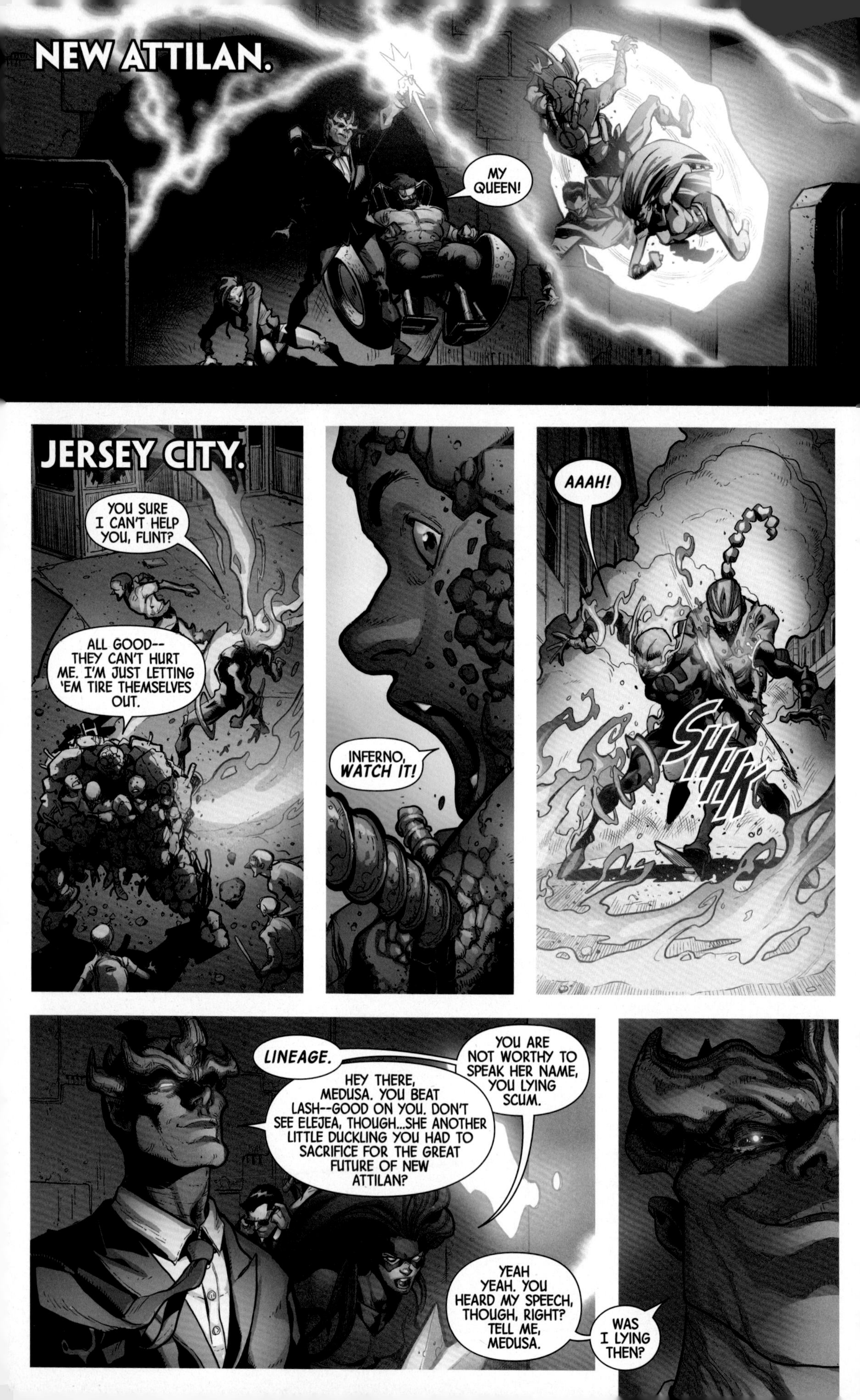
NEW ATTILAN.
MY QUEEN!
JERSEY CITY.
YOU SURE I CAN'T HELP YOU, FLINT?
ALL GOOD-- THEY CAN'T HURT ME. I'M JUST LETTING 'EM TIRE THEMSELVES OUT.
INFERNO, WATCH IT!
AAAH!
SHHK
LINEAGE.
HEY THERE, MEDUSA. YOU BEAT LASH--GOOD ON YOU. DON'T SEE ELEJEA, THOUGH...SHE ANOTHER LITTLE DUCKLING YOU HAD TO SACRIFICE FOR THE GREAT FUTURE OF NEW ATTILAN?
YOU ARE NOT WORTHY TO SPEAK HER NAME, YOU LYING SCUM.
YEAH YEAH. YOU HEARD MY SPEECH, THOUGH, RIGHT? TELL ME, MEDUSA.
WAS I LYING THEN?

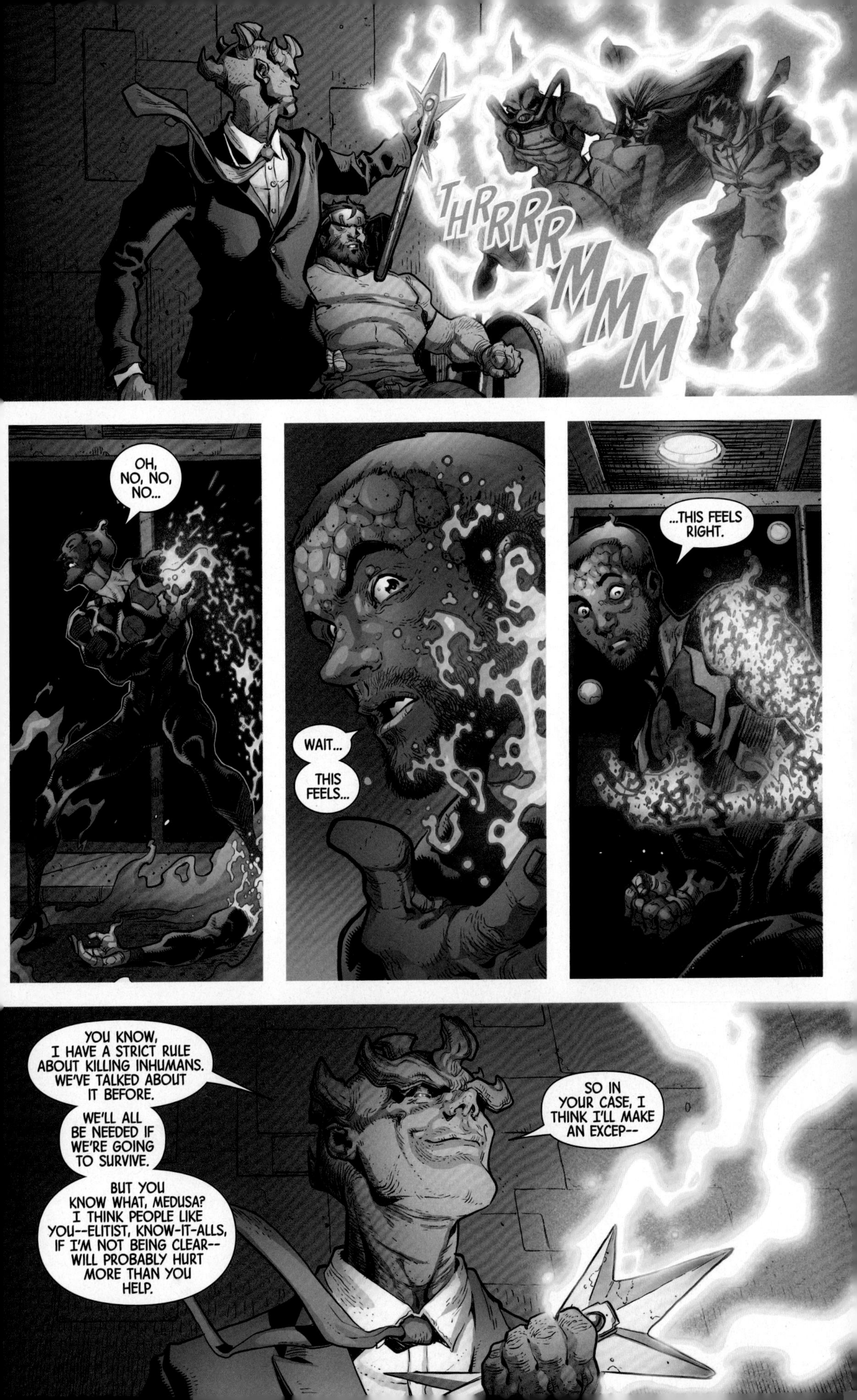
THRRRRMMMM
OH, NO, NO, NO...
WAIT...
THIS FEELS...
...THIS FEELS RIGHT.
YOU KNOW, I HAVE A STRICT RULE ABOUT KILLING INHUMANS. WE'VE TALKED ABOUT IT BEFORE.
WE'LL ALL BE NEEDED IF WE'RE GOING TO SURVIVE.
BUT YOU KNOW WHAT, MEDUSA? I THINK PEOPLE LIKE YOU--ELITIST, KNOW-IT-ALLS, IF I'M NOT BEING CLEAR--WILL PROBABLY HURT MORE THAN YOU HELP.
SO IN YOUR CASE, I THINK I'LL MAKE AN EXCEP--

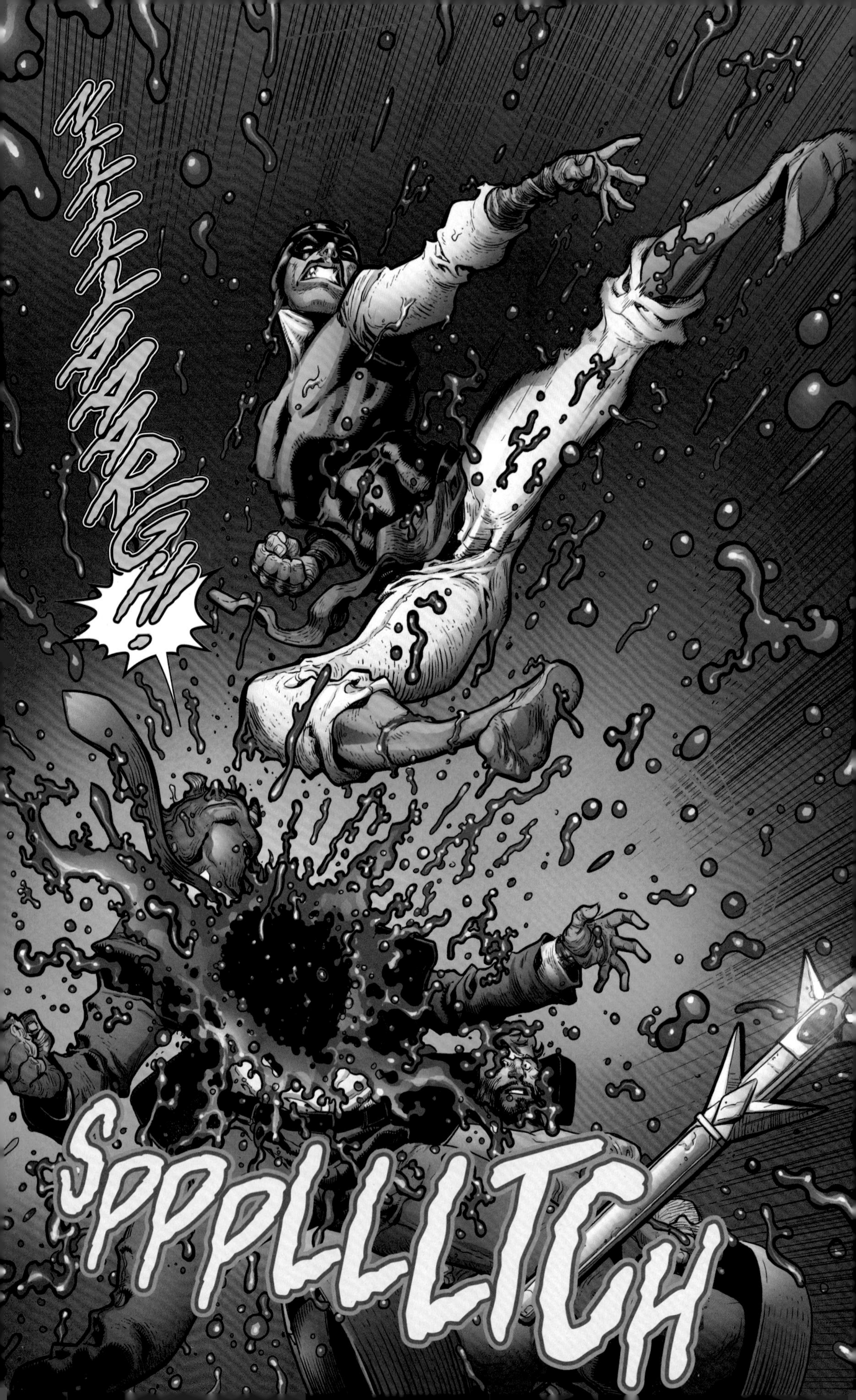
NYYYYAARGH!
SPPPLLLTCH

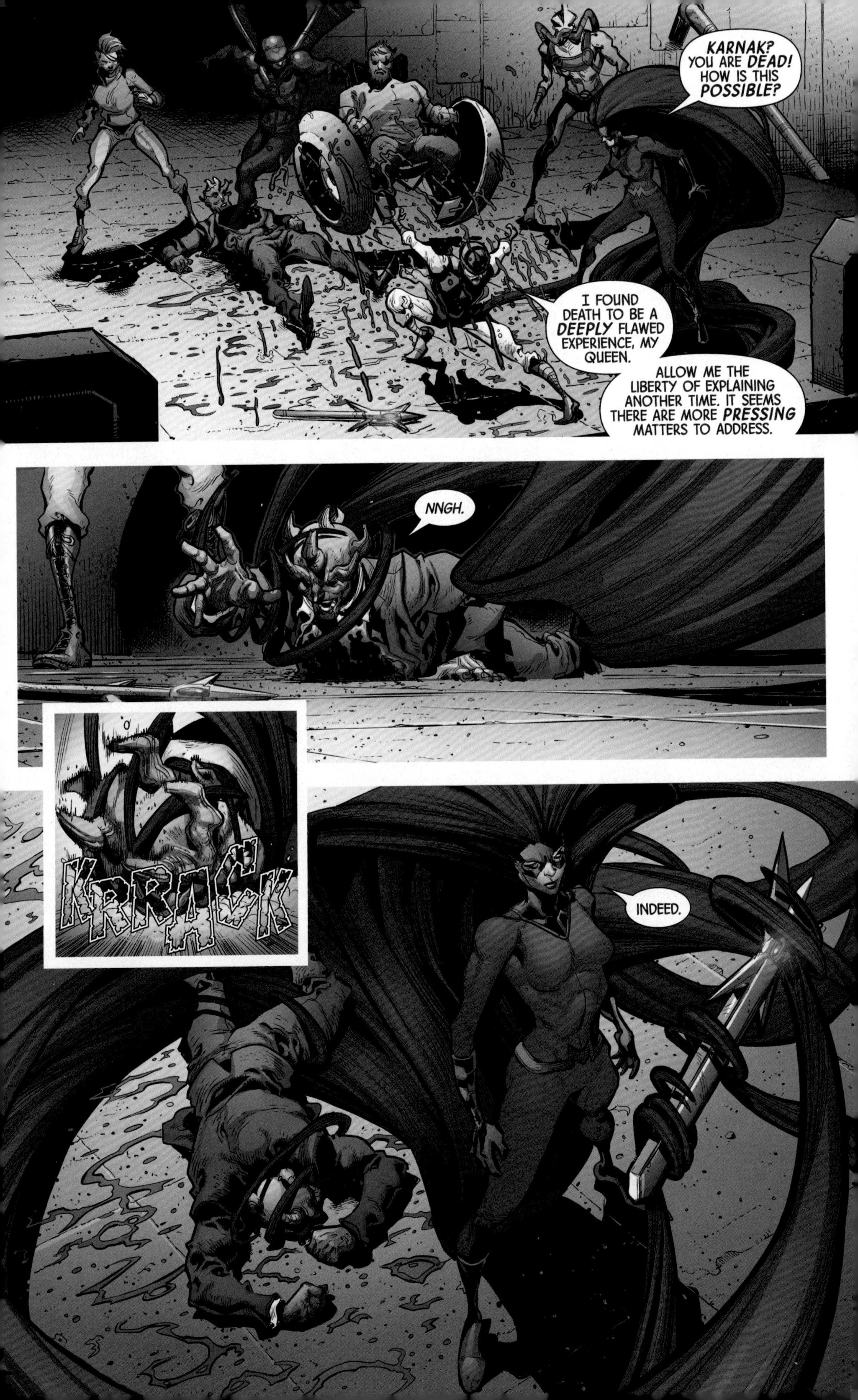
KARNAK? YOU ARE DEAD! HOW IS THIS POSSIBLE?
I FOUND DEATH TO BE A DEEPLY FLAWED EXPERIENCE, MY QUEEN.
ALLOW ME THE LIBERTY OF EXPLAINING ANOTHER TIME. IT SEEMS THERE ARE MORE PRESSING MATTERS TO ADDRESS.
NNGH.
KRRACK
INDEED.

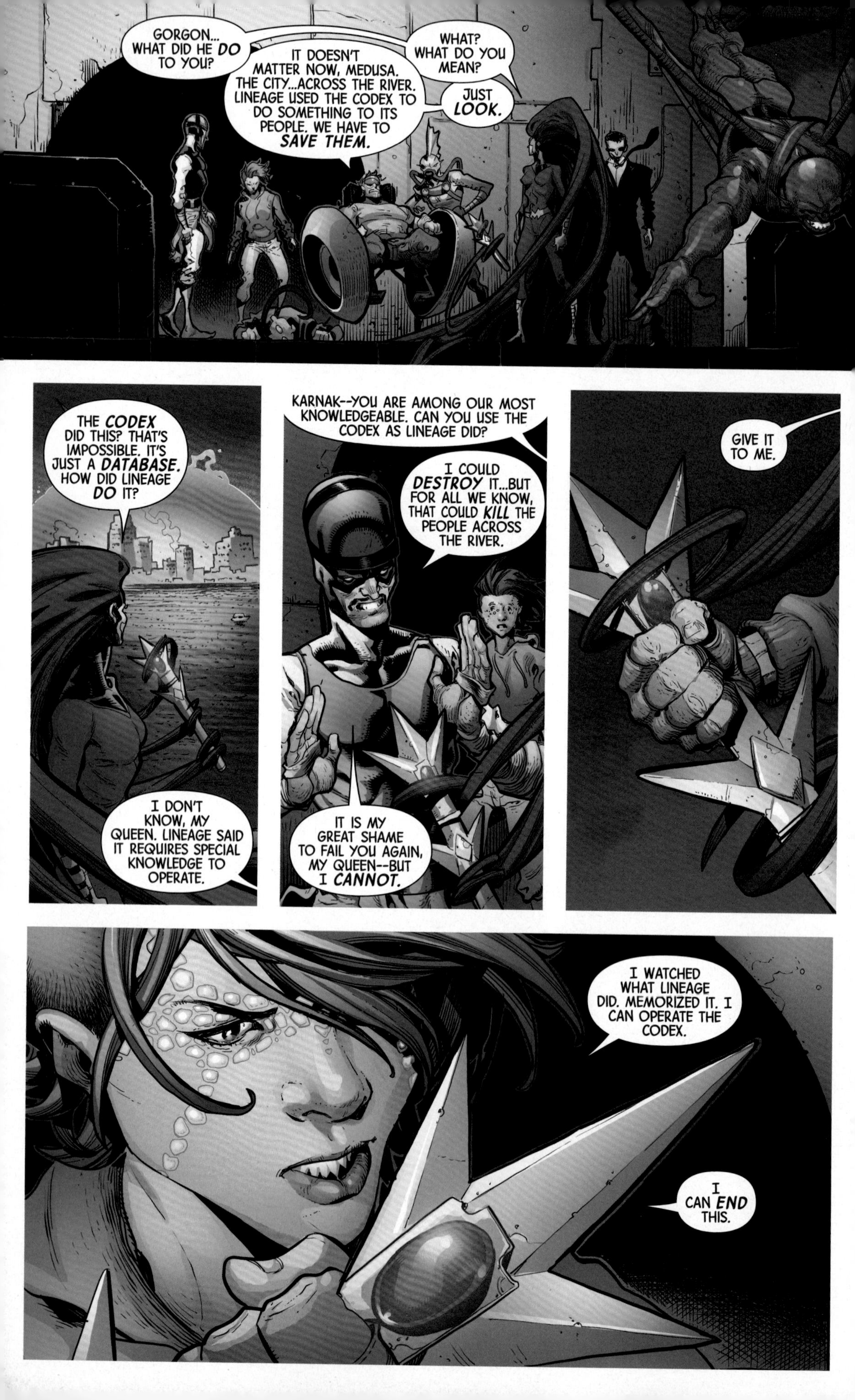
GORGON... WHAT DID HE DO TO YOU?
IT DOESN'T MATTER NOW, MEDUSA. THE CITY...ACROSS THE RIVER. LINEAGE USED THE CODEX TO DO SOMETHING TO ITS PEOPLE. WE HAVE TO SAVE THEM.
WHAT? WHAT DO YOU MEAN?
JUST LOOK.
THE CODEX DID THIS? THAT'S IMPOSSIBLE. IT'S JUST A DATABASE. HOW DID LINEAGE DO IT?
I DON'T KNOW, MY QUEEN. LINEAGE SAID IT REQUIRES SPECIAL KNOWLEDGE TO OPERATE.
KARNAK--YOU ARE AMONG OUR MOST KNOWLEDGEABLE. CAN YOU USE THE CODEX AS LINEAGE DID?
I COULD DESTROY IT...BUT FOR ALL WE KNOW, THAT COULD KILL THE PEOPLE ACROSS THE RIVER.
IT IS MY GREAT SHAME TO FAIL YOU AGAIN, MY QUEEN--BUT I CANNOT.
GIVE IT TO ME.
I WATCHED WHAT LINEAGE DID. MEMORIZED IT. I CAN OPERATE THE CODEX.
I CAN END THIS.

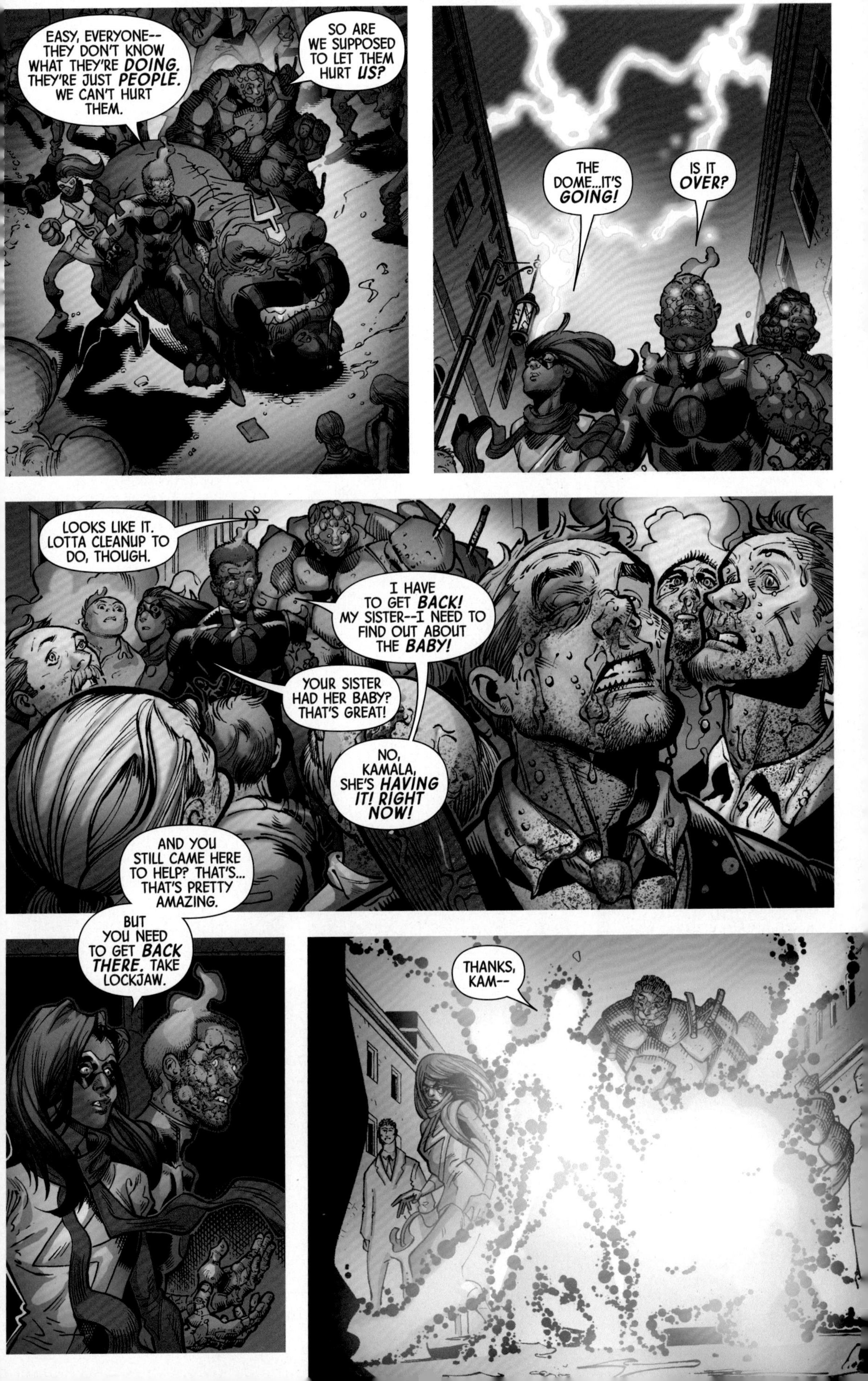
EASY, EVERYONE-- THEY DON'T KNOW WHAT THEY'RE DOING. THEY'RE JUST PEOPLE. WE CAN'T HURT THEM.
SO ARE WE SUPPOSED TO LET THEM HURT US?
THE DOME...IT'S GOING!
IS IT OVER?
LOOKS LIKE IT. LOTTA CLEANUP TO DO, THOUGH.
I HAVE TO GET BACK! MY SISTER--I NEED TO FIND OUT ABOUT THE BABY!
YOUR SISTER HAD HER BABY? THAT'S GREAT!
NO, KAMALA, SHE'S HAVING IT! RIGHT NOW!
AND YOU STILL CAME HERE TO HELP? THAT'S... THAT'S PRETTY AMAZING.
BUT YOU NEED TO GET BACK THERE. TAKE LOCKJAW.
THANKS, KAM--

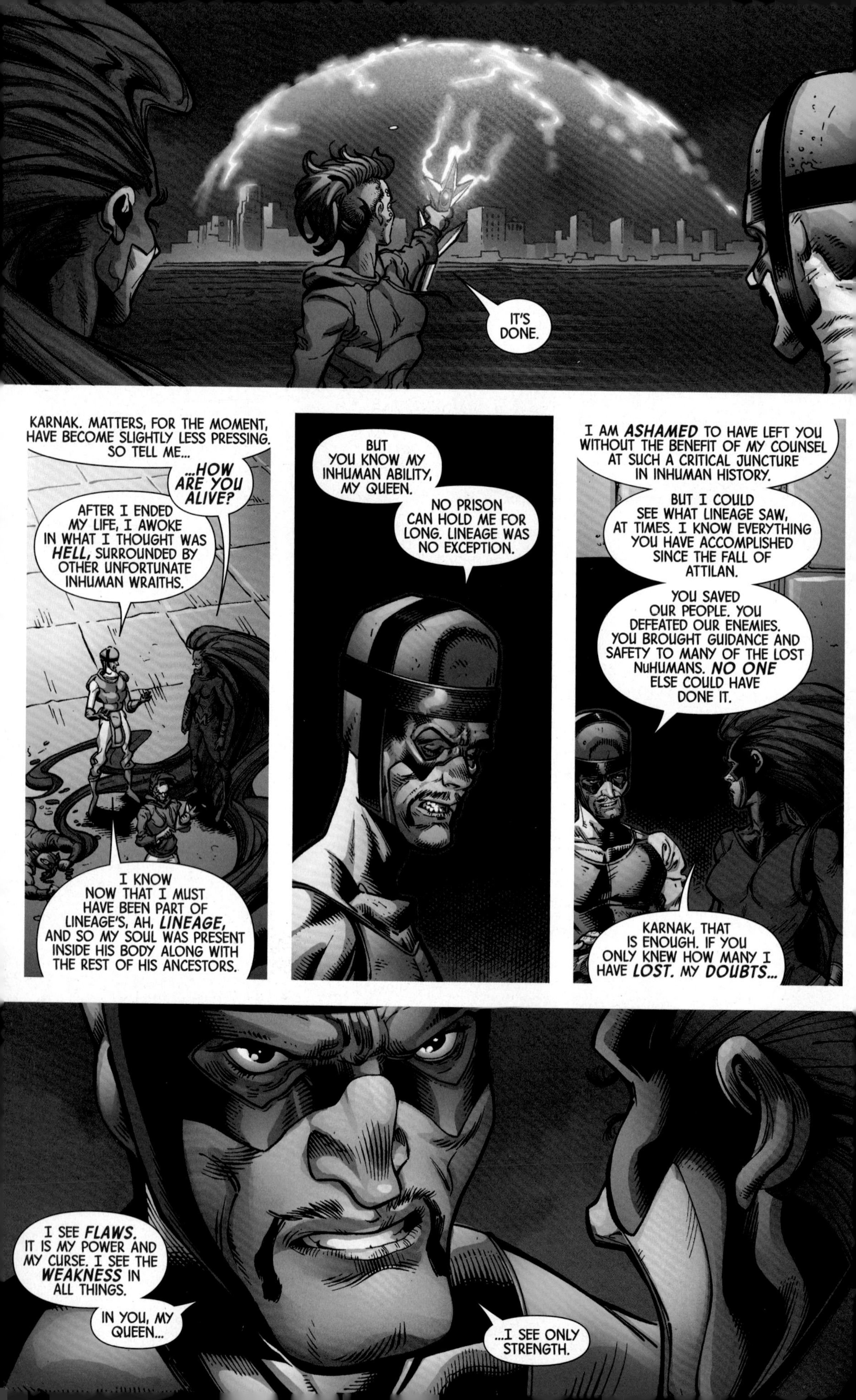
IT'S DONE.
KARNAK. MATTERS, FOR THE MOMENT, HAVE BECOME SLIGHTLY LESS PRESSING. SO TELL ME...
...HOW ARE YOU ALIVE?
AFTER I ENDED MY LIFE, I AWOKE IN WHAT I THOUGHT WAS HELL, SURROUNDED BY OTHER UNFORTUNATE INHUMAN WRAITHS.
I KNOW NOW THAT I MUST HAVE BEEN PART OF LINEAGE'S, AH, LINEAGE, AND SO MY SOUL WAS PRESENT INSIDE HIS BODY ALONG WITH THE REST OF HIS ANCESTORS.
BUT YOU KNOW MY INHUMAN ABILITY, MY QUEEN.
NO PRISON CAN HOLD ME FOR LONG. LINEAGE WAS NO EXCEPTION.
I AM ASHAMED TO HAVE LEFT YOU WITHOUT THE BENEFIT OF MY COUNSEL AT SUCH A CRITICAL JUNCTURE IN INHUMAN HISTORY.
BUT I COULD SEE WHAT LINEAGE SAW, AT TIMES. I KNOW EVERYTHING YOU HAVE ACCOMPLISHED SINCE THE FALL OF ATTILAN.
YOU SAVED OUR PEOPLE. YOU DEFEATED OUR ENEMIES. YOU BROUGHT GUIDANCE AND SAFETY TO MANY OF THE LOST NuHUMANS. NO ONE ELSE COULD HAVE DONE IT.
KARNAK, THAT IS ENOUGH. IF YOU ONLY KNEW HOW MANY I HAVE LOST. MY DOUBTS...
I SEE FLAWS. IT IS MY POWER AND MY CURSE. I SEE THE WEAKNESS IN ALL THINGS.
IN YOU, MY QUEEN...
...I SEE ONLY STRENGTH.

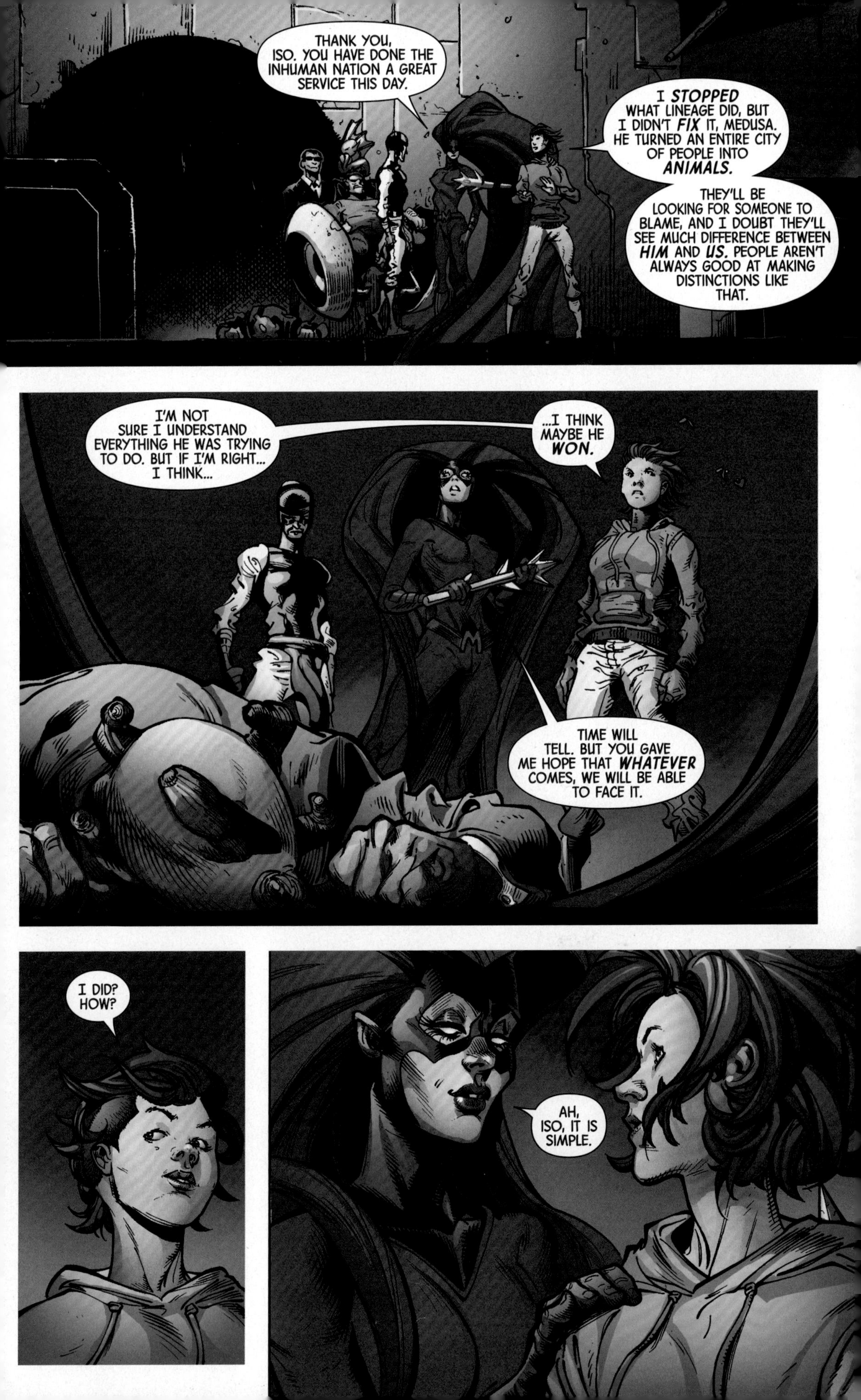
THANK YOU, ISO. YOU HAVE DONE THE INHUMAN NATION A GREAT SERVICE THIS DAY.
I STOPPED WHAT LINEAGE DID, BUT I DIDN'T FIX IT, MEDUSA. HE TURNED AN ENTIRE CITY OF PEOPLE INTO ANIMALS.
THEY'LL BE LOOKING FOR SOMEONE TO BLAME, AND I DOUBT THEY'LL SEE MUCH DIFFERENCE BETWEEN HIM AND US. PEOPLE AREN'T ALWAYS GOOD AT MAKING DISTINCTIONS LIKE THAT.
I'M NOT SURE I UNDERSTAND EVERYTHING HE WAS TRYING TO DO. BUT IF I'M RIGHT... I THINK...
...I THINK MAYBE HE WON.
TIME WILL TELL. BUT YOU GAVE ME HOPE THAT WHATEVER COMES, WE WILL BE ABLE TO FACE IT.
I DID? HOW?
AH, ISO, IT IS SIMPLE.

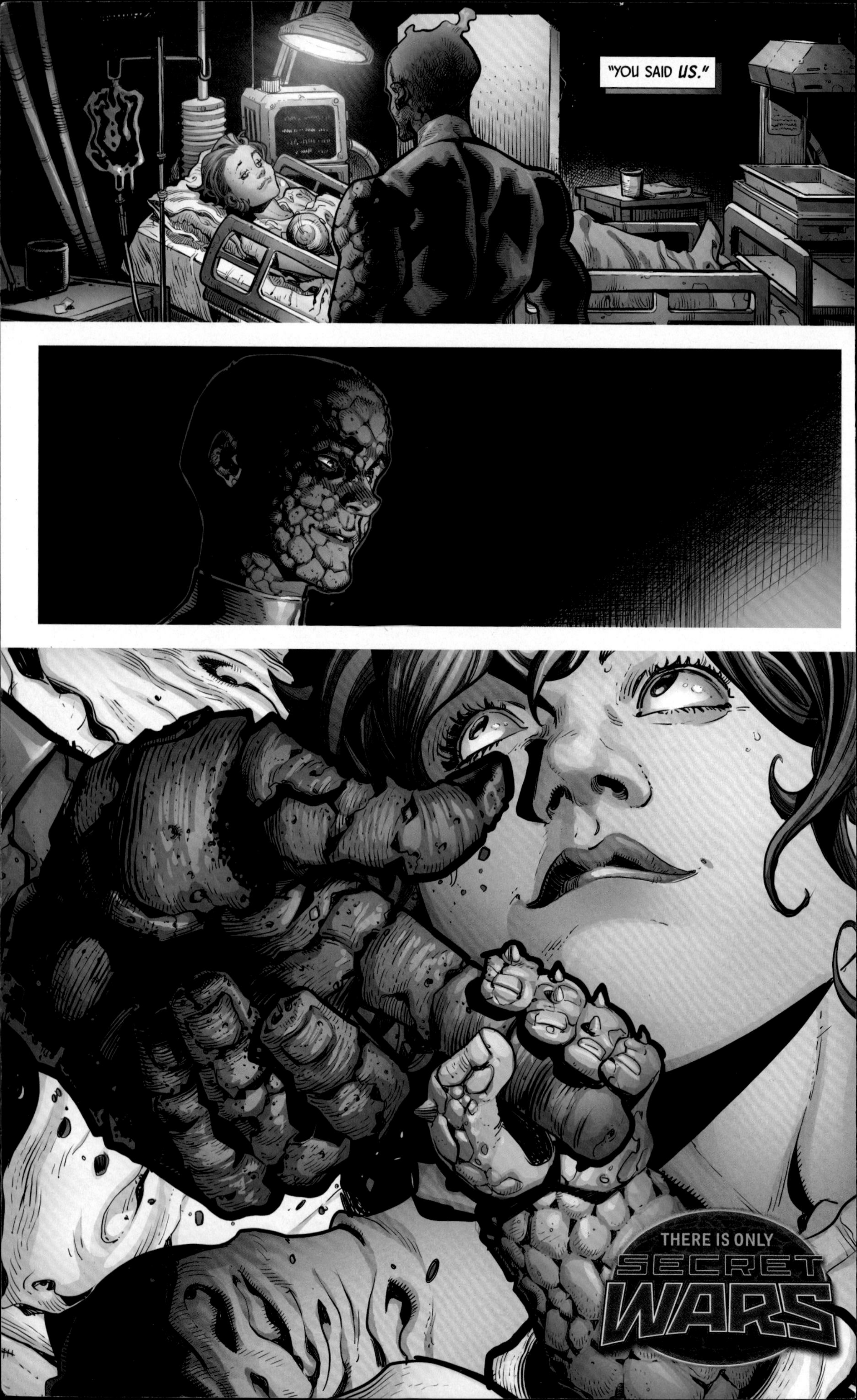
"YOU SAID US."
THERE IS ONLY
SECRET
WARS

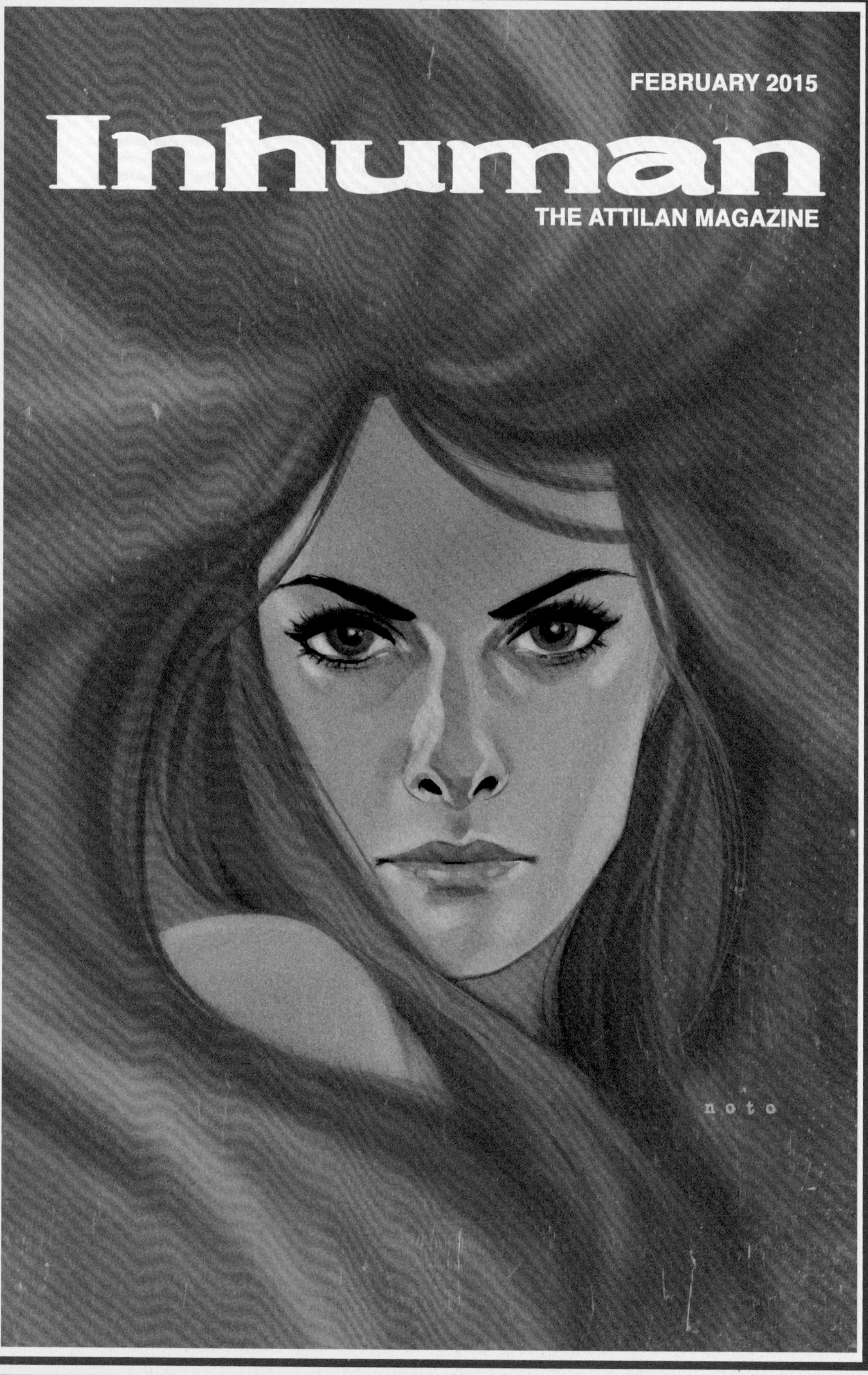

FEBRUARY 2015
Inhuman
THE ATTILAN MAGAZINE
noto

 VARIANT BY PHIL NOTO

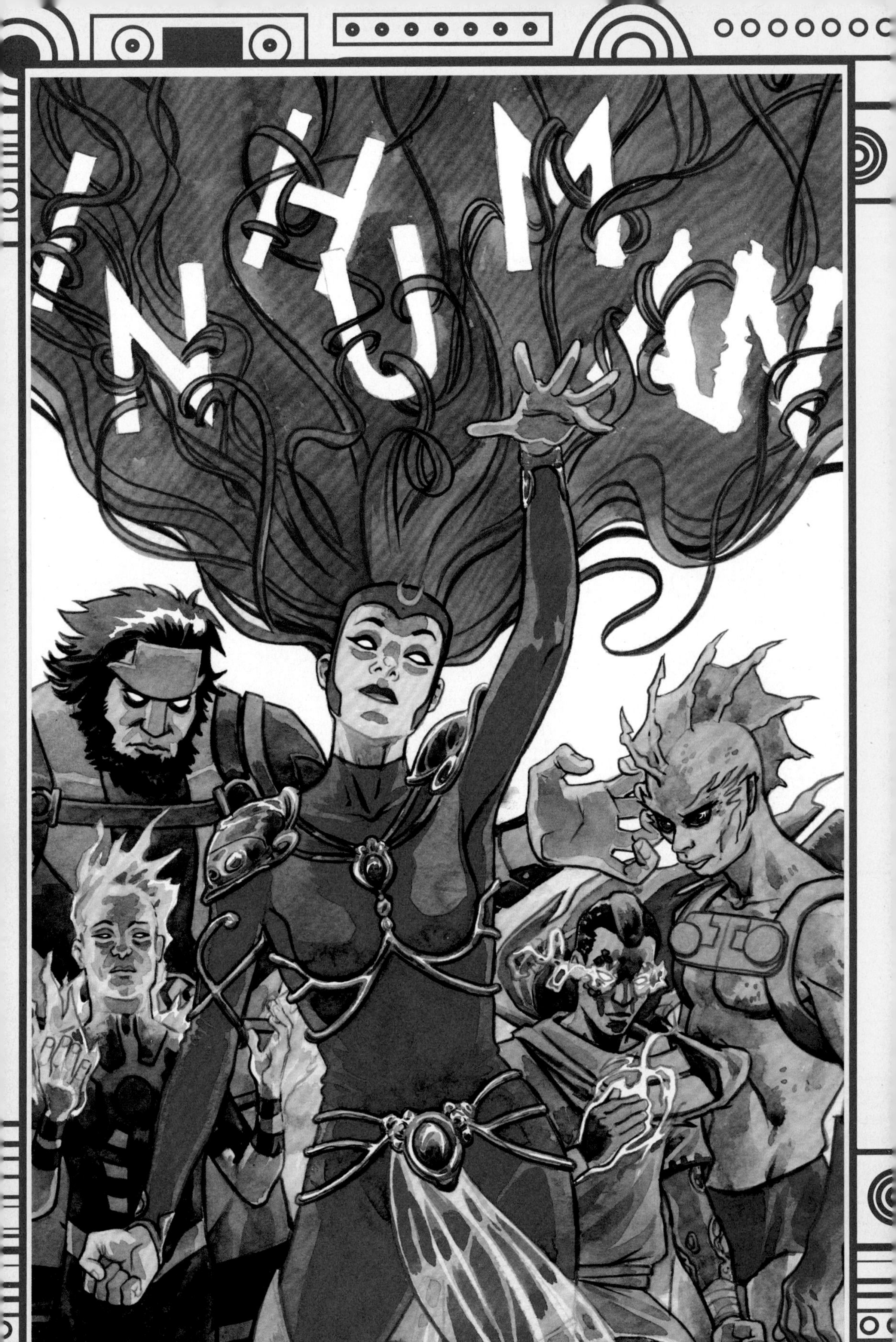

WOMEN OF MARVEL VARIANT
BY JILL THOMPSON

13

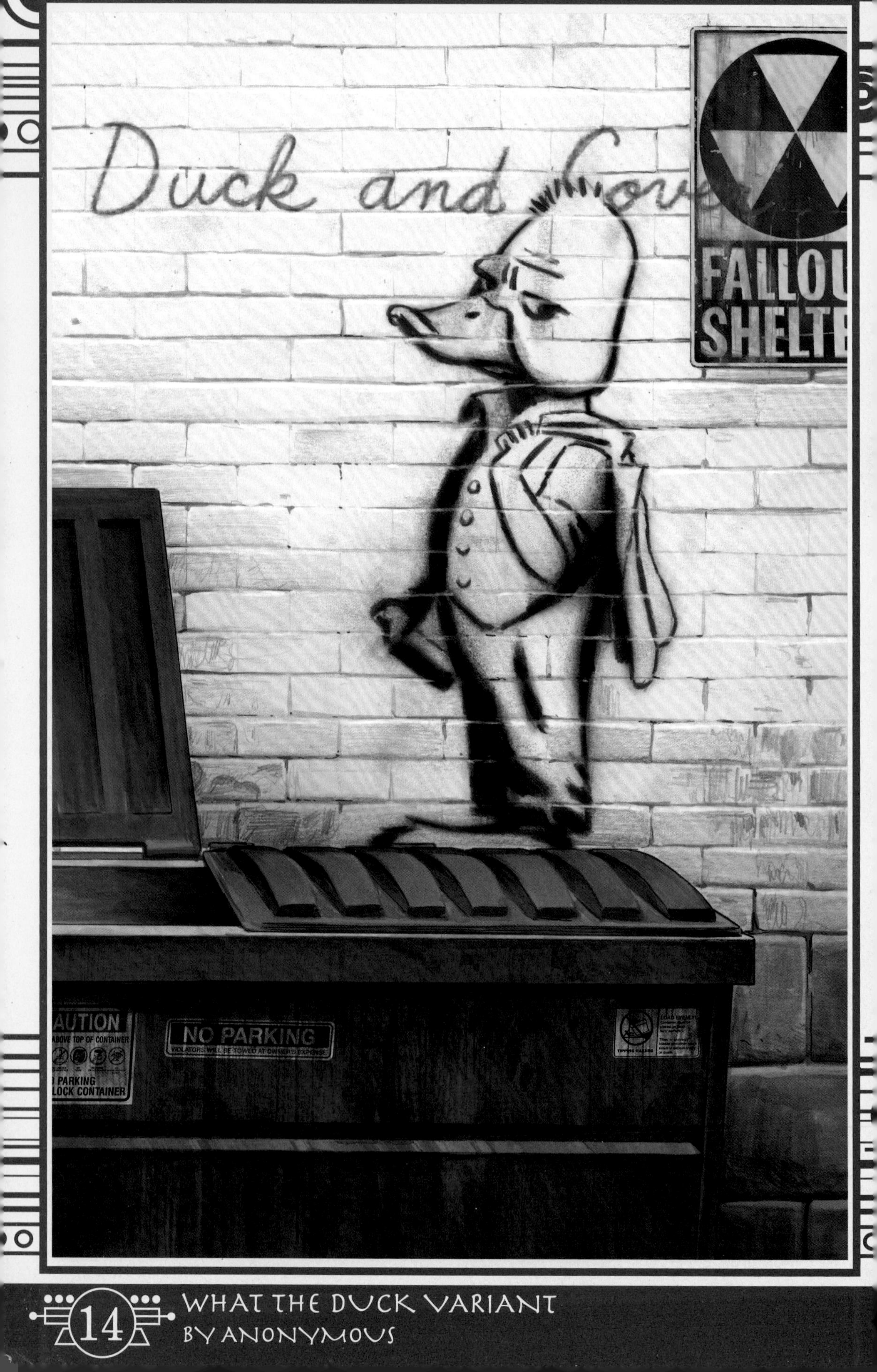
Duck and
NO PARKING

WHAT THE DUCK VARIANT
BY ANONYMOUS

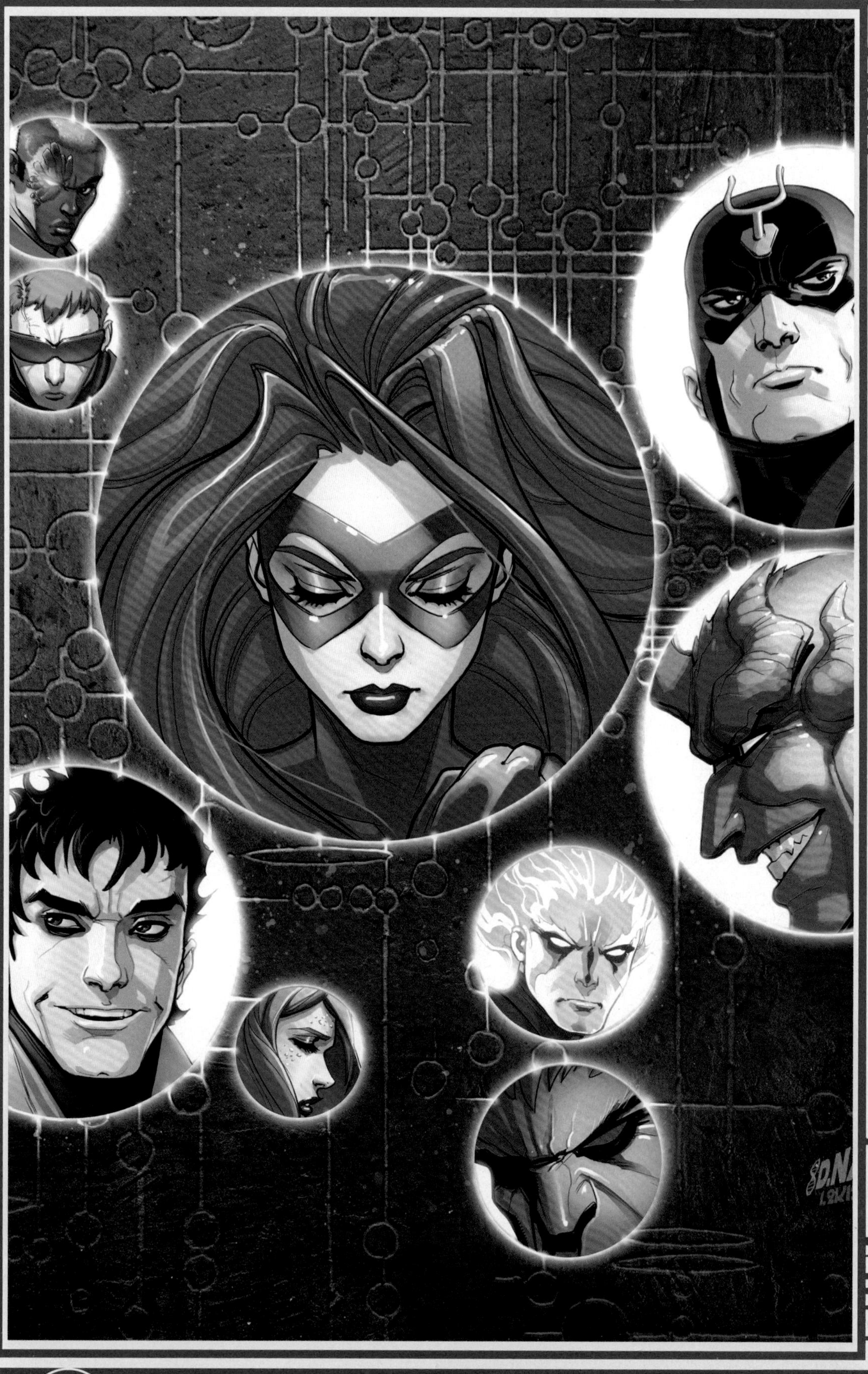

ANNUAL 1 VARIANT BY DAVID NAKAYAMA